FROM SINAI TO ROME

From Sinai to Rome

Jewish Identity in the Catholic Church

Edited by Angela Costley and Gavin D'Costa

IGNATIUS PRESS SAN FRANCISCO

Cover image:
© Cross and Star of David/iStock/Lisalson

Cover design by Enrique J. Aguilar

ISBN 978-1-62164-799-7 (PB)
ISBN 978-1-64229-361-6 (eBook)
Library of Congress Control Number 2025937875
Printed in the United States of America ♾

CONTENTS

INTRODUCTION

Angela Costley and Gavin D'Costa

This book is aimed at Catholics who are studying and exploring the Catholic faith. It is concerned with recovering the Jewish dimensions of the Gospel and the Church so that Catholicism may recover its full ecclesial dimensions as consisting of Jews and gentiles under the Messiah of Israel.[1] This is the primary concern of the book. At the same time, its aim is also to help Catholics understand their present relationship to the Jewish people, especially in light of recent Church teaching.

In three sections, our authors explore the following topics: the Jewish context of the New Testament and the presence of the "church of the circumcision" in the earliest period of the Church's formation; the way in which "Jews" have been understood and sometimes misunderstood in the Tradition and how Jewish Catholics were considered anachronistic; and finally, the emergence of Hebrew Catholics—Catholics who retain their Jewish identity—after the Shoah. This final section shows a recovery of the early patrimony of the Church, its roots in Vatican II, and its many forms and challenges.

The first section of the book turns to the New Testament to locate the importance of the Jewish dimensions of Catholicism. In some scholarship and in elements in the Tradition, the New Testament has been contrasted with the Old in a supersessionist manner. Supersessionism suggests that the Jewish covenant has been abrogated or nullified and is somehow not a significant part of salvation history.[2] This means that the Church has slowly become detached from its Jewish roots from the fourth century on. Christians began to read the New Testament increasingly as a text that had turned its back on its Jewish roots, rather than being grounded in Jewish Messianic theology. However, the contributions in this section show us that being aware of the Jewish roots of the New Testament narratives allows us to read the texts more richly. In the repression of the Jewish dimensions of the biblical texts, there is a repression of the gospel and the full dimensions of the good news. Jesus was a Jew and so were his first disciples, and the authors in section 1 underline the continuity and fulfillment of Israel's hopes and aspirations in the New Testament writings. This neither denigrates living Judaism today nor eradicates the significance of the Jewish covenantal church that formed around Jesus, the Jewish Messiah. It was this new Jewish covenantal community that messianically gathered in the gentiles that constituted the Church of the New Testament: a church of Jews and gentiles. Our authors argue that it is only in taking seriously the Jewish context of Jesus and his disciples and teachings that we come to see the Church for what it is: a Jewish covenantal community established in Abraham and welcoming the gentiles, the nations, to share this great promise and gift from God.

Indeed, there are some important parts of the Catholic faith that are fully grasped only when the New Testament is read in the light of its Jewish background. Brant Pitre opens our collection of essays and shows that the roles of Mary and Jesus are truly understood only in the light of the Jewish Scriptures and tradition. Through examining the traditions of the Ark of the Covenant and the expectation of its return to the people, Pitre shows how Mary is depicted as the return of the Ark, within whom God's presence resides. The New Testament texts use the same terms as the Hebrew scriptural texts, and Pitre argues that this identification was honored and developed in the early Church before finding its final formulation in the *Catechism of the Catholic Church*. The same treatment is extended to the manna from heaven that is given in Exodus to Israel as they travel to the Promised Land. This understanding is applied to Jesus both to configure him and to explain the Eucharist. Pitre shows that we find this in the early Church's reception, and it, too, is eventually firmly underlined in the *Catechism*. In short, the central figures of the Gospel are both Jewish and best comprehended within a Jewish paradigm that at the same time expands and fulfills that paradigm to include the nations and the gentiles.

Angela Costley, a Hebrew Catholic scholar, challenges the "traditional" historical-critical view that the book of Acts represents the beginning of a gentile-based universal community of followers of Christ. She shows, with careful attention to the text and its intra-Jewish dynamics, that instead we should see the gentile church as an insertion into Israel and see the Jewish covenant as established by God. She also argues that the prophetic discourse haranguing the Jewish people provides a better view of the fact that Israel is not rejected for not accepting Jesus as the Messiah as previously thought, but that gentiles are instead incorporated into Israel. This paradigm change calls for a different view of Jews, in keeping with Vatican II, but also for a different attitude to contemporary Jewish Catholics. The latter is implied in some of the Council teachings, but Costley, in a prophetic manner, helps to unfold the implications of the reality of Jewish Catholics.

Scott Hahn then examines the centrality of Temple Christology to the depiction of Jesus in the Fourth Gospel. Hahn goes beyond the usual scholarly consensus that Jesus is merely depicted as the fulfillment of the Temple. The usual consensus could easily lead people to believe that because Christ has ascended, the Christian Temple must also be gone, but a closer look reveals that the Temple is fulfilled not only in Christ but also in the Church and her sacraments. Having reviewed the depiction of the Temple in the Old Testament, Hahn goes on to look in depth at the Passover narrative in John 2:13—3:21, the second Passover narrative in John 6, and the narrative of the feast of Tabernacles in John 7–9. He demonstrates that Jesus indeed functions as a new Temple, but that the signs Jesus performs point forward to the Church's sacraments, namely the Eucharist and baptism. Hahn then moves to the final Passover narrative of John in 11:55—20:31, strengthening his thesis. Placing an emphasis on the farewell discourse, Hahn demonstrates that Christ confers on the disciples his own "Templeness" by commissioning them to continue his mission and perform "even greater works" than his own—works that precisely include the sacraments of baptism and the Eucharist. He thus demonstrates the importance of understanding the Jewishness of the Scriptures for understanding Catholic theology and sacramental practice.

Father David Neuhaus revisits and questions, like Costley, the supersessionist reading of the books of the New Testament. Neuhaus focuses on the Epistle to the Hebrews. This epistle has often been used to further supersessionist ends. In contrast, Neuhaus argues that Jesus comes to fulfill and transform the Levitical priesthood, not to abolish or negate its value. With close attention to the role of the priest in Leviticus regarding purification, sacrifice, and representation, Neuhaus shows that the author of Hebrews views Jesus as being an eschatological priest, requiring and demanding a priestly character of his followers, who in doing the will of God enact the priestly vocation.

The second section of the book, "Tradition", looks at two pillars of Catholic theological Tradition: the Angelic Doctor, Thomas Aquinas, and magisterial teachings in the form of the Council of Florence and the papal encyclical *Ex quo primum*. These aspects of the Tradition have often been rendered as grave obstacles to a Catholic appreciation of the Jewish elements within itself—or of the Jewish people. This section of the book does not call Tradition into question but rather shows how it has sometimes been misunderstood and is the source from which we can renew our Catholic faith today.

Bruce Marshall turns to Thomas Aquinas to show that he is far from a straightforward supersessionist, teaching a replacement theology. Marshall is deeply sensitive to the inherent tensions within Aquinas that also run through the Catholic Tradition: Jesus' life, death, Cross, and Resurrection are the hoped-for salvation of the world by both Jews and gentiles; and yet the very people from whom Jesus comes, the Jewish people, do not accept this salvation today. Marshall shows that despite strong currents to the contrary, Aquinas' works contain teachings that echo Vatican II in insisting that Paul's teaching in Romans about the "irrevocable promises" made to God's people is "without repentance", whatever Jews say or do. Along with this profound affirmation of the Jewish covenant as being entirely oriented toward salvation, Aquinas holds an almost contrary position: that Jewish rituals carried out after the coming of Christ are dead and deadly. Marshall makes clear that despite modern attempts, trying to free Aquinas from the latter reading will not work if one is loyal to the internal logic of his thinking. This struggle within the Tradition profoundly encapsulates the issues being thought through in this collection. Marshall shows that we cannot simply escape Tradition but must gratefully wrestle with it in the light of the Church's teaching today.

Robert Fastiggi takes the baton from Marshall's Aquinas and shows how the Magisterium's teachings at Florence, and through Pope Benedict's encyclical *Ex quo primum*, continue to wrestle constructively with these tensions. Fastiggi carefully contextualizes these magisterial teachings and also distinguishes between prudential judgments (which can be changed) and doctrinal magisterial teachings (which cannot be changed). He shows that the context of Jewish proselytism toward Christians (or the assumed danger of it) and the conversions of convenience by Jews who became Christians was determinative for the resistance toward allowing any Jewish rituals to be practiced within Christian circles. Fastiggi shows how Pope Benedict, much later on, noted these contextualizations and also observed how successful Jewish practices, which did not in any way deny the exclusive salvific efficacy of Christ's Cross, allowed for Jewish practices that were Christologically understood. From this, Fastiggi concludes that Jewish Catholics of today might well be permitted to celebrate Jewish rites within the modern context—with benefit rather than loss to the ecclesial community.

The third section of the book turns to the modern period, examining the ways in which ethnic (or what used to be called "carnal") Jews within the Church raise important questions about the nature of the Church and its practices and fullness.

Roy Schoeman presents a mapping exercise that helps the reader to place the remaining essays of the collection into context. He explores how those who are Jewish and Catholic view the options ahead of them, since after the Shoah, retaining Jewish identity became more existentially important and theologically viable. This followed from the Second Vatican Council's teachings in *Nostra aetate* no. 4. His title amusingly illuminates the complexity of the situation and the spectrum of opinions, none of whose outcomes are officially affirmed or denied within the Catholic Church. Schoeman is unambiguous about the baseline: Jewish identity is vital and central for most Jewish Catholics. Nothing in the Gospel demands they should eradicate that identity. He cites cardinals, popes, nuns, and saints to make this point forcefully. How continuing to be Jewish and Catholic plays out can vary according to place, history, and context, and while outlining the key issues, Schoeman makes his own position clear.

Gavin D'Costa brings the theological implications of the various topics covered in this section of the volume together. D'Costa points out that recognition of the visible elements of the Jewish ecclesia that began at Vatican II was not the emergence of a new ecclesiology, a fact established repeatedly in this volume. Rather, it was both a recovery of the Pauline view that God's calling of Israel is irrevocable and a recognition that the Church has *literally* comprised Jews and gentiles since its earliest days. He carefully discusses the unfolding of the developments of doctrine in and after the Council through a close examination of key Council documents and the subsequent teaching of Saint John Paul II. D'Costa draws out their implications for Jews in the Catholic Church who wish to retain their Jewish identities, and his essay does much to highlight how the existence of the Jewish ecclesia responds to the Jewish criticism that conversion to Christianity is an eradication of Jewish identity, while also prompting the Church to consider carefully her own internal Jewish dimension. D'Costa ends with a careful discussion of the practical working out of this theology in ecumenical terms, especially in relation to Messianic Judaism, and the practicalities of the establishment of a more carefully defined Jewish community in the Church, drawing on the work of another author in the collection, Father Antoine Levy.

Levy, who has written extensively on the establishment of a Jewish community within the Catholic Church, here addresses the controversial question of mission to the Jewish people. Levy also registers that since the creation of the nation state of Israel, the dynamics of interaction and engagement between Christians and Jews has radically altered, and he calls for fresh thinking on the question of mission. Levy outlines the different historical periods and strategies related to mission to the Jews deployed by both Catholics and Protestants. The Shoah forced Christians to focus on the problematic aspects of their attitudes toward Jews. He argues that traditionally, mission had required the stripping of Jewish identity as a precondition for becoming a Christian. Hitler was also focused on destroying Jewish identity. Levy focuses on post-Shoah Catholic and Protestant approaches to mission in the light of the establishment of a Jewish nation, Israel. He questions the Messianic Jewish strategies in Israel and develops an alternative Catholic model of silent witness that could be found in a truly Jewish church in Israel, identifying with the nation and the Jewish people, while being resolutely Catholic.

To some extent, the work proposed by Levy has already begun. Our next author, Father Elias Friedman, was the founder of the Association of Hebrew Catholics, and we insert a chapter on the important theology that inspired him to create this association, whose work continues today and on whose board of directors Costley sits. Born in 1916 into a Jewish family in South Africa as Jacob Friedman, he joined the Catholic Church in 1943 and later became a Discalced Carmelite and entered the Stella Maris Monastery of Mount Carmel. Friedman never lost his sense of Jewishness and began to work out what it meant to be a Jew in the Catholic Church. His book, *Jewish Identity*, is a modern classic and contains the formulation of his theological and practical understanding of what it means to share these two identities. This book led to the formation of the Association of Hebrew Catholics. We reprint, with permission of the Association, his chapter on the move from Mosaic Judaism, called "biblical Judaism" elsewhere in our book, to the Church. In this chapter, Friedman carefully outlines the theological outcomes of true respect for the Jewishness of Jesus. His basic claim is that Jesus did no violence to Mosaic Judaism, keeping its Law during his earthly life in a perfect manner. With regard to the prescriptions of the Torah, he claims that Mosaic Judaism did indeed die when Jesus died, but it also rose again with him, transfigured. Friedman discusses the transformation of Mosaic Judaism into Christianity, and, relying heavily on the theology of Cardinal John Henry Newman, he outlines how the Jewish "Church" of the Old Testament and the Christian Church are really one. Friedman touches on important issues such as the keeping of the Torah's legal prescriptions by Jewish Christians and posits that the situation for modern Jews embracing Christianity is different from those in the early Church. Jews who today embrace Christianity are considered excluded from the Jewish community by most Jews, whereas the first Christians were free to continue their Jewish forms of worship. Jews who followed Jesus remained Israelites, or Hebrews, the outworking of which is the identity of Jews in the Catholic Church as *Hebrew Catholics*.

Indeed, the phenomena of Jews coming to faith in Christ requires the working out of how Jews are to retain their identity once they have entered the Church. Father David Neuhaus, in his second essay, outlines the emergence of Jewish discipleship to Christ from the eighteenth century to contemporary forms of Messianic Judaism and Jewish Catholicism, including Hebrew Catholics. Neuhaus, who has been involved in the official and semiofficial dialogues between the Catholic Church and Messianic Jews, gives an account of those meetings, which have taken place since 1990. The challenge to Catholics is whether to view these Jewish Messianic congregations as part of the Holy Spirit's work and to see in them the germ of the Jewish ecclesia that is part of the Church itself. The challenge to Messianic congregations is with regard to the universal community of disciples of Yeshua/Jesus, called to visible unity. Neuhaus outlines the special contributions of Rabbi Mark Kinzer, a leading Messianic Jew, and Levy, a critic and colleague of Kinzer. Neuhaus also locates his own position in contrast to these two. This essay shows the live and open vistas to be explored by Jewish and gentile Christians—as Schoeman has already noted.

Lawrence Feingold, like Costley, represents and is part of the Association of Hebrew Catholics founded by Father Friedman that is mentioned in every essay in section 3 of this collection. Feingold develops Elias Friedman's view and shows why biblically and magisterially such an association is both timely and theologically vital for the Church. He also engages with the traditions discussed by Marshall and Fastiggi and shows how the Association of Hebrew Catholics both honors and carries forward Catholic Tradition while also historically contextualizing and distinguishing between the prudential judgments and doctrinal commitments of the Church. He uses Vatican II to renegotiate Aquinas. As with all writers in this section, Feingold sees messianically transformed Jewish rituals as serving a positive biblical vision and serving the Catholic gentile Church in an important manner.

We offer these essays in the hope of deepening our Catholic appreciation of the Jewish church that is within the precious Body of Christ and are very grateful to all our contributors for their generous participation in the project.

Section 1

Roots

I

The Jewish Roots of Jesus and Mary

Brant Pitre

When discussing the existence of Hebrew Catholics and the place of Jews in the Church today, it is important to realize the deeper understanding of the Catholic faith that arises when we consider it in a context of continuity with ancient Judaism. This can only be done when we see how the Old and New Testaments mutually illuminate each other when they are read in light of the mystery of Jesus Christ. As the Second Vatican Council taught in its Dogmatic Constitution on Divine Revelation: "The economy of the Old Testament was deliberately so orientated that it should prepare for and declare in prophecy the coming of Christ, ... and should indicate it by means of different types (cf. 1 Cor. 10:11).... God, the inspirer and author of the books of both Testaments, in his wisdom has so brought it about that *the New should be hidden in the Old and that the Old should be made manifest in the New*" (*Dei Verbum* nos. 15–16).[1]

If the New Testament is truly concealed in the Old and the Old is revealed in the New, then any attempt to understand the Catholic faith must pay close attention to the Jewish roots of Christian practice and belief. This is especially true if we want to understand Jesus of Nazareth and Mary, his mother, both of whom lived, moved, and had their being in a first-century Jewish context.

Throughout the centuries, the figures of Jesus and Mary have played a central role in Catholic faith and piety. One excellent example of this is a third-century fresco from the catacomb of Priscilla in Rome, which depicts the Virgin Mary holding the infant Jesus in her arm while a man to her left points at a star in the sky above them.[2]

The official *Catechism of the Catholic Church* uses this icon to introduce its section on the Creed with these words: "This image, among the most ancient in Christian art, expresses a theme that lies at the heart of the Christian faith: the mystery of the incarnation of the Son of God born of the Virgin Mary."[3]

This ancient image is a particularly appropriate introduction to this essay, because the man pointing at the star above Mary and Jesus has long been identified as the prophet Balaam. According to Jewish Scripture, at the time of Moses, Balaam prophesied that one day "a star" would "come forth out of Jacob" and "a scepter" would "rise out of Israel" (Num 24:17). By the first century A.D., the oracle of Balaam was interpreted in some Jewish circles as a prophecy of the long-awaited "anointed one" (Hebrew *mashiach*), the Messiah.[4] Seen in this light, the icon depicts an important theological truth: In order to understand the mystery of Jesus and Mary, one must see them in the "light" of Jewish Scripture, especially the words of the prophets. In other words, we must pay close attention to *the Jewish roots of Jesus and Mary*.

That is what I will attempt to do in this essay. Of course, an entire book could be devoted to this subject; I have written a few myself.[5] Within the confines of this essay, however, I simply want to highlight briefly four episodes in the Gospels that typologically link the figures of Jesus and Mary with the fulfillment of ancient Jewish hopes for the future:

1. The Annunciation (Lk 1:26–35)
2. The Visitation (Lk 1:39–56)
3. The Lord's Prayer (Mt 6:9–13)
4. The Bread of Life Discourse (Jn 6:48–59)

As we will see, when key elements from each of these episodes are interpreted in the light of both Jewish Scripture and ancient Jewish tradition, we will discover that Jesus and Mary are being identified as much more than just the long-awaited Messiah and his royal mother. The Gospels reveal that Mary is the *new Ark of the Covenant* and Jesus is the *new manna from heaven*. Seen in this light, both Jesus and Mary fulfill ancient Jewish hopes for a new exodus, in which certain aspects of the first exodus from Egypt will be recapitulated and fulfilled in new ways.

The Jewish Roots of the Ark of the Covenant

Since Mary comes before Jesus in the history of salvation, we will begin with her. In order to see clearly how Mary is depicted by the Gospels as fulfilling ancient Jewish expectations regarding the Ark of the Covenant, we need to take a few moments to review briefly what Jewish Scripture and tradition have to say about the Ark of the Covenant, especially regarding its disappearance and eventual return.[6]

The Ark of the Covenant and the Dwelling Place of God

The Ark of the Covenant is first mentioned in Jewish Scripture in the biblical account of the exodus from Egypt. After the Israelites arrive at Mount Sinai and receive the Ten Commandments (see Ex 19–20), God instructs them to build a portable sanctuary, known as the Tabernacle, and to place within it a sacred chest, known as the Ark:

> Let them make me a sanctuary, that I may dwell in their midst. According to all that I show you concerning the pattern of the tabernacle, and of all its furniture, so you shall make it. They shall make an ark of acacia wood.... And you shall overlay it with pure gold.... And you shall put the poles into the rings on the sides of the ark, to carry the ark by them.... And you shall put into the ark the covenant which I shall give you.... And you shall put the mercy seat on the top of the ark; and in the ark you shall put the covenant that I shall give you. There I will meet with you, and from above the mercy seat, from between the two cherubim that are upon the ark of the covenant, I will speak with you of all that I will give you in commandment for the sons of Israel. (Ex 25:8–11, 14, 16, 21–22)

For our purposes here, three aspects of this description of the Ark are worth emphasizing.[7]

First, the Tabernacle in which the Ark is kept is explicitly identified as the dwelling place of God on earth. Indeed, the primary reason for the sanctuary is so that it can be the place where God will "dwell" in the "midst" of his people (25:8).

Second, the Ark is a sacred "box" or "chest" (Hebrew *'aron*) in which the Ten Commandments are to be kept. This is the meaning of God's command "You shall put into the ark the covenant which I shall give you" (25:16); the "covenant" refers to the tablets of the Decalogue (see 31:18). According to Jewish Scripture, eventually, in addition to the two tablets, a golden bowl of manna and the miraculous staff of the high priest Aaron that "budded" would also be kept inside the Ark (see 16:34; Num 17:10).

Third, the Ark is covered in "pure" or "clean" (Hebrew *zahab*) gold—that is, free from any impurities.[8] Here the purity of the gold functions to signify the absolute holiness of the Ark.[9] That is why the Ark can only be carried using golden poles; it is too sacred for sinful humans to touch it.

Fourth and finally, the Tabernacle and the Ark are together the place where the "cloud" of God's glory comes down from heaven. As the book of Exodus describes it: "[Moses] brought the ark into the tabernacle.... *Then the cloud covered the tent of meeting, and the glory of the* L*ORD* *filled the tabernacle.* And Moses was not able to enter the tent of meeting, because the cloud abode upon it, and the glory of the LORD filled the tabernacle" (40:21, 34–35).[10]

It is hard to overemphasize the significance of the presence of the cloud of God's "glory" (Hebrew *kabod*) within the Tabernacle. In Jewish Scripture, the glory cloud is not just a visible sign that God has descended to earth to be with his people. It is also the means by which he will visibly lead the Israelites through the desert to the Promised Land (see 40:36–38).

The Ark, the Jerusalem Temple, and the Glory Cloud

Although the description of the Ark of the Covenant ends in the book of Exodus, the story of the Ark does not. Once the Israelites are in the Promised Land, the Ark moves around quite a bit.[11] During the time of Joshua and thereafter, the Ark is housed at various sanctuaries throughout the land (see Josh 4:19; 7:6; 18:1; Judg 20:26–28). Eventually, according to the book of Samuel, King David "arose and went" with the people of Israel "to bring up ... the ark of God" to Jerusalem (2 Sam 6:1–2). Tragically, while the Ark is being brought up to Jerusalem, a man named Uzzah inadvertently touches it and is struck dead. Here is what follows: "And David was afraid of the LORD that day; *and he said, 'How can the ark of the* L*ORD come to me?'* So David was not willing to take the ark of the LORD into the city of David; but David took it aside to the house of Obed-edom the Gittite. *And the ark of the* L*ORD remained in the house of Obed-edom the Gittite three months*" (6:9–11).

Once David sees that Obed-edom's household is blessed because of the presence of the Ark, he again decides to bring it up to Jerusalem. This time, the Ark is carried in proper procession: "So David and all the house of Israel brought up the ark of the LORD with shouting, and with the sound of the horn" (6:15; cf. Ps 132:1–10).[12]

Although David brings the Ark up to the Tabernacle in Jerusalem, it is only with the completion of the permanent Temple by Solomon that we once again hear of the "cloud" of God's glory descending from heaven and filling the sanctuary:

> Then Solomon assembled the elders of Israel and all the heads of the tribes ... to bring up the ark of the covenant of the LORD out of the city of David, which is Zion.... Then the priests brought the ark of the covenant of the LORD to its place, in the inner sanctuary of the house, in the most holy place.... *And when the priests came out of the holy place, a cloud filled the house of the* L*ORD, so that the priests could not stand to minister because of the cloud; for the glory of the* L*ORD filled the house of the* L*ORD.* (1 Kings 8:1, 6, 10–11)

The upshot of this account is simple: Once the Ark is brought into the Jerusalem Temple where it belongs, God fills the sanctuary with his presence.[13] Of course, after the death of Solomon, the kingdom of Israel would eventually split in two (see 1 Kings 11–12), and the Temple itself along with the city of Jerusalem would be destroyed by the Babylonian Empire in 587 B.C. (see 2 Kings 25). According to the prophet Ezekiel, before the Jerusalem Temple is destroyed, the glory cloud departs from the city and the sanctuary (see Ezek 10:18–22; 11:22–23).

The Prophecy of the Return of the Lost Ark

With all this background in mind, we can now ask the question: What happens to the Ark of the Covenant *after* the destruction of the Temple? How is it lost, and where does it go?

Theories about the location of the lost Ark abound.[14] Many assume the Ark was stolen by the Babylonians, but the Scriptures do not list it among the objects taken to Babylon (see 2 Kings 25:13–17; Jer 52:17–23). Others speculate that it is hidden in some unknown location to this day.[15] One thing many such theories have in common is that they tend to ignore the oldest account we possess of the disappearance of the Ark. According to 2 Maccabees, usually dated to the second century B.C., the prophet Jeremiah removed the Ark from the Temple and hid it in a cave on Mount Nebo, where Moses had been permitted by God to see the Promised Land before his death:

> It was also in the writing that the prophet [Jeremiah] ... ordered that the tent and the ark should follow with him, and that he went out to the mountain where Moses had gone up and had seen the inheritance of God. And Jeremiah came and found a cave, and he brought there the tent and the ark and the altar of incense, and he sealed up the entrance. Some of those who followed him came up to mark the way, but could not find it. When Jeremiah learned of it, he rebuked them and declared: "The place shall be unknown until God gathers his people together again and shows his mercy. And then the Lord will disclose these things, and the glory of the Lord and the cloud will appear, as they were shown in the case of Moses, and as Solomon asked that the place should be specially consecrated." (2:4–8)

Although this tradition is well-known to scholars, it is not as widely known as one might expect, perhaps because it is found only in the Catholic Old Testament.[16] For our purposes here, it is important because it bears witness to the ancient Jewish belief that one day, *the location of the lost Ark will be revealed*. When will this happen? According to Jeremiah's oracle, when the cloud of "the glory of the Lord" finally returns (2:8).

In other words, at the time of Jesus and Mary, the Jewish people were still waiting for the reappearance of the lost Ark. Should there be any doubt about this, it is important to recall that, during the Second Temple period, the sanctuary in Jerusalem lacked two important features. First, as we have already seen, it was missing the glory "cloud" of God's presence (cf. Ezek 10–11). Second, as the first-century Jewish historian Josephus notes, it was also bereft of the Ark itself: "The innermost recess ... was screened in like manner from the outer portion by a veil. *In this stood nothing at all*: unapproachable, inviolable, invisible to all, it was called the Holy of Holies."[17] Indeed, according to the Greco-Roman historian Tacitus, when the Roman general Pompey conquered Jerusalem in the first century B.C., he entered the Temple but found that "the place was empty and the secret shrine contained nothing."[18]

In summary: At the time of Mary and Jesus, any Jew familiar with the Scriptures and ancient traditions about the Ark would have known that the Jewish people were waiting not only for the coming of the Messiah. They were also waiting for *the revelation of the location of the Ark* and *the return of the glory cloud of God's presence*. With these two expectations in mind, we can now turn to what the New Testament reveals about the relationship between the Annunciation to Mary, the Visitation to Elizabeth, and the revelation of the new Ark.

Mary, the New Ark of the Covenant

When we take everything we have learned about the Ark of the Covenant from Jewish Scripture and Jewish tradition and turn to the pages of the New Testament, we discover that Mary, the mother of Jesus, is much more than simply the woman who gives birth to Jesus the Messiah. She is also depicted as *the new Ark of the Covenant*—that is, the living dwelling place of God on earth. Within the Gospels, this is especially clear in the accounts of the Annunciation to Mary and the Visitation to Elizabeth in the Gospel of Luke.[19]

The Annunciation and the Return of the Glory Cloud

The first key passage for tying Mary to the Ark is the famous account in which Gabriel appears to her and announces that she will miraculously conceive and give birth to Jesus (see Lk 1:26–38). Taken at face value, the primary significance of the Annunciation is that Gabriel is declaring to the Virgin Mary that Jesus will be conceived miraculously and revealing his identity as "the Son of the Most High" and heir to "the throne of his father David" (1:32)—that is, as "the messianic king".[20]

At the same time, when seen through first-century Jewish eyes, there is more going on in this episode. When we interpret the Annunciation in the light of Jewish Scripture and traditions about the Ark, we discover that it depicts the return of the long-absent glory cloud. After the angel makes his declaration and Mary asks how it is going to take place, Gabriel responds as follows:

> And the angel said to her,
> "The Holy Spirit will come upon you,
> and the power of the Most High will overshadow you;
> therefore the child to be born will be called holy,
> the Son of God. (1:35)

Although it is easy to miss the Old Testament allusions, when we compare the Greek text of Luke's account with the ancient Greek Septuagint (the LXX), there is a striking parallel between the language used to describe the descent of the *glory cloud* upon the Ark in the Tabernacle and the descent of the *Holy Spirit* upon Mary:

The Tabernacle	The Virgin Mary
The cloud of the Lord's glory	The Holy Spirit
"overshadows" (*epeskiazen*)	"overshadows" (*episkiasei*)
the Tabernacle.	the Virgin Mary.
(Ex 40:35–35 LXX)	(Lk 1:35)

In light of the distinctive use of the verb "overshadow" (Greek *episkiazō*) in the Greek Bible, scholars from a variety of perspectives—Jewish, Protestant, and Catholic—agree that the imagery of the Holy Spirit overshadowing Mary is meant to call to mind the glory cloud of the exodus.[21] In the words of John McHugh's classic study of Mary in the New Testament: "St Luke, when he wrote the word 'overshadow,' must have known what associations it would evoke in the Jewish mind. *No Jew, reading the words, 'A Power of the Most High will overshadow thee', could fail to think of the Divine Presence or Shekinah.*"[22]

In other words, just as the Ark of the Covenant was the special place of God's presence in the Tabernacle of Moses at the time of the exodus from Egypt, so now, through the virginal conception of Jesus, Mary's womb has become the special dwelling place of God's glory in the new exodus spoken of by the prophets.

The Visitation and the Revelation of the New Ark

Should there be any doubt about this connection, several more parallels between Mary and the Ark are present in the account of the Visitation to her cousin Elizabeth (see Lk 1:39–56).[23] Again, on the surface, the basic meaning of this episode is the recognition of Jesus by the infant John, who "leaped for joy" in his mother's womb (1:44). However, if we compare the account of the Visitation with what the Old Testament says about the Ark of the Covenant, we discover once again that more is going on than at first glance meets the eye:

> *In those days Mary arose and went with haste into the hill country, to a city of Judah,* and she entered the house of Zechariah and greeted Elizabeth. And when Elizabeth heard the greeting of Mary, the child leaped in her womb; and Elizabeth was filled with the Holy Spirit *and she exclaimed with a loud cry,* "Blessed are you among women, and blessed is the fruit of your womb! *And why is this granted me, that the mother of my Lord should come to me?* For behold, when the voice of your greeting came to my ears, *the child in my womb leaped for joy.* And blessed is she who believed that there would be a fulfilment of what was spoken to her from the Lord." And Mary said, "My soul magnifies the Lord, and my spirit rejoices in God my Savior, for he has regarded the low estate of his handmaiden. For behold, henceforth all generations will call me blessed.... *He has helped his servant Israel, in remembrance of his mercy,* as he spoke to our fathers, to Abraham and to his posterity for ever." *And Mary remained with her about three months,* and returned to her home. (1:39–49, 54–56)

When the Gospel account of Mary's visit to Elizabeth is compared with the biblical account of King David's bringing the Ark of the Covenant up to Jerusalem, a number of striking parallels emerge:

The Ark of the Covenant	The Virgin Mary
The glory of the Lord and the cloud cover the Tabernacle (containing the Ark) and *"overshadow"* (*episkiazen*) them (Ex 40:34–35, cf. v. 3)	The Holy Spirit comes upon Mary and the power of the Most High *"overshadows"* (*episkiasei*) her (Lk 1:35)
David *"arose and went"* to the hill country of *Judah* to bring up "the ark of God" (2 Sam 6:2)	Mary *"arose and went"* into the hill country of *Judah* to visit Elizabeth (Lk 1:39)
David admits his unworthiness to receive the Ark by exclaiming: "How can *the ark of the* LORD *come to me*?" (2 Sam 6:9)	Elizabeth admits her unworthiness to receive Mary by exclaiming: "And why is this granted to me, that *the mother of my Lord* should *come to me*?" (Lk 1:43)
David *"leaped"* before the Ark as it was brought in *"with shouting"* (2 Sam 6:15–16)	John *"leapt"* in Elizabeth's womb at the sound of Mary's voice and Elizabeth cried *"with a loud cry"*: (Lk 1:41–42)
The Ark remained in the hill country, in the house of Obed-edom, for *"three months"* (2 Sam 6:11)	Mary remained in the hill country, in Elizabeth's house, for *"three months"* (Lk 1:56)

Although some interpreters ignore these parallels as if they did not exist[24] or try to simply dismiss them,[25] neither approach is convincing. Instead, when the cumulative evidence from the accounts of the Annunciation and Visitation is given due weight, the most plausible explanation is that Luke is indeed depicting Mary as the new Ark of the Covenant.[26] In the words of Pablo Gadenz, quoting Pope Benedict XVI:

> Elizabeth's question ... suggests that *Mary is being presented as the new ark of the covenant*, an image or theme similar to her being presented as *the new tent of meeting* overshadowed by God's presence (Luke 1:35).... The Greek verb translated "cried out" (*anaphoneō*), found only here in

> the whole New Testament, is used in the parallel account of David's transport of the ark in 1 Chronicles (1 Chron 15:28 LXX).... In summary, "Luke, with various allusions, makes us understand that Mary is the true Ark of the Covenant, that the mystery of the temple—God's dwelling place here on earth—is fulfilled in Mary."[27]

If this is correct, then the implications for who Mary is and what role she will play in salvation history are enormous. Far from being just the mother of Jesus, or even just the mother of the Messiah, Mary is being depicted by the New Testament as *the dwelling place of God on earth*.

Mary and the New Ark in Ancient Christian Tradition

Should there be any doubt about Mary's identification with the Ark, it is worth noting that this is how the Gospel portraits of Mary have been interpreted for centuries. Consider, for example, the words of two ancient Christian writers, one from the Latin West and the other from the Greek East:

> The Lord was made without sin, made in His human nature of *incorruptible wood, that is to say, of the Virgin and the Holy Spirit*, overlaid within and without, as it were, by *purest gold* of the word of God.... Tell me, O Blessed Mary, what it was that was conceived by thee in the womb; what it was that was borne by thee in a Virgin's womb. It was *the Word of God*, firstborn from Heaven.[28]

> O noble Virgin, truly you are greater than any other greatness. For who is your equal in greatness, O dwelling place of God the Word? ... O [Ark of the] Covenant, clothed with purity instead of gold! You are the Ark in which is found the golden vessel containing the true manna, that is, the flesh in which divinity resides.... You carry within you the feet, the head, and the entire body of the perfect God ... you are God's place of repose.[29]

Notice how these ancient Christian writers derive their beliefs about Mary from the Old Testament and not just the Gospels. Notice also that they base their beliefs about Mary on what they believe about Jesus. Nor has this ancient identification of Mary as the true Ark of the Covenant disappeared. It continues to be taught in the official *Catechism of the Catholic Church*, which states: "Mary, in whom the Lord himself has just made his dwelling, is ... *the ark of the covenant*."[30] In order to see this typological identification clearly, however, we must strive to see Mary through ancient Jewish eyes. If, however, we attempt to view the New Testament portrait of Mary in isolation from its Old Testament background, we will render ourselves unable to understand just how deeply Jewish the Catholic understanding of Mary truly is. As Joseph Ratzinger (who later became Pope Benedict XVI) once wrote: "The image of Mary in the New Testament is woven entirely of Old Testament threads."[31]

The Jewish Roots of the Manna from Heaven

As with Mary, so with Jesus: In order to see more clearly how the words and actions of Jesus fulfill ancient expectations regarding the manna from heaven, we will need to take a few moments to review what Jewish Scripture and Jewish tradition outside the Bible have to say about the manna.[32] Then we will be better able to see the words and actions of Jesus through ancient Jewish eyes.

The Miraculous Manna from Heaven

Although the manna is mentioned multiple times in the Old Testament, the foundational account of its appearance comes from the book of Exodus. Immediately after Israel's triumphant crossing of the Red Sea (see 14–15), the people of Israel begin to grow hungry and to "murmur" against Moses and Aaron (16:1–3). In response to their complaints of hunger, God promises to give the Israelites a miraculous gift:

> Then the LORD said to Moses, "Behold, *I will rain down bread from heaven* for you; and the people shall go out and gather a day's portion every day, that I may test them, whether they will walk in my law or not. On the sixth day, when they prepare what they bring in, it will be twice as much as they gather daily...." And the LORD said

> to Moses, "I have heard the murmurings of the sons of Israel; say to them, '*At twilight you shall eat flesh, and in the morning you shall be filled with bread*; then you shall know that I am the LORD your God'." *In the evening quails came up and covered the camp; and in the morning dew lay round about the camp.* And when the dew had gone up, there was on the face of the wilderness a fine, flake-like thing, fine as hoarfrost on the ground. When the sons of Israel saw it, they said to one another, "*What is it?*" For they did not know what it was. And Moses said to them, "*It is the bread which the Lord has given you to eat.*" (16:4–5, 11–15)

Although the biblical account of the manna is very familiar, for our purposes here, several features need to be highlighted.

First, according to the book of Exodus, the manna is no ordinary phenomenon but *miraculous bread from heaven*. One reason this needs to be stressed is because in our own day it has become rather popular to identify the manna with a natural substance secreted by the tamarisk plant or by one of the desert insects that feeds on its leaves.[33] However, in the biblical account itself, the miraculous nature of the manna is indisputable. Not only is it explicitly described as "bread from heaven" (Ex 16:4), but the biblical account stresses that the Israelites "did not know what it was" (16:15). That is why they call it "*manna*", from the Hebrew words *man hu*, or, "What is it?"[34] If it were a common natural occurrence, this response would make no sense. Indeed, later biblical texts go on to refer to the manna as "the bread of heaven" (Ps 78:24), the "bread of angels" (Greek *artos angelōn*) (Ps 77:25 LXX). Indeed, any first-century Jew familiar with the Scriptures would have recognized that the manna was not ordinary bread but "heavenly food" (Wis 19:21).

Second, the manna is a *daily miracle*. It appears each day with the coming of the "dew" (Ex 16:13), and the people are commanded each day to go out and gather the appropriate amount (see 16:16–21). Here, too, we see the miraculous character of the bread, since no matter how much the Israelites gather, it always measures out as an omer's worth (about a liter), and it never lasts more than a day (see 16:16–20).

Third, and equally important, the manna was a *double miracle*. In the morning, God promises to give the Israelites "bread" from heaven, but in the evening, he promises to give them "flesh" to eat, in the form of quail that cover the camp: "At twilight you shall eat *flesh*, and in the morning you shall be filled with *bread*; then you shall know that I am the LORD your God" (16:12). Bread from heaven and flesh from heaven: that is the twofold miracle of the manna. Again, the Jewish Scriptures reiterate the point elsewhere: "He rained flesh upon them like dust, winged birds like the sand of the seas" (Ps 78:27).

Fourth, the Israelites not only eat the manna as daily food; they also preserve it by *placing it in the Tabernacle*. As we saw earlier, the Tabernacle is the portable temple and dwelling place of God on earth (see Ex 25–40). It is divided into three parts, and the Holy of Holies stands at its center, enshrining the golden Ark of the Covenant. According to the book of Exodus, God commands Moses to place some of the manna there: " 'This is what the LORD has commanded: "Let an omer of [the manna] be kept throughout your generations, *that they may see the bread* with which I fed you in the wilderness, when I brought you out of the land of Egypt." ' And Moses said to Aaron, 'Take a jar, and put an omer of manna in it, and place it before the LORD, to be kept throughout your generations.' As the LORD commanded Moses, *so Aaron placed it before the covenant*, to be kept" (16:32–34).

By means of this command, God is revealing that the manna is not only miraculous but also holy—so sacred indeed that it is to be reserved in the Holy of Holies itself.[35] It is indeed no ordinary bread.

The Manna: A Foretaste of the Promised Land

One final aspect of the manna that merits our attention is its taste. According to Jewish Scripture, it has a distinctive flavor: "Now the house of Israel called its name manna; it was like coriander seed, white, and *tasted like wafers made with honey*" (16:31). Why "wafers made with honey"? In context, the most plausible explanation is that the manna is a *foretaste of the Promised Land*—the "land flowing with milk and honey" (3:8). Should there be any doubt about this, it is important to remember that the manna was a *temporary miracle*. This is yet another sign that it is no ordinary substance.[36] According to the book of Joshua, as soon as the Israelites reach the Promised Land, the manna ceases: "On the next day after the Passover, on that very day, they ate the produce of the land, unleavened cakes and parched grain. *And the manna ceased* on the next day . . . and *the sons of Israel had manna no more, but ate of the fruit of the land of Canaan*" (5:11–12).

The upshot of this passage is simple: Once the exodus is complete, the manna is no longer necessary.[37] Now that the people have tasted the fruit of the land, they no longer need the foretaste.

The Manna of the Messiah

When we turn from the Jewish Scriptures to ancient Jewish literature outside the Bible, we discover one final tradition that is important for our purposes: namely, the expectation that when the Jewish Messiah finally came, he would bring back the miracle of the manna. Consider, for example, the words of the early Jewish apocalypse known as 2 Baruch: "And it will happen that when all that which should come to pass in these parts is accomplished, *the Messiah* will begin to be revealed.... And those who are hungry will enjoy themselves and they will, moreover, see marvels every day.... *And it will happen at that time that the treasury of manna will come down again from on high*, and they will eat of it in those years because these are they who will have arrived at the consummation of time" (29:3, 6–8).[38]

This text, which is commonly dated to the first century A.D., is an important witness to the fact that this belief was held around the time of Jesus. It also clearly shows that the coming of the future manna was expected to be miraculous: Indeed, the righteous would see miracles ("marvels") every day, because they would eat the manna every day.

Jesus and the New Manna

With this background in mind, we can now turn to the two key passages in which Jesus refers to the ancient Jewish hope for the new manna to illuminate the mystery of his identity and mission: the Lord's Prayer (see Mt 6:9–13) and Jesus' famous Bread of Life Discourse in the Jewish synagogue at Capernaum, in which he uses the imagery of the manna to teach his disciples that they must eat his "flesh" (Jn 6:35–59, esp. 48–51). I have written at some length about both these passages elsewhere.[39] For our purposes here, I simply want to make a few basic points about how the Jewish roots of the manna can shed fresh light on the meaning of Jesus' teachings.

"Give Us This Day Our Epiousios *Bread"*

Although the words of the Lord's Prayer are recorded in two places in the Gospels (see Mt 6:9–13; Lk 11:2–4), their most familiar form is in the First Gospel:

> Our Father who art in heaven,
> Hallowed be thy name.
> Thy kingdom come.
> Thy will be done, on earth as it is in heaven.
> *Give us this day our daily bread;*
> And forgive us our trespasses,
> As we forgive those who trespass against us;
> And lead us not into temptation,
> But deliver us from evil. (Mt 6:9–13)

For our purposes here, a couple of key questions need to be asked: (1) What exactly is the object of the fourth petition: "Give us this day our daily bread"? Is Jesus simply telling his disciples to pray for ordinary food and drink? (2) Why does Jesus appear to repeat himself in this line? Why does he say "Give us this *day* our *daily* bread"? Why does he put so much emphasis on the *daily* nature of the bread for which the disciples are to pray?

In my view, the answer to both these questions lies in the mysterious Greek word *epiousios*, which is used in this line of the prayer. Although most English translations of the prayer suggest that the word "day" or "daily" occurs twice, this is somewhat misleading. The normal word for "day" in Greek is *hēmera*. Behind the English word "daily" in the Lord's Prayer lies another word, found in both versions:

"Give us this day our *epiousios* bread" (Mt 6:11).

"Give us each day our *epiousios* bread" (Lk 11:3).

What is the meaning of *epiousios*? Unfortunately for contemporary scholars, this question is difficult to answer, since the only time this word occurs in ancient Greek literature is in the Lord's Prayer (or in ancient writers quoting or alluding to the Lord's Prayer).[40] Because of the ambiguity of the term, commentators have suggested four major interpretive options: (1) *"daily bread"* (Greek *epi* + *tēn ousan*), as in "for the current [day]"; (2) "natural bread" (Greek *epi* + *ousia*), as in "for existence"; (3) "supernatural bread" (Greek *epi* + *ousia*), as in "above nature"; (4) "for the coming day" (Greek *hē epiousa*), as in "that which is coming".[41]

This is not the place to try to adjudicate between these options. For our purposes here, the main point is that whatever interpretation one favors, each of them coheres quite well with an allusion to *the manna* of the exodus:

1. *Daily Bread*: The manna is daily bread, in that the Israelites are given "a day's portion every day" (Ex 16:4).
2. *Bread for Existence*: The manna is necessary for existence, since it sustained the Israelites by filling them (see 16:1–3, 8, 12).
3. *Supernatural Bread*: The manna is miraculous "bread from heaven" (16:4, 13–30).
4. *Bread for the Coming Day*: The manna is bread for the coming day, including the Sabbath rest (see 16:5).

In light of such connections, however one interprets the exact meaning of the word *epiousios*, one thing seems certain: When Jesus' words are interpreted in a first-century Jewish context, he is teaching his disciples to pray for the long-awaited *new manna from heaven*. This is especially clear when we recall that the request for the *epiousios* bread takes place in the context of a prayer for the eschatological advent of the "kingdom" of God (Mt 6:10).

In sum, Jesus places the hope for the new manna from heaven at the very center of the Lord's Prayer, the one prayer he is recorded as having taught to his disciples. Before his disciples are to ask for anything else for themselves—the forgiveness of their trespasses, protection from temptation, or deliverance from evil—they are to ask for the new manna of the kingdom of God, which will be their daily "supernatural" bread.

Jesus and the Bread of Life Discourse

After Jesus' allusion to the manna in the Lord's Prayer, by far the most explicit reference to the Jewish hope for the new manna can be found in one of Jesus' most famous (and most controversial) teachings: the so-called Bread of Life Discourse (see Jn 6:35–58). Again, I have written about this in much more detail elsewhere.[42] Here I simply want to emphasize that Jesus frames his momentous teaching on the necessity of eating his flesh with allusions to *the manna from heaven*. Consider, for example, the final words of his discourse in the Capernaum synagogue:

> [Jesus said:] "I am the bread of life. Your fathers ate the manna in the wilderness, and they died. This is the bread which comes down from heaven, that a man may eat of it and not die. I am the living bread which came down from heaven; if any one eats of this bread, he will live for ever; and the bread which I shall give for the life of the world is my flesh."
>
> The Jews then disputed among themselves, saying, "How can this man give us his flesh to eat?" So Jesus said to them, "Amen, Amen, I say to you, unless you eat the flesh of the Son of Man and drink his blood, you have no life in you; he who eats my flesh and drinks my blood has eternal life, and I will raise him up on the last day. *For my flesh is real food, and my blood is real drink.* He who eats my flesh and drinks my blood abides in me, and I in him. As the living Father sent me, and I live because of the Father, so he who eats me will live because of me. *This is the bread which came down from heaven, not such as the fathers ate and died; he who eats this bread will live forever.*" This he said in the synagogue, as he taught at Capernaum (6:48–59, adapted).

It is widely recognized by New Testament commentators of various perspectives that Jesus is speaking here about what he will give the disciples at the Last Supper.[43] For one thing, he explicitly says that his flesh and blood are "real food" and "real drink" (6:55).[44] Moreover, there are striking parallels between the two events:

Bread of Life Discourse	The Last Supper
The bread which I will give	This
is my flesh	is my body
for the life of the world	which is for you
(Jn 6:51)	(1 Cor 11:24)[45]

In light of such parallels, Raymond Brown wrote: "*If Jesus' words in [John] 6:53 are to have a favorable meaning, they must refer to the Eucharist.*

They simply reproduce the words we hear in the Synoptic account of the institution of the Eucharist (Matt xxvi 26–28): 'Take, eat, this is my body.'"[46]

The question, however, remains: What does Jesus *mean* when he speaks about eating his flesh? Is he speaking literally or merely symbolically?

It is here that I think paying close attention to how Jesus uses ancient Jewish beliefs about the manna of the exodus can help answer this highly debated question. Although many interpreters recognize Jesus is pointing forward to what he will do at the Last Supper, one important point often goes overlooked: *When Jesus gives his most explicit and realistic teaching about the Eucharist, he directly identifies it with the new manna from heaven.* Note it well: Jesus *begins* the final portion of the discourse speaking about the manna when he says, "Your fathers ate the manna in the wilderness" (Jn 6:49), and he *ends* it by contrasting the food he will give with the old manna: "This is the bread which came down from heaven, not such as the fathers ate and died; he who eats this bread will live for ever" (6:58). This manna-focused *inclusio* is extremely significant. Jesus could have chosen any number of images or events from Jewish Scripture to illuminate the mystery about what he would do at the Last Supper, but when he wants to emphasize the necessity of eating his flesh and blood and the fact that it will be "real food" and "real drink", he chooses *the manna from heaven* to shed light on the mystery.

Once this link between the manna and the Last Supper is solidly established, the logic behind the realism of Jesus' language becomes easier to explain. In short: *If the old manna of the exodus was miraculous bread from heaven, then the new manna Jesus will give cannot be merely a symbol.* The Eucharist must also be *miraculous bread from heaven.* Otherwise, the old manna would be greater than the new! And that is simply not how biblical typology works; Old Testament prefigurations are never greater than their New Testament fulfillments. Consider in this vein the words of Rudolf Bultmann and Johannes Beutler:

> He takes up again the concept of the "bread which comes down from heaven." ... This *miraculous bread* is indeed *the sacrament of the Lord's Supper.*[47]

> Jesus repeats his statement that his flesh is truly food and his blood is truly drink (v. 55). The adverb "truly" can have different meanings....

In John 6:55, the sense is rather: *my flesh is really food to eat, not just a symbol.*[48]

In other words, the Eucharist is no mere symbol, but the miraculous manna of the Messiah. That is why it has the power to give something much greater than physical life: "He who eats my flesh and drinks my blood has eternal life" (6:54). Indeed, if Jesus had wanted his Jewish disciples to regard the Eucharist he would give them at the Last Supper as ordinary food and drink, he would never have identified with the new manna of the Messiah, the miraculous bread from heaven.

Jesus and the New Manna in Ancient Christian Tradition

Again, lest there be any doubt about the importance of the new manna as a key to understanding Jesus' eucharistic teaching, it is worth emphasizing that this is no modern exegetical innovation.[49] Rather, for centuries, Christian writers have identified the Eucharist with the manna from heaven. Consider, for example, the words of Ambrose of Milan and Augustine of Hippo regarding the relationship between the manna and the Eucharist:

> Great and venerable indeed is the fact that manna rained upon the Jews from heaven. But understand! *What is greater, manna from heaven or the body of Christ? Surely the body of Christ, who is the Author of heaven.* Then, he who ate the manna died; he who has eaten this body will effect for himself remission of sins and "shall not die forever" (John 6:58).[50]

> "I am the living bread that came down from heaven" (John 6:48).... *Manna also came down from heaven; but manna was the shadow, this is the truth.* "If anyone eats of this bread, he will live for ever; and the bread which I shall give is my flesh for the life of the world" (John 6:51). When would flesh be able to grasp that he called bread flesh? ... *O sacrament of piety, O sign of unity, O bond of charity!*[51]

As with Mary and the Ark, so with Jesus and the manna: This typological interpretation of the New Testament continues to be part of official Catholic teaching. As the official *Catechism of the Catholic*

Church teaches: "Manna in the desert prefigured the Eucharist, 'the true bread from heaven.'"[52]

In sum, when we look at the Lord's Prayer and the Bread of Life Discourse through the lens of Jewish Scripture and ancient Jewish traditions regarding the manna, we discover the new manna of the kingdom of God that Jesus promises to give his disciples is much more than ordinary bread; it is miraculous bread from heaven that gives the gift of eternal life.

Conclusion

In light of everything we have seen in this essay, what can we say by way of conclusion regarding the Jewish roots of Jesus and Mary?

The first point that needs to be made is one worth repeating: namely, that in order to comprehend fully the identity and mission of both Jesus and Mary, it is absolutely crucial that we interpret the New Testament accounts of their words and actions in the light of ancient Jewish Scripture and tradition. When we do, we discover that Jesus and Mary are not simply the long-awaited Messiah and his mother but the fulfillment of ancient Jewish expectations regarding the return of the lost Ark of the Covenant and the coming of the new manna of the Messiah. In other words, a deeply *biblical* Christology and Mariology is one that is also deeply *Jewish*.

Second, the typological connections between Mary and the Ark and Jesus and the manna have manifold implications that go well beyond Christology and Mariology. They also have a direct impact on *devotion to Mary* and belief in the *real presence* of Jesus in the Eucharist. With regard to the former, it is no coincidence that the ancient Christian writers cited previously who see Mary as the new Ark of the Covenant—Hippolytus and Athanasius—also bear witness to two of the earliest extant Christian *prayers* to Mary, asking for her powerful intercession. Likewise, it is no coincidence the same ancient Christian writers cited previously who see Jesus as giving the new manna from heaven—Ambrose and Augustine—also have a robust theology of his real presence in the Eucharist.[53]

Finally, but by no means least significantly, when we look at the Jewish roots of Jesus and Mary together, we discover that Mary's identity as the new Ark of the Covenant sheds light on Jesus' identification of his own body with the manna from heaven. Taken together, they help us to understand that salvation in the New Testament is not merely the forgiveness of sin or deliverance from eternal separation from God; rather, it is the inauguration of a new exodus, a new journey to a new promised land. Seen in this light, we cannot fully understand who Jesus is claiming to be without situating his claims in the context of the identity of his Jewish mother. This entails reading Scripture in the direction of Old Testament to New Testament, as well as "backward" (from New to Old). Likewise, we cannot fully understand who the Church believes Mary to be without reference to what she believes about Christ. In the words of the *Catechism of the Catholic Church*: "*What the Catholic faith believes about Mary is based on what it believes about Christ*, and what it teaches about Mary illumines in turn its faith in Christ."[54] In other words, Catholic beliefs about Jesus and Mary are mutually illuminating. It is my hope that this essay has offered some brief insights into how our understanding of this mutual illumination can be broadened and deepened by paying closer attention to the Jewish roots of both Jesus and Mary.

2

The Ecclesiology of the Book of Acts: A Hebrew Catholic Perspective

Angela Costley

The Acts of the Apostles is widely recognized as a sequel to Luke's Gospel. It picks up where Luke leaves off, namely at the Ascension of Our Lord into heaven. Also addressed to Theophilus, like the Third Gospel, the opening lines tell of Jesus' post-Resurrection appearances to his apostles and his final order to them not to leave Jerusalem but to wait there for the baptism with the Holy Spirit "before many days" (1:3–5). Jesus then ascends heavenward, taken up by a cloud. What follows are the details of that baptism in the Holy Spirit at Pentecost and the subsequent spreading of the Gospel.[1] Essentially, Acts is a historical monograph that details the earliest days of the Church, beginning as a small Jewish sect but rapidly expanding, even by increments of three thousand (2:41) and five thousand (4:4). The key word here is "expanding"—both en masse acceptances of Jesus are of Jesus as the *Jewish* Messiah. Much New Testament scholarship, and indeed Church history, is centered on the coming to faith of gentiles, often with a transfer of God's favor from his people, Israel, to the nations. However, Acts serves to remind us that the early Christians were, of course, Jews and that the early leaders such as Peter and Paul did not see themselves as breaking from their ancestry and inventing some new kind of religion. In this chapter, we will look at the difference this latter understanding makes to a reading of Act's ecclesiology as I offer a Hebrew Catholic perspective on this important book.

Hebrew Catholics are Jews in the Catholic Church who wish to retain our Jewish identity while being faithful to the Magisterium.

The term was first coined by Father Elias Friedman, O.C.D., a chapter of whose book, *Jewish Identity*, is reprinted here. This work helpfully distinguishes those who are in full communion with Rome from our Messianic Jewish brethren. The term "Hebrew" also avoids confusion with Jews who do not hold Jesus to be the Messiah while still emphasizing our heritage. The movement is a growing one. Members keep Torah observance to various degrees or not at all, in line with the understanding that prophecy has been fulfilled in Christ and that such practices constitute private devotion; but all of us wish to share the richness of our people's history to enlighten the interpretation of Scripture and to explain the faith and practices of the Catholic Church so that the faith lives of all may be deepened, to the glory of God and for the salvation of souls.

Critical Views on the (Non-)Jewishness of Acts

Perhaps surprisingly, for over one hundred years, much scholarship has depicted Luke-Acts as detailing the emergence of the *gentile* church. This mindset was particularly common in the early days of historical criticism and is often associated with Franz Overbeck, who was in conflict with the Tübingen school. The Tübingen school saw Acts as reconciling Jewish and gentile Christians via the apostolic council in chapter 15, but Overbeck argued instead that Luke was anti-Jewish and proposed the books were *nationale Antijudaismus*. Key to his argument was the theory that God had rejected "the Jews"—in Paul's words "turn[ed] to the Gentiles" (13:46; see also 18:6 and 28:28).[2] Overbeck was followed by Loisy in the early 1900s, and the trend continued for the next few decades with the likes of Ernst Haenchen also proposing anti-Semitic bias in Luke.[3] There are several places where the Jews appear hostile to followers of Jesus, especially Paul, and appear to be depicted as a distinct and hostile group, and this led such scholars to think that Luke saw Christians and Jews as distinct religious groups. For instance, in Acts 13:50, "the Jews" incite women of high standing and leading men of the city to persecute Paul and Barnabas, causing them to flee to Iconium, and in 13:51 and 9:23 "the Jews" plot to kill him. Furthermore, "the Jews" are depicted as "filled with jealousy; and blaspheming", as Paul preaches in

Acts 13:45 (NRSV). In Acts 14:4, the residents of the city are said to be divided, some siding with "the Jews" and others with the apostles, supposedly indicating that the Jews are here depicted as an antagonistic group, collectively understood as contrary to the apostles. The trend of Jewish persecution of Christians seems to continue in Thessalonica in 17:13, in Syria in 20:3, and pretty much wherever Paul preached. Christians were therefore "distinct" from Jews, receiving this name for the first time in 26:28.

Yet the depiction of Jews in Acts is not straightforward. What of those mass conversions we mentioned earlier, for instance? Haenchen posited that the Church enjoyed conversions of Jews in the early days and was persecuted only by Jewish leaders at first, as represented in Acts 3–5, but that the tide turned with the martyrdom of Stephen, whose speech was directed angrily against the Jews of his own day and represented a split between Christians as the true heirs to the promises made to the Israelites and "the Jews".[4] For Haenchen, this speech was part of a progression of negativity toward "the Jews" in the narrative of Acts, and Acts 8–11 then switched focus from the mission to Jews to the (more successful) mission to the gentiles. By Acts 12, he claimed that "the Jews" were in complete opposition to Christianity and thus Paul's missionary activity became redirected toward the gentiles, beginning at Antioch in 13:46.[5] Gerhard Lohfink similarly posited that Stephen's speech marked a turning point.[6] Taking Luke 2:34, the declaration that Jesus will be for the fall and rise of many in Israel, as his starting point, Lohfink suggested that Luke and Acts were detailing the early Church's response to the *krisis* [crisis] of what constituted the "true Israel" as many Jews rejected Jesus. The conversions of thousands of Jews constitute the "ingathering" of Israel that became the Church, with those who rejected Jesus losing their "right" to be called God's people, ceasing to be "Israel" and instead becoming "the Jews".[7] The initial ingathering represented only an initial period of apostolic preaching, and the failure to convert all Israel resulted in the gospel message going to the gentiles, the adoption of whom into the Church resulted in the formation of the "true Israel".[8] Ideas of a "divided Israel" are also found in the work of Conzelmann, George, and Gnika.[9]

This debate was taken up in the final quarter of the last century by Jack T. Sanders.[10] Sanders argues that the blame for the Crucifixion is in some places leveled at the Jewish officials, the chief priests and scribes plotting to kill Jesus in Luke 22:2, and the Temple authorities and Temple soldiers arresting Jesus and crucifying him, respectively.[11] At other times, though, Luke blames the Jewish people as a whole. Again, Stephen's speech was key, for at the end, just before his martyrdom at Jewish hands, Stephen declares: "Which of the prophets did not your fathers persecute? And they killed those who announced beforehand the coming of the Righteous One, whom you have now betrayed and murdered, you who received the law as delivered by angels and did not keep it" (Acts 7:52–53). By this, Sanders says, Stephen intends for all Jews to receive the blame for the Crucifixion.[12]

Sanders does admit, however, that things are not as clear-cut as Haenchen and Lohfink present them because the references to Jewish conversions do not stop in the early chapters of Acts—for instance, some Jews "believed" in Acts 14:1 and 17:11–12.[13] This leaves Luke's attitude toward Jews a bit of a mystery. Sanders claims that Luke was redefining what it was to be the "People of God". The traditional Jewish view was that Israel and Israel alone was God's people, but in Acts, God is said to take a people for himself out of the gentiles instead (see, for example, 15:14; 18:7–10).[14] Rather than suggest a divided Israel, however, Sanders insists that there was an initial "Jewish" incoming but that the overall depiction of "Jews" in Luke-Acts is of a rejected and spurned people, as evidenced in the speeches in Acts in particular. He, too, drawing on Lohfink, argues that the Stephen event marks a turning point.[15] Sanders claims this specifically against the backdrop of Roman occupation and persecution in the late-first/early-second century and states that Luke's anti-Jewish stance is essentially a polemic intended to draw a distinction between Jews and Christians, protecting the latter from accusations of being seditious. He even goes so far as to say that "Christian Jews can be valid Christians, in Luke's opinion, only to the degree that they are willing to recognize that Christianity is not a part of Judaism, is not Judaism, is in fact a Gentile religion."[16] He bases this view on the decision of the Jerusalem council not to impose Torah observance on gentile converts save to abstain from fornication, food sacrificed to idols, blood, and the meat of strangled animals (see 15:20), claiming that were Jewish Christians to impose any more on gentile followers than what that council decided, it would earn them the title "hypocrite" like the Pharisees.[17] Here, he perhaps finds a friend in Conzelmann, who saw the "Law" as being replaced by the apostolic decree of the council, thus rendering the time when the Torah was observed before Christ an epoch that had reached its conclusion.[18]

In Defense of Jewish Christianity in Acts

For the Hebrew Catholic reading such accounts, it seems all might be lost for our spirituality. According to these interpretations, we are an aberration, something that was supposed to have died out at the Church's very inception. Acts is not always read as a philo-semitic text, much less a Jewish-Christian one. How else, then, could a Hebrew Catholic approach Luke's ecclesiology?

Firstly, not all scholars have thought the same way. Jacob Jervell takes a very different view of Luke-Acts. He concedes that one of the main problems in scholarship is a tendency to think that the Church is in some way "the New Israel" when, in fact, this term is not present anywhere in the New Testament.[19] For Jervell, the story of Luke-Acts is not one of the *rejection* of Jesus by the Jews, but rather their *acceptance* of him.

Jervell also accepts that the coming of the Messiah created a crisis for God's "people", but his resolution for understanding Luke-Acts is very different from that of Lohfink, Overbeck, or Sanders. Firstly, the term "the people" is important in that there are only two exceptions where "the people" are mentioned apart from Israel as the People of God: in 15:14, which we have already seen refers to God's taking a people from among the gentiles for his name, and 18:10, where God says there are a number of his "people" in Corinth.[20] The overall usage would indicate that there is only really one "People of God" and that gentiles are assimilated into it, though he says that it is specifically *God-fearer gentiles* who are allowed in: a group of gentiles that had already partially integrated with Jews, keeping part of the Torah.[21] This view finds some support in the Council of Jerusalem in chapter 15. It has been argued that when the apostles decree that gentiles should abstain from things polluted by idols, blood, the flesh of strangled animals, and fornication (see 15:20), this was a kind of bare minimum of the Torah that was going to be retained for the sake of peace, for Jewish or gentile "converts" alike, even though the text itself makes it explicit that these commands were intended only for gentile believers.[22]

However, the precepts that gentiles are told to retain as a result of the Council of Jerusalem are, in fact, derived from the Holiness Code in Leviticus 17–18, which made provisions for sojourners with Israel, among which were detailed prohibitions on consuming blood or animals not killed according to ritual, sacrificing to idols, and fornication (see especially Lev 18:26).[23] That is to say, when gentiles dwelt with Israelites, under the Law, they were put under certain restrictions, and these are now retained by the early Christian community—not in contradistinction to the Law, as is often assumed, but *because this is what the Law itself required gentiles to do* when mixing with Israelites. This ruling would seem to indicate that gentiles are seen to be *dwelling with Israelites* as part of God's people. "Taking a people from among the gentiles" thus refers not to the formation of a new people apart from Israel but to the creation of a believing gentile community that is in some way absorbed into the preexisting Israelite one, a kind of people within a people.[24]

Furthermore, as Jervell continues, throughout Acts, the Messiah is the fulfillment made to this one people, Israel. He is going to restore the kingdom to Israel (see Acts 1:6), rebuilding the House of David (see 2:30; 15:16–17) despite all their sins against God's action in history (see 7:9, 25; 13:26–31).[25] Rather than break his promises to Israel, God renews them, and God is always faithful, despite their unfaithfulness (see 7:5–8, 10, 33–60).[26] As the rejection of Israel does not appear to be envisaged at these points, why would rejection of "the Jews" suddenly occur when they reject another prophet, even if that "prophet" is the Messiah himself? If anything, this is a very Jewish paradigm![27]

For gentile Christians, it is easy to think of "Jews" as outsiders wherever they see the word in the New Testament, because from their vantage point, "the Jews" are a distinct group, other from themselves. However, as Hebrew Catholics in the Church, we are more keenly aware that this was not the situation for early Christians. They were, like us, Jews who came to faith in Jesus and were then confronted by those of our own community who had not come to such faith. However, we were, and are, still one people, in much the same way a member of a highly observant Chasidic group, like Chabad, would still recognize a Reform Jew as a Jew, but perhaps just one who needs to focus more on *Gemarah* or Torah learning. What gentiles describe as a "divided Israel" is not far off, but this does not mean that "the Jews" suddenly become "the enemy". As Marilyn Salmon points out, how one reads Luke-Acts and understands "the Jews" really depends on whether one sees Luke as an outsider or an insider of that community.[28] Outsiders form opinions of people collectively, creating stereotypes, but an insider does not have the necessary distance to do this.[29] Luke is clearly an "insider", knowledgeable about various types of Jews, Sadducees to Pharisees, which is precisely what causes Salmon to think that he must have some kind of "inside knowledge"[30]—this is not a gentile looking in; it is a Jew looking around. Furthermore, sometimes insiders might use the same words as outsiders to describe the group, for example, "the Jews", but they do not necessarily mean the same thing by it or lose their own identification with it; and sometimes language that might seem abusive when spoken by an outsider might be prophetic when spoken by an insider.[31] Stephen's speech is actually a good case in point, here: "You stiff-necked people, uncircumcised in heart and ears, you always resist the Holy Spirit. As your fathers did, so you do. Which of the prophets did not your fathers persecute? And they killed those who announced beforehand the coming of the Righteous One, whom you have now betrayed and murdered, you who received the law as delivered by angels and did not keep it" (Acts 7:51–53).

For Sanders, Luke was saying through Stephen that by nature Jews oppose God's will and have therefore lost all hope of salvation, but this is because he sees Luke as an outsider.[32] Once we see Luke as an insider, that position becomes untenable. We should be more likely to read it with David Tiede, who rightly acknowledges that this is a very Jewish indictment. He gives the example of Deuteronomy 31–34, where Moses announces a "destruction which verges on the utter annihilation of Israel", but we might also cite numerous passages from any one of the prophets, and the thrust of such prophetic "callings out" is usually to elicit repentance.[33] Indeed, Peter himself points to a generalized fulfillment of prophecy in 3:24: "And all the prophets who have spoken, from Samuel and those who came afterwards, also proclaimed these days." While there is no specific call to repentance in Stephen's speech, such is the usual reason for Luke's beratement of Israel in Acts 2:37–38; 3:19; 5:31; 17:30; and 26:20, and so it is likely that Stephen speaks in a similar vein.[34]

Oracles of punishment for rejecting the Lord, especially through idolatry, are common in the prophetic books in the Bible, starting with eighth-century prophecy in Amos (see, for example, Amos 2–5). However, also common are promises of restoration (see, for example, Amos 9), a pattern that persists down to the latter prophets (for example, Ezek 2; 37), often with Israel's land, that is, its promise, being handed over to gentiles as part of the punishment so that God will eventually be glorified when he restores his people as they turn to him. Such is the overall thrust of the book of Isaiah, for instance, and its view of the Day of the Lord, which is at once terrifying (see, for example, 13:9; 17:4–10; 24:21) and also heralds a glorious vindication of Israel's faithful and even a new era of peace (see 4:2–3; 10:20–27; 11:10; 25:9; 27:13; 29:18). Among the latter is also Isaiah 40:3, cited in Luke 3:3–4, and Jesus is presented by Luke as a prophet specifically like Isaiah in Luke 4:16–21, which references Isaiah 61:1–2, and, crucially, has a reference to the Day of the Lord:

> And he came to Nazareth, where he had been brought up; and he went to the synagogue, as was his custom, on the sabbath day. And he stood up to read; and there was given to him the book of the prophet Isaiah. He opened the book and found the place where it was written.
>
> "The Spirit of the Lord is upon me, because he has anointed me to preach good news to the poor. He has sent me to proclaim release to the captives and recovering of sight to the blind, to set at liberty those who are oppressed, to proclaim the acceptable year of the Lord."
>
> And he closed the book, and gave it back to the attendant, and sat down; and the eyes of all in the synagogue were fixed on him. And he began to say to them, "Today this Scripture has been fulfilled in your hearing." (Lk 4:16–21)

Compare this to the passage from Isaiah:

> The spirit of the Lord God is upon me, because the Lord has anointed me to bring good tidings to the afflicted; he has sent me to bind up the brokenhearted, to proclaim liberty to the captives, and the opening of the prison to those who are bound; to proclaim the year of the Lord's favor, and the day of vengeance of our God; to comfort all who mourn. (61:1–2)

Stephen also makes a reference to Isaiah in the final part of his speech in Acts 7:48–50, quoting Isaiah 66:1–2, before he berates his Jewish accusers, as above, which is evidence that this prophet is still in mind at this juncture. The influence of Isaiah is also apparent in the surrounding co-text. Shortly after, in Acts 8:28–33, Philip encounters the Ethiopian eunuch, who is reading from Isaiah 53:7–8, a significant messianic prophecy regarding the suffering servant too. From a discourse-analysis perspective, it is clear that Luke has in mind the salvific prophecies in Isaiah *after* Stephen's speech, and those who claim that he suddenly switches to favoring gentiles on the basis of Stephen's speech miss the fact that Luke continues to work within the framework of Israelite prophecy.

This "insider" framework is still present right until the end of the book. In Acts 28:17, Paul requests an audience with the Jewish leaders in Rome. On meeting them, he immediately lays out his Jewish credentials, saying, "I had done nothing against the people or the customs of our fathers, yet I was delivered prisoner from Jerusalem into the hands of the Romans." Here, he clearly identifies with "the Jews", before going on to speak about "the Jews" as a collective who are against him in verse 19, which would suggest that while those particular Jews might be against him, he is not thinking of himself as an outsider "Israelite" as distinct from a Jew, but rather as an "insider", referring to others of his own grouping. This is certainly true when we consider that he actually calls himself a Jew in Acts 21:39 and 22:3. It is notable that at this very point, in Acts 28:26–27, Paul then goes on to quote none other than Isaiah to berate his fellow Jews, quoting 6:9–10 about being dull of heart and hard of hearing when it comes to heeding the Lord. Whereas scholars favoring a supersessionist approach to Acts, whereby Christianity replaces Judaism, might point to the fact that Paul makes this statement and then immediately turns to the gentiles in verse 28, nevertheless, some of the Jewish leaders are convinced by him (see verse 24). Others are not, true enough, but nonetheless, they are not depicted as Israelites as apart from Jews, but as Jewish leaders to whom Paul the Jew shows reverence, and the argument Paul makes is clearly Jew-on-Jew, even at the end of the book. Interestingly, there is perhaps a hint at hope for the belief of all Israel, as Paul is allowed by them to continue preaching without hindrance (see verse 30). One might argue this is possible only because he has said he has turned to the gentiles and so is allowed by the leaders to continue on his way, but this is not explicitly stated in the text, and he is said to welcome *all* who come to him and to preach to them about the coming of the kingdom and Jesus Christ. Given his history of preaching in synagogues, this likely includes Jews.

There is, in fact, a prophetic precedent for the ingathering of the gentiles, into whose power faithless Israel and Judah were pushed in days of exile. In the Bible are various prophecies about the Day(s) of the Lord or an upcoming era of peace and ingathering/return of the nation following exile. What is more, they sometimes specifically include the idea of gentiles simultaneously turning to the Lord as per Isaiah 19:21. A restoration of Israel that somehow incorporates gentiles as part of the People of God is, I consider, somewhat most visible in Isaiah, where in the peaceful times to come, gentiles take up Israelite worship of God, on God's holy mountain and so with his original nation, specifically in their temple—that is, alongside Israelites in union with them, where the gentiles bring offerings:

> On this mountain the LORD of hosts will make for all peoples a feast of fat things, a feast of choice wines—of fat things full of marrow, of choice wines well refined. And he will destroy on this mountain the covering that is cast over all peoples, the veil that is spread over all nations. He will swallow up death for ever. (25:6–7)

> These I will bring to my holy mountain,
> and make them joyful in my house of prayer;
> their burnt offerings and their sacrifices
> will be accepted on my altar;
> for my house shall be called a house of prayer
> for all peoples. (56:7)

Another prophet to the gentiles was Jeremiah, who in Jeremiah 1:4–10 is designated as such even before his birth and indeed addresses his prophecies to both God's people and the gentiles throughout the book. He, too, is concerned with the Day of the Lord (see, for example, 46:10) and with the institution of a New Covenant (see Jer 31). In both cases, this era is not possible save for the sins of Israel, which is exactly how Paul and Barnabas respond when rejected by Jews in Acts 13:46–47, this time quoting Isaiah 49:6: "Both Paul and Barnabas spoke out boldly, saying, 'It was necessary that the word of God should be spoken first to you. Since you thrust it from you, and judge yourselves unworthy of eternal life, behold, we turn to the gentiles. For so the Lord has commanded us, saying, "I have set you to be a light for the Gentiles, that you may bring salvation to the uttermost parts of the earth."'"

Notably, this does not mean they are turning solely to gentiles. Indeed, they go on to preach in various synagogues (see Acts 13:5, 14, 43; 14:1; 17:1, 10; 18:7, 26). The overall depiction of their mission is that it is twofold and that the idea they argue, that Jewish prophecies have been fulfilled, also seems to be behind 17:11, where the Berean Jews eagerly receive the good news and examine the Scripture every day to see whether what Paul said was true.

There is a clear sense in Acts that what has happened in the coming of Jesus is the fulfillment of Israelite prophecy, and it therefore makes sense to consider the rejection of Jesus on the part of some Jews in this light, not to perceive the nation itself as being rejected.[35] Indeed, even if many were destroyed by God's wrath during the exile, there is a promised remnant that will bring about the salvation of the nation, even if not everyone makes it back to the Holy Land (see Is 10:19–21; 11:11, 16; 37:11, 31; but cf. 2 Kings 19:31; Ezra 9:13–14; Jer 6:9; 23:3; 50:20, to name a few). Arguably, the apostles and Jewish believers may even form such a remnant from which the nation of Israel is rebuilt in the Church. Importantly, at no point in Hebrew prophecy is it ever envisaged that this remnant is a separate nation from Israel. Rather, it represents the surviving shoot from which the bush regrows.[36]

It would seem that the paradigm of Old Testament prophecy should be the basis for understanding Luke's ecclesiology. The Church is not something distinct from Israel; it is rather the renewed Israel after the coming of the Messiah, which now also sees gentiles as part of its fold.

Thus far, we have essentially been discussing the idea of the restoration of Israel after the exile, when the people would return to the land. The paradigm of post-exilic restoration is found even in the earliest chapters of Acts. We said at the very start that Acts begins its narrative just after the Ascension and with the promise of the coming of the Holy Spirit, which happens at Pentecost, or Shavuot. Firstly, it should be noted that the Pentecost events take place on a Jewish festival, which in later tradition is seen by Jews as the day on which the Torah was given on Sinai (*b.T Pes.* 68b). While the relevance of this is sometimes questioned, given the later dating of the Talmud, Jubilees, dated to around 135–105 B.C., sees this festival as a renewal of the covenant in 6:17–21 and so the tradition appears much older.[37] Moses is, for Jews, the prophet of prophets, and this feast represents the anniversary of the most significant date in Israel's history, on which he communicated directly with God. Indeed, when the Spirit descends as tongues of fire, the appearance of fire is important because it was often a sign of the Torah, as in *b.T Ta'anith* 7a; *Bab. Bath.* 78b.[38] When we look at Philo, *On the Decalogue* 33, we see that in the late first century B.C. and first century A.D., the Torah was thought to have been given through flame, and so the Pentecost event is presented as an equally important encounter with God. What is more, the people hear God's voice in their own language: "Then from the midst of the fire that streamed from heaven there sounded forth to their utter amazement a voice, for the flame became articulate speech in the language familiar to the audience, and so clearly and distinctly were the words formed that they seemed to see rather than hear them."[39]

Now, to Philo, this probably means the collective language of the nation, Hebrew, but there could well be a similar idea underlying the *glossolalia* of Acts 2:4 when the apostles begin to speak in other languages and are understood by the crowd. Now I can get to the point. At Sinai, of course, the nation was united, but in Luke-Acts, it is clear the people are presented as divided and having been scattered and then regathered in what comes next. In terms of what was said previously, that the fulfillment of Israelite exilic prophecy is envisaged here, we may note, too, the nations from which the "pious Jews in Jerusalem" have come. The list is extensive: "Parthians and Medes and Elamites and residents of Mesopotamia, Judea and Cappadocia, Pontus and Asia, Phrygia and Pamphylia, Egypt and the parts of Libya belonging to Cyrene, and visitors from Rome, both Jews and proselytes, Cretans and Arabians" (Acts 2:9–11).

The list represents the fact that these pious Jews, prior to gathering in Jerusalem at the new Sinai, were scattered throughout the Roman Empire in exile.[40] Now, Shavuot was a pilgrim festival, so this may have simply been a historical fact, but it is a convenient one that hints at the ingathering of Israel back into one nation. This is the rebirth of the nation, the bringing of it back into God's presence in his holy city with an event every bit as important as the one on Sinai. Might this be the fulfillment of Jeremiah's promise of a New Covenant to be established after the exile in Jeremiah 31:31–34? It is indeed intriguing that Jeremiah said this covenant would be written on their hearts, and indeed the gentiles' hearts are said to have been cleansed *like those of the Jews* in Acts 15:8.[41] Although not citing Jeremiah, Peter's speech alludes to the "last days" by quoting Joel 2:28–32. He also goes on to reference prophecies made through David (see Acts 2:25–31), stating that the answer to the prophecies has now arrived in Jesus (see 2:22–35), most notably with the command to "repent, and be baptized" (2:38) in the name of Jesus so that they, too, will receive not only forgiveness but also the Holy Spirit. This same Spirit has just been represented as fire, just like the Torah (see 2:38); and so just as the Torah was given to the nation as a whole, here representatives of that nation, the remnant that will rebuild Israel, also receive a theophany. Interestingly, the idea of gentiles now being among the Israelites is also present, for some of these men are proselytes, those who had converted to Judaism (see 2:10).[42]

Let us summarize the position so far. We saw at the beginning how some scholars, starting with the early historical critics, believed that Acts is, essentially, an anti-Semitic document that posited a break between Jews and Christians from the earliest days. Central to this is Stephen's speech, which the likes of Haenchen, Lohfink, and Sanders saw as a turning point whereby God's favor switched to the gentiles. However, a closer examination of Acts reveals, in fact, that it is a very Jewish document, written by Luke, the Jewish insider. Luke placed the apostles' actions within the context of Israelite prophecy so as to stress that the time of exile had indeed ended and that the end times, which would include the incorporation of gentiles into the People of God, had arrived. So, what does Acts' post-exilic ecclesiology have to do with Hebrew Catholicism today? Importantly, it does not seem to be envisaged that these "pious Jews" give up their Jewishness, and especially not their Torah observance. Jervell also acknowledges that according to Luke, the early Christians live as pious Jews, and not just in the first few chapters, as some would have it. This was, in fact, the very reason that the Council of Jerusalem was called in the first place (see 15:5). However, whereas the scholars we first assessed saw that council as insisting that the Jewish Law was obsolete following that council, Acts itself does not present the same picture. Indeed, even after that declaration, in 16:3, Paul even has Timothy circumcised.[43] This is not lost on Salmon, either, who notes that Luke's heroes are Torah-observant (see, for example, Acts 21:22–26; 23:4–5),[44] and Jesus himself acts in accordance with the Law (see Luke 2:22, 27; 13:14), which goes back to what we said earlier about how the decree of the council that gentiles should abstain from certain things but not be circumcised itself comes from the holiness code. We can now add that nowhere is it suggested that Jews should not be circumcised. With regard to Timothy, as Bryan points out, his circumcision seems strange if circumcision has been reduced to naught at the council.[45] Indeed, Timothy's mother is identified as Jewish in Acts 16:1, and, questions over when a Jewish mother's identity resulted in a Jewish child's Jewish identity aside, he has Jewish heritage.[46] Luke's need to defend Jewish Christians as Torah-observant also stands behind Acts 21:20: "When they heard it, they glorified God. And they said to him, 'You see, brother, how many thousands there are among the Jews of those who have believed; they are all zealous for the law.'" The depiction of Paul in Acts has also been widely discussed since he depicts himself as Torah-observant (see, for example, 21:17–23; 25:8)—indeed, we saw earlier that Paul, far from rejecting his identity, still identifies as a Pharisee and faithful Jew and offers this as his defense when on trial:[47] "I am a Jew, born at Tarsus in Cilicia, but brought up in this city at the feet of Gamaliel, educated according to the strict manner of the law of our fathers, being zealous for God as you all are this day" (22:3).

Torah observance might also be troubling for those trying to interpret Peter's vision in Acts 10:1—11:8. Peter is shown a vision from heaven of all manner of animals, which he is commanded to kill and eat. Peter piously declines because he has never eaten anything unclean but is again told to kill and eat, a total of three times. David B. Woods rightly points out that the almost uniform understanding of this passage is that it pertains to the making clean of all food. While I am willing to concede that there are other biblical passages that suggest such a thing (see, for example, Mk 7:19), this is not necessarily the case in Acts.[48] Scholars like Mark Kinzer, D.A. Carson, D.J. Moo, and David Stern have all noted the possibility.[49] The argument here goes that the Greek does not actually have "what God has made clean, you must not call unclean" in Acts 10:15, but rather "the things ...", leaving open the question of what, or who, exactly was meant.[50] Unlike in other biblical visions where the prophet then does what he has been shown in the visions (see, for example, Hos 1:2–3; Is 20:2–3), Peter does not then go and eat nonkosher food.[51] Rather, he goes shortly after to meet a gentile who appears to be a God-fearer—that is, someone sympathetic to Jews who lives among them and thus, Jervell argues, likely obeys dietary laws![52] In verse 28, Peter actually states that the vision pertained to gentiles.[53] Indeed, he has hitherto seen them as "unclean" (v. 28), but as he says at the council in 15:11, they have been made clean.[54] In Peter's vision, there are also clean animals, but he *will not eat* the unclean ones. The fact that he does not go on to eat nonkosher food suggests that he held those animals still to be unclean. However, it is different with people, for they have been made clean and so are not to be counted like unclean animals. Even though the charge is that he ate with gentiles in Acts 11:3, Peter possibly did not understand the vision to mean he should eat nonkosher food, but rather that people were of a different order from unclean animals, and so it was fine to mix with them. Indeed, it is people who are made clean in verses 15–17 through baptism. This is not the only possible reading, but if the vision did not pertain to making all things edible, this would make sense in the context of Acts when Paul can still keep the Law (and indeed insists on it). In fact, he even goes to extra stringencies when he takes a vow, presumably that of a Nazirite, in Acts 18:18—they were to abstain from hair cutting and alcohol and certainly from things unclean (see Num 6:2–18).

For Hebrew Catholics, these observations are vitally important. For centuries, Jews entering the Church have been made to assimilate on the assumption that the Church replaced the Jewish people. This is what lies behind not only the supersessionist interpretations of Acts that we saw in the first section of this chapter but also the harsh writings of the apostolic fathers and, even more importantly, Church councils like Florence, which is covered elsewhere in this volume. While the harsh edicts like those of session 16, which forced unbearable penalties on those who wished to continue with Jewish customs in the Church, have since been softened with the publication of *Ex quo primum* and Vatican II, and subsequent documents have sought to cast Judaism in a more positive light, it is still the case that Hebrew Catholics are generally expected to give up their Jewish identity. Once the reality has arrived, why bother with the shadows? Why would you want to keep up older rites when the newer rite is here? However, once we realize that the Church is by nature Jewish, those shadows cease to be shadows and become guiding lights for understanding the faith: The anamnesis of the Mass as resulting from the anamnesis of the Seder can help deepen the sense of being on the Cross with Christ and raised with him from the tomb, as we understand that it is *we* who are being led out of Egypt *and* up Calvary; the need for the confession of sin and its connection to sacrifice can similarly highlight the importance of the sacrament of reconciliation. Certainly, too, the connection between the giving of the Law and God's imparting of his Spirit can spur us to a new life of obedience to the divine will as we realize that we are united to the Divine through keeping his commandments.

A proper understanding of Acts goes a long way to proposing an ecclesiology that sees the Church not in supersessionist terms but in terms of the fulfillment of the promises made to Israel and thus recenters the Church on its innately Jewish identity. This affords the Hebrew Catholic a chance to live out his Jewish vocation to be a light to the gentiles, and the wider Church the opportunity to learn from the oldest Christian spirituality for the benefit, and thereby salvation, of souls.[55]

3

Christ as Temple in John: From Signs to Sacraments?

Scott W. Hahn

The significance of the Jerusalem Temple in John's Gospel has been the subject of many monographs and articles in recent decades. As a result of this work, scholars now generally accept not only that the Temple is a central theme in the Fourth Gospel but also that John is advancing what might be characterized as a "Temple Christology"—that is, John wishes to show how the Temple and its liturgy and feasts find their fulfillment in Jesus Christ, especially in his death and Resurrection.[1]

However, if our interpretation of John stops with that scholarly consensus—that John portrays Jesus as the fulfillment of the Temple—we are left with an apparently disconcerting situation; for, since Christ is now ascended, our Temple must be gone. If this is true, the Church's situation would be not unlike that of Judaism after A.D. 70 and the destruction of the Temple.[2] But John's Temple Christology is not conceived so narrowly as to limit it to Christ's immediate person and earthly ministry. Rather, the evangelist insists that Jesus' ministry continues in and through the intermediaries of the Spirit and the apostles.

At issue here is a significant but hitherto underappreciated aspect of the "Jewishness" of Jesus and the Church. In this essay, I want to pursue these broader lines of the Temple fulfillment theme in John. In particular, I want to explore how John envisions Christ's ongoing fulfillment of the Temple and its festivals as taking place through the sacraments celebrated by the power of the Spirit, especially the sacraments of baptism and the Eucharist.[3]

I will begin by briefly reviewing the depiction of the Temple in the Old Testament and its significance for the Old Covenant People of God. This may enable us to understand better how John's first-century Jewish readers would have received his identification of Jesus as the replacement of the Temple and its festivals.

Following that, I will examine the first Passover narrative in John (2:13—3:21). This will show three things: first, that John depicts Jesus as the "new Temple" at the outset of his public ministry, a theme he pursues throughout his Gospel; second, that Jesus performs his "signs" in the context of this broader fulfillment of the Temple and the Temple festivals; and third, that in the dialogue with Nicodemus, Jesus moves from his "signs" to the sacrament of baptism, that is, rebirth by the Spirit (see Jn 3:3, 5).

I will then consider John's narratives of the second Passover (Jn 6) and the feast of Tabernacles (Jn 7–9). I hope to show that in these accounts, too, Jesus functions as the new Temple, that the Temple festivals are the context for Jesus' "signs", and that the "signs" he performs point forward to the sacraments of baptism and the Eucharist.

Moving to the third and final Passover narrative of the Gospel (Jn 11:55—20:31), I will focus on Jesus' farewell discourse (Jn 13–17), in which he confers on the disciples his own "Templeness" and commissions them to continue his mission—indeed, to perform "greater works than these" (14:12). I will suggest that the sacraments fall under this category of "greater works" and that this interpretation is supported by consideration of John 19:34, which symbolically depicts the sacraments flowing from the death and Resurrection of Christ, and John 20:22–23, in which the apostles receive the Spirit in order to perform the "greater work" of remitting sins.

This exploration will allow me to suggest the conclusion that if one follows the logic and symbolism of John's Gospel, the sacraments, primarily baptism and the Eucharist, truly are the specific times and places in which the believer continues to experience Christ as the new Temple.

New Testament "fulfillment" of the Old is, as Pope Benedict XVI stated, a "complex" topic.[4] The subject of fulfillment implies that "*the New Testament itself acknowledges the Old Testament as the word of God* and thus accepts the authority of the sacred Scriptures of the Jewish people."[5] The events of the New Testament, then, find their background and authority in the pages of the Old: "The New Testament itself claims to be consistent with the Old and proclaims that in the mystery of the life, death and resurrection of Christ the sacred Scriptures of the Jewish people have found their perfect fulfilment."[6] There is, therefore, profound continuity in the midst of development and fulfillment of the promises. We will see, in what follows, how John's Temple Christology is true to this pattern.

The Centrality of the Temple in Ancient Israel

The literature on both the historical role of the Temple in ancient Israel and its literary importance in the Scriptures is enormous.[7] From this literature, I wish briefly to make the following points:

First, the Temple was *the dwelling place* of God's "name" (see Deut 16:2; Ps 74:7), his "glory" (see 1 Kings 8:10–11; Ezek 43:2–5), and finally, God himself (see Ps 68:16; Ezek 43:6).

Second, the Temple was *the embodiment of God's covenant with David*.[8] The central text of the divine covenant with David (see 2 Sam 7:8–16) focuses on a son of David who will build a "house" for God (that is, the Temple), and for whom God will build a "house" (that is, a dynastic kingdom). The immediate, though penultimate, fulfillment of this covenant was found in David's son, Solomon, who, like David, was an "anointed" one—that is, a "Messiah" (Hebrew) or "Christ" (Greek) (see 1 Kings 1:34, 39). He also enjoyed the status of "son of God" according to the terms of the covenant (see 2 Sam 7:14; Ps 2:6–7). In King Solomon we have a "christ", a Temple-builder, and the first *individual* in the canon of Scripture to be described as "son of God".

Third, the Temple was *the place of pilgrimage and priestly ministry*. Three times a year, all the men of Israel were required to journey to the Temple to celebrate the feasts of Passover, Pentecost, and Tabernacles (see Deut 16:1–17). For Israelites, participating in these feasts meant undergoing water washings (ablutions) to enter a state of ritual purity (see Ex 19:10–11; 2 Chron 30:17–20; Lev 11–15; and especially 15:31).[9] Only then were Israelites able to offer sacrifice (see Deut 16:2, 6; Lev 23:8) and participate in the feast, which principally involved eating and drinking (see Deut 16:3, 7–8; see also Lev 7:11–17; 2 Chron 30:22; Is 25:6): usually the meat of the sacrifice (see Deut 16:4, 7), with bread (see Deut 16:3; Lev 23:6) and wine (see Is 25:6; Lk 22:18, 20), the fruits of the Promised Land (see Deut 16:13).[10] Through participation in these Temple sacrifices, Israelites made atonement for their sins (see, for example, Lev 4:20, 26, 35; 5:10, 13; 19:22; 15:25). The entire experience of the Temple—the ritual washings, the sacrifice, the eating and drinking, and the remission of sin—was possible only because of the work of the Temple ministers: the high priest, his fellow priests, and the Levites.

Finally, a new Temple, often with divine properties, is a *central feature of the eschatology* of some of the prophets (see, for example, Ezek 40–4; Joel 3:17–18) and at least an important feature in several others (cf. Zech 6:12–15; 8:9–12; 14:16–21; Is 2:1–4; 56:3–6; 66:18–22; Jer 33:10–11; Hag 2:1–9, 15–19; Dan 8:14; 9:17, 24–27; Mic 1:1–4)—especially when one takes into account the relationship of the Temple, Zion, and Jerusalem.[11] It will be useful to bear in mind these points concerning the Temple as we proceed to explore John's deployment of Temple and Temple-festival motifs in his Gospel, especially in relation to Jesus.

The First Passover and the Cleansing of the Temple

While the Synoptic tradition describes the public ministry of Jesus as beginning in Galilee, John chooses instead to show Jesus revealing himself first in Judea, beginning in Jerusalem, at the Temple during the Passover (see Jn 2:13—3:21).[12] Moreover, during these opening public scenes, John depicts Jesus proclaiming himself to be the new Temple (see 2:19–21). Indeed, the majority of John's Gospel is set in Jerusalem, and specifically in the Temple.[13] Moreover, most of the events in John take place during seven Temple feasts, the succession of which serve to structure much of the narrative:[14] Passover (see 2:13—3:21); a Sabbath feast, possibly Pentecost (see 5:1–47); Passover again (see 6:1–71); Tabernacles (see 7:1—10:21); Sabbath (see 9:14); Dedication (see 10:22–39); and the final Passover (see 11:55—20:31). The account of Jesus' cleansing of the Temple thus announces themes that are unique to John and will continue to be emphasized throughout his Gospel: Jerusalem, the Temple, and the Temple feasts.[15]

Jesus' teachings and "signs" during these liturgical festivals often correspond to the central themes of the festivals themselves; some scholars have gone so far as to argue that they relate specifically to the Jewish lectionary readings for those feasts.[16] What is John's intention in emphasizing the Temple and the festivals? I would argue that it is to demonstrate that Christ is the fulfillment of the Temple and the worship performed there.[17]

Since Deuteronomy specified that the Passover lamb must be sacrificed at the central sanctuary (see Deut 16:2), the celebration of Passover became inextricably bound to the Tabernacle and later to the Temple. The Passover was arguably the greatest pilgrim feast of Judaism in the period of the First and Second Temple.[18] Its importance is reflected in the fact that John records three Passover celebrations during Jesus' public ministry. John may have known of Jewish traditions that anticipated the arrival of the Messiah at Passover.[19]

In John 2:13–25, we see Jesus, recently identified as king of Israel (see 1:49), showing his solicitude for the well-being of the Temple. Driving out the merchants and money changers, he rebukes them for making his "Father's house" (*oikon tou patros mou*) a "house of trade" (*oikon emporiou*). Jesus' actions and words here should be understood in light of Zechariah 14:21, which says of the eschatological Temple: "There shall no longer be a trader in the house of the LORD of hosts on that day."[20] The Judeans question Jesus: "What *sign* have you to show us for doing this?" to which Jesus responds: "Destroy this temple, and in three days I will raise it up." They misunderstand, but the evangelist clarifies: "He spoke of the temple of his body" (Jn 2:18–19, 21).

Although the literature on this passage is vast,[21] here we should summarize just some salient points. First, by beginning Jesus' public ministry with the Temple cleansing, John casts his whole ministry in light of the concept that he is the new Temple.[22] Second, by calling the destruction and raising of his Temple-body a "sign", John establishes a strong link between this narrative and the account of Jesus' death and Resurrection. This suggests that his death and Resurrection should be interpreted as a Temple-(re)building account, while at the same time identifying in advance these events as the climactic "sign" in the sequence of "signs" that help to structure the narrative.[23] The "sign" of his death and Resurrection—the "destruction" and "raising up" of his Temple-body—is the definitive "sign" toward which all the others are ordered.

Thus, we can see that John introduces the theme of Jesus as the new Temple in John 2:13–21 in order to pursue that theme at key points throughout the remainder of his Gospel. As numerous scholars have noted from the strong literary connections, the Passover and new Temple contexts of John 2:13–25 are carried over to the next passage, Jesus' dialogue with Nicodemus (see 3:1–21).

The Temple cleansing culminated in a discussion of the "signs" (*semeia*) that Jesus performed and how "men" (*anthropoi*) came to believe in his name because of the signs. This leads directly into Jesus' conversation with Nicodemus, who is presented in the very next verse (3:1) as a "man" (*anthropos*) who has come to believe because of the "signs" (*semeia*). Thus, the conversation with Nicodemus should be understood against the context of Jesus having indicated himself to be the new Temple during Passover.

Nicodemus comes to Jesus to discuss the "signs". The use of the term *semeia* ("signs") to describe Jesus' miracles is characteristic of John's Gospel. The Synoptics typically use the term *dynameis* ("mighty deeds") to describe the same phenomena. The difference in terminology seems intentional. John employs "signs" because he wishes to stress the role of the miracles not as ends in themselves but as indicators or pointers to a deeper reality—such as Jesus' identity as Messiah, Son of God, indeed, God himself.[24] The signs do point to Jesus' messianic and divine identity, to be sure; but, as I will argue, they also point to something greater than themselves—the coming activity of the Spirit in the sacraments, which continues the presence and work of Christ himself.

The Gospel, as scholars have suggested, is structured according to a succession of Jesus' signs that are all associated with Israel's liturgical feasts.

Nicodemus wants to discuss Jesus' signs, which he understands as physical miracles indicating divine power at work through Jesus:

> This man came to Jesus by night and said to him, "Rabbi, we know that you are a teacher come from God; for no one can do these signs that you do, unless God is with him." Jesus answered him, "Truly, truly, I say to you, unless one is born anew [*anōthen*], he

> cannot see the kingdom of God." Nicodemus said to him, "How can a man be born when he is old? Can he enter a second time into his mother's womb and be born?" Jesus answered, "Truly, truly, I say to you, unless one is born of water and the Spirit, he cannot enter the kingdom of God." (3:1–5)

Nicodemus interprets Jesus' words in terms of *physical miracles*—this is as much as he has been able to comprehend about the "signs" to this point. His incomprehension is detected in his inquiry about how a man can return to his mother's womb. He is understandably baffled because even granted that Jesus has miraculous powers over the physical world, the physical requirements for a rebirth in the natural sense seem not only supernatural but also counternatural and positively absurd. Jesus continues: "Unless one is born of water and the Spirit, he cannot enter the kingdom of God."

This statement clarifies his meaning, and now the reader, if not Nicodemus, begins to understand that Jesus is talking about baptism.[25] John has prepared the reader to associate water, baptism, the Spirit, and divine sonship almost from the beginning of the Gospel. In his prologue, he emphasized the need to become "children of God" by being "born ... of God"—as opposed to natural birth "of blood ... of the will of the flesh [or] the will of a man" (1:12–13). In addition, John has already given the reader an account of Jesus' own baptism in water, in which the Spirit descends and marks Jesus out, not only as child but also as "Son of God" (1:31–34).

Here in his audience with Nicodemus, the motifs of water, baptism, Spirit, and divine sonship are all correlated. Jesus' words about being "born again (anew)", that is, becoming a child once more, and being "born of water and the Spirit" pick up on those motifs of divine begetting associated with water and the Spirit announced earlier in the Gospel.[26] John's Christian readers would have understood the reference to rebirth by "water and the Spirit" as a reference to Christian baptism, as the evangelist no doubt intended them to.[27] It is not accidental that the Nicodemus dialogue is followed immediately by references to Jesus and the disciples baptizing (see 3:22), further description of John the Baptist's baptismal ministry, and a discussion of ritual washing leading to affirmation of Jesus' divine sonship (see 3:23–36), and yet another account of Jesus' baptismal ministry (see 4:1–3).

There is a discernible effort made by Jesus in this dialogue to lead Nicodemus from an "earthly" sphere of reference to a "heavenly" one. Jesus' conversation implies a dualism between the "Spirit" (*pneuma*) and the "flesh" (*sarx*), between the "heavenly" (*epourania*) and the "earthly" (*epigeia*). Clearly, his intent is to guide Nicodemus from the lower to the higher, from the earthly to the heavenly,[28] with the earthly regarded as precondition of the heavenly: "If I have told you earthly things and you do not believe, how can you believe if I tell you heavenly things?" (3:12).[29] This form of pedagogy from the "earthly" to "heavenly" may aptly be described by the term "mystagogy".[30] In particular, in the Nicodemus dialogue, there is a mystagogy that leads from the *signs* that Jesus performs to the activity of the Spirit in the *sacraments*—in this case, the sacrament of baptism.

Jesus' words and actions in this Passover narrative, then, point forward to a great "sign" yet to come—the destruction and raising of his body, also during the Passover. By this great sign, Jesus will replace the stone Temple (with his body, the new Temple—see 2:21) and will fulfill the Passover (himself becoming the "Lamb of God"—see 1:29, 36). But the fulfillment of Temple and Passover is not the final *terminus* toward which this climactic finish to his "signs" points. This reading is supported by the mystagogical catechesis given to Nicodemus. All this suggests that John envisions the fulfillment of the Temple and the Passover continuing in the sacramental signs of the Church, which themselves point to the work of the Spirit.[31]

"The Holy Place" and the Temple of the Church

The account of the first Passover in John (2:13—3:21) has prepared the reader to interpret the death and Resurrection of Jesus in the third Passover (11:55—20:31) as the destruction and rebuilding of the true Temple, and nothing less. The clearest references to the Temple motif in the last discourse is to be found in John 14:2–3: "In my Father's house [*oikia tou patros mou*] are many rooms [*monē*]; if it were not so, would I have told you that I go to prepare a place [*topos*] for you? And when I go and prepare a place [*topos*] for you, I will come again and will take you to myself, that where I am you may be also."

We have here several significant deployments of Temple terms and images.[32] First, the phrase "Father's house" recalls the nearly identical description of the Temple in John 2:16 ("my Father's house"). The two expressions are certainly close enough for the connection to be made easily, yet there is a subtle, theologically significant alteration. In John 2:16, the phrase *oikos tou patros mou* employs the expected term, *oikos*, used in the Septuagint translation to describe the Temple, the palace, and other large buildings in the Temple complex. In John 14:2, however, the phrase is *oikia tou patros mou*, using *oikia*, which also means "house" but frequently tends toward a more personal and familial rather than architectural sense—"household", "home", or even "family". I concur with the detailed arguments of Mary Coloe and James McCaffrey that a shift is taking place in John 14:2–3 as compared with John 2:16: The sense of the new Temple is being extended from Jesus' physical body to the community of God—that is, to God's "household" or "family".[33]

The Temple reference in the phrase "Father's house" is confirmed by other Temple allusions in these verses. The reference to a "house" with "many rooms" could not fail to bring to mind the Jerusalem Temple, the largest and most multichambered edifice known to the Jewish reader. Indeed, the Temple's "many rooms" are immortalized in certain passages of the Old Testament (see Ezek 40–42).[34]

Jesus goes on to speak of preparing a "place" (*topos*; *mâqôm*) for the disciples. It is not coincidental that the last employment of "place" (*topos*) was in John 11:48, where Caiaphas, the high priest, used it as shorthand for "holy place", a meaning it bears frequently throughout the Old Testament, especially in Deuteronomy and related texts.[35] Furthermore, the Septuagint translation employs the exact phrase John uses—"prepare a place" (*etoimazō ton topon*)—exclusively with respect to the tent-shrine of the Ark of the Covenant (see 1 Chron 15:1, 3) or the Temple itself (see 2 Chron 3:1).

Thus, Jesus is telling his disciples that his departure is necessary to prepare a Temple sanctuary for them in which they will dwell with him. Frequently this is understood in terms of a heavenly, eschatological fulfillment—the disciples will dwell with Jesus forever in the "Temple" of heaven. While an eschatological sense should not be excluded, one must also take into account that in the chapter that follows this, Jesus clearly speaks of the disciples "abiding" (*menō*) in

Christ even now, in this life. The sense of "abiding" should not be isolated from the sense of the "abiding places" (*monē*) that Jesus will prepare for the disciples in John 14:2. One also must be cognizant of 14:23: "If a man loves me ... my Father will love him, and we will come to him and make our home [dwelling, *monē*] with him."

Thus, Jesus goes to prepare a (holy) "place" for the disciples, with dwellings (*monē*) for them, but simultaneously the Father and Son will come to the faithful disciple and make their dwelling (*monē*) with him. Therefore, John 14 taken as a whole describes a mutual indwelling of Father and Son with the disciples, a mutual indwelling that is treated at greater length and more explicitly in the (eucharistic) vine discourse of John 15:1–17, with its stress on "abiding" or "dwelling" (*menō*). All this suggests that Jesus' promise to prepare a Temple in which the disciples shall abide will be realized now, in this age, through the divine indwelling in the midst of the believing community as a living Temple.[36] The disciples will be constituted a Temple by the Spirit, whom the Father and the Son will send after Jesus departs.

The idea of the believing community as Temple—a concept also present in the scrolls found at Qumran[37]—resonates on a deep level with other themes of the last discourse, especially when these are understood in light of Old Testament Temple traditions. As I noted earlier, the Temple was the dwelling place of the name of God (see, for example, Deut 16:2; Ps 74:7), the glory of God (see, for example, 1 Kings 8:1; Ezek 43:2), and indeed, of God himself (see Ps 68:16; Ezek 43:6). Compare these characteristics of the Temple with what is said about the disciples during the last discourse: They are the locus of the *name* of God: "I have manifested your name to the men whom you gave me out of the world.... I have made known to them your name" (Jn 17:6, 26). They have received the *glory*: "The glory which you have given me I have given to them, that they may be one even as we are one" (17:22). They are the dwelling of God: "The Spirit of truth ... dwells with you, and will be in you" (14:17); "If a man loves me ... we will come to him and make our home with him" (14:23). As Jesus spoke of the Father having "consecrated" (*hagiazō*) him as the new Temple during the feast of Dedication (see 10:36), so now Jesus prays for the Father to consecrate ("sanctify") the apostles (17:17, *hagiazō*) to continue the ministry of Jesus, the new Temple in the world.[38]

In sum, a close reading of the last discourse indicates that the role of the Temple is being communicated from Jesus to the disciples. It follows that they will continue to fulfill the function of the Temple after his departure.[39]

Signs and the "Greater Works" of the Disciples

A major theme in the last discourse is the commissioning of the disciples for ministry apart from the physical presence of Jesus. Jesus is "sending out" the disciples just as he was sent from the Father (see Jn 13:16, 20; 15:15; 17:18). This theme is reinforced by statements affirming that the experiences of Jesus will be replicated in those of his disciples (see 13:15; 15:20). One statement in particular deserves special attention: "He who believes in me will also do the works that I do; and greater works than these will he do, because I go to the Father" (14:12). The term "works" (*erga*) is used as a synonym for "signs"—that is, referring to Jesus' miracles, in many places in the Gospel (see 5:20, 36; 7:3, 21; 9:3; 10:25, 32, 38; 14:11; 15:24). What could it possibly mean that the disciples will do the same "works" and even greater "works" than Jesus?

It could mean that the apostles would perform miracles, even more spectacular ones than those Jesus performed. There are two problems with this interpretation. First, there is a historical problem. While Acts does record the apostles, especially Peter and Paul, performing miracles similar to those of Jesus himself, one would be hard-pressed to argue that they exceeded the "grandeur" of, say, the raising of Lazarus or the Resurrection itself. Second, there is a theological problem. The "signs" and "works" Jesus performed were never ends in themselves. In fact, his comment, hinting at a kind of exasperation, in John 4:48 ("Unless you see signs and wonders, you will not believe") suggests that the performance of miracles was a concession to a lack of faith among his contemporaries (see 20:29), but not a practice Jesus thought should be normative. Thus, the thesis that the "greater works" refers to miracles performed by the disciples that would "outdo" those of Jesus himself faces some formidable objections. But what other interpretive options are available?

One clue to the nature of the "greater works" is the explanation given at the end of Jesus' statement, "because I go to the Father". Taken at face value, this is not much of an explanation: There seems to be no reason why Jesus' departure to the Father would result in the disciples accomplishing greater works than those of Jesus himself. The statement must be taken in conjunction with John 16:7: "It is to your advantage that I go away, for if I do not go away, the Counselor will not come to you; but if I go, I will send him to you." The reason the disciples will perform "greater works" is not because of the absence of Jesus but because Jesus' departure will result in the *gift of the Spirit, through which the disciples will be empowered to perform these works*.

Another clue is the pattern we have observed—that, in the aftermath of performing signs, Jesus attempts to move those who have witnessed the sign from the "earthly" to the "heavenly"—from the physical miracle to that to which it points. In John 3, Jesus tries to move Nicodemus from thinking of the "signs" in terms of "earthly things" (a physical rebirth) to "heavenly things"—rebirth by the Spirit, inseparably tied to baptism. In John 6, Jesus urges the people not to seek earthly bread through another multiplication miracle, but heavenly bread—himself and his eucharistic presence, through which the Spirit gives life. And without doubt, in Jesus' hierarchy of significance, the eucharistic bread of his "flesh" is "greater" than the bread created by the multiplication of loaves.

Could the "greater works" that the disciples will perform include the divine works of baptism and the Eucharist carried out by the power of the Spirit? This was noted long ago by Oscar Cullmann: "The sacraments have this in common, that in the time after the resurrection they take the place of the miracles performed by the incarnate Christ."[40] That is to say, they do not merely point to the reality of God's presence on earth but also contain it. As Leo the Great put it, "That which till then was visible of our Redeemer was changed into a sacramental presence."[41]

At least the following conclusions may be warranted exegetically: Whatever the "greater works" will be, they will not be performed apart from the power of the Paraclete sent by Jesus; and whatever they are, they will not be unrelated to the rebirth of baptism and the nourishment of the Eucharist, toward which Jesus' own "works" pointed.

Sign, Spirit, and Sacrament

John presents Jesus as the new Temple promised by Israel's prophetic Scriptures and as the personal fulfillment of all the feasts celebrated in the Temple. In fact, this is one theological idea: Jesus' fulfillment of the feasts is an aspect of his role as the new and eternal Temple.[42]

Yet for Christian readers of John's Gospel—whether in the first century or the twenty-first—it is not satisfactory to stop at the affirmation that "Jesus is the new Temple." Christ has ascended; how is he still the Temple for us? How, where, and through what means is this fulfillment continued?

In these "greater works" of the sacraments, we see Jesus' ultimate fulfillment of the Temple and its festivals and liturgy.[43] Indeed, it was through the Temple festivals and liturgy that the people of the Old Covenant experienced the Temple for what it really was—the site of reconciliation and communion with God; thus, they bear an analogy to the sacraments of the New Covenant.[44] In the sacraments of the New Covenant, we come to the new Temple, the Body of Christ, his Church.[45] And in the sacramental liturgy of the new Temple, we experience the healing, life-giving, and reconciliatory reality of dwelling with God, receiving the promise he made to his people from of old.[46]

Conclusion: Fulfillment as Transcendence, Transformation, and Sublation

Must John's Temple Christology, then, be labeled "supersessionist"? Not if this means revocation, cancellation, replacement, or annulment. God calls his people into his holy presence and into relationship with him, and he does not revoke that call (see Rom 11:29). But the Temple, in all its various forms (for example, desert Tabernacle, Solomonic Temple, Second Temple), reaches its term and completion in the death and Resurrection of Christ (see Jn 2:19–22). In sum, Christ gives the Temple its definitive meaning; at the same time, this meaning brings about a transformative fulfillment.

How is this fulfillment to be understood? Obviously, this question is too complex to resolve in one essay, and the literature too vast.

To begin, however, the mystery of transformative fulfillment may be described in terms of transcendence, as Pope Benedict XVI observes in *Verbum Domini*:

> *The concept of the fulfilment of the Scriptures is a complex one*, since it has three dimensions: a basic aspect of *continuity* with the Old Testament revelation, an aspect of *discontinuity*, and an aspect of *fulfilment and transcendence*. The mystery of Christ stands in continuity of intent with the sacrificial cult of the Old Testament, but it came to pass in a very different way.... The paschal mystery of Christ is in complete conformity—albeit in a way that could not have been anticipated—with the prophecies and the foreshadowings of the Scriptures; yet it presents clear aspects of discontinuity with regard to the institutions of the Old Testament.[47]

What calls for further study beyond this essay is how this process of fulfillment by transcendence was already well underway throughout the periods of ancient Israelite history.[48] The Old Testament bears witness, for instance, to the transformative fulfillment of the desert Tabernacle, where the twelve tribes assembled for sacrificial worship, to the Jerusalem Temple(s), where gentiles were also invited and included (see 1 Kings 8–10).[49] But in all three periods—Moses, Solomon, and Ezra—what remained central was a sanctuary, a high priest, an altar, and sacrifice.[50]

At each stage, however, God's people were required to adapt to a new situation. With the destruction of the Herodian Temple, this process reached an inflection point—for both Rabbinic Judaism and New Covenant believers. Baruch A. Levine describes, on the one hand, a "transformation from sacrificial worship ... to the alternative modes of worship and different religious institutions that became vital in later Judaism"—what he calls "new Judaism".[51] The central sanctuary gives way to the synagogue; the high priests give way to rabbis; altar and sacrifice give way to scroll and interpretive teaching.[52] Both continuity and discontinuity are evident.

Levine notes, however, that the Christian alternative also involves both continuity and discontinuity. With the transposition of sacrificial worship in terms of Temple Christology, "Christianity adopted the policy of sanctifying space, as [biblical] Judaism had done. Christian worship in the form of the traditional Mass affords the devout an experience of sacrifice, of communion, and proclaims that God is present. *The Christian church, then, is a temple.*"[53]

With Christ's death, Resurrection, and Ascension into heaven, Christ is now sanctuary, high priest, altar, and sacrifice. The transposition effected by the Christ event was not merely geographical, but universal (that is, catholic). Neither was it merely heavenly or ethereal, but also earthly and tangible, culminating in the gift of the Paraclete to the apostles for the doing of "greater works".

Hence, there is arguably no less continuity in the Christian worship that flows from John's Temple Christology than in Rabbinic Judaism. Both involved continuity and discontinuity, where elements of the prior arrangement gave way to new things (see Is 65:17). Where Rabbinic Judaism preserves what could be preserved of the arrangement prior to 70 A.D.,[54] for John, the prior arrangement has been transformatively fulfilled in the sacrificial ministry of Israel's resurrected and ascended Messiah.

In this light, Bernard Lonergan's notion of "sublation", while hailing from a different theological context, may prove useful. Lonergan defines "sublation" as follows: "What *sublates* goes beyond what is sublated, introduces something new and distinct, yet so far from interfering with the sublated or destroying it, on the contrary *needs it, includes it, preserves all its proper features and properties*, and carries them forward to a fuller realization within a richer context."[55]

For William Wright, Jesus' teaching during the feast of Tabernacles/ Sukkot in John 8 can be seen in terms of "sublation": "When *Jesus 'sublates' these liturgical rites by incorporating them into his deeper revelation of the God of Israel*, then new, previously unseen aspects of the liturgy become visible, for example, the ways in which the liturgy participates in Jesus' mission. These Christological dimensions of a biblical reality like Sukkot remain hidden until they are revealed in light of Christ and the explanatory activity of the Holy Spirit in the disciples."[56]

For John, the Herodian Temple is holy and yet penultimate—soon to pass away, as its imminent destruction confirms. But God's sacramental presence in the midst of his people is an integral part of every stage of Israel's history. When fulfillment is understood in terms of sublation, rather than annulment and supersession, we can see that God's tangible, life-giving, sacramental presence must be integral to the New Covenant promised by Israel's prophets.

This, in turn, confirms our reading of John's understanding of Temple Christology whereby the apostles will be enabled by the Paraclete to perform the "greater works" that constitute the fulfillment of the Old Covenant and its Temple(s).[57]

4

Understanding the Jewish Priesthood of Hebrews: Lessons for the Catholic Priesthood Today

David Neuhaus

The Epistle to the Hebrews has been seminal in the history of Christian thinking about how a new, substantially different and superior priesthood replaces the old one. Catholic discourse on Christ as priest has tended to regard the Old Testament priesthood as obsolete.[1] In this, the epistle has often been mobilized to ground a "theology of supersessionism" by which the Church replaces Israel. However, this reading has tended to ignore the striking continuity between the old and the new, the Old Testament priesthood and Jesus' priesthood, firmly rooted in it. The relationship between the old and the new in the epistle is not one of opposition or negation. In fact, the newness of Christ's priesthood is not foreign to the Old Testament, which is the precise context for understanding it.

The central section of the Epistle to the Hebrews, chapters 8–10, describes Jesus as "high priest", a theme that runs through the entire epistle. The Gospel writings underline his role as king,[2] sage,[3] and prophet.[4] However, the intimation that the death of Jesus is a sacrifice for the sins of the world does evoke priesthood, at least implicitly.[5] Hebrews is the only New Testament writing that explicitly focuses on Jesus as a priest. A major obstacle for Hebrews is that Jesus was not from a priestly family; thus, Christ's priesthood is related to the priesthood of Melchizedek in the words of Psalm 110:4: "You are a priest for ever according to the order of Melchizedek" (cf. Heb 5:6,

10; 6:20; 7:11, 17). Traditional readings of Hebrews have underlined how the epistle focuses on the differences between Jesus' priesthood and priesthood in the Old Testament.[6] The epistle explicitly describes the priesthood of Melchizedek as superior to that of the Levitical priesthood: "Now if perfection had been attainable through the Levitical priesthood (for under it the people received the law), what further need would there have been for another priest to arise according to the order of Melchizedek?" (Heb 7:11).

Old and New in Hebrews

In the opening of the central section of Hebrews (8:1—10:16),[7] the author states:

> Now the main point in what we are saying is this: we have such a high priest, one who is seated at the right hand of the throne of the Majesty in the heavens, a minister in the sanctuary and the true tent that the Lord, and not any mortal, has set up. For every high priest is appointed to offer gifts and sacrifices; hence it is necessary for this priest also to have something to offer. Now if he were on earth, he would not be a priest at all, since there are priests who offer gifts according to the law. They offer worship in a sanctuary that is a sketch and shadow of the heavenly one; for Moses, when he was about to erect the tent, was warned, "See that you make everything according to the pattern that was shown you on the mountain." But Jesus has now obtained a more excellent ministry, and to that degree he is the mediator of a better covenant, which has been enacted through better promises. For if that first covenant had been faultless, there would have been no need to look for a second one.
>
> God finds fault with them when he says:
>
> "The days are surely coming, says the Lord,
> when I will establish a new covenant with the house of Israel
> and with the house of Judah;
> not like the covenant that I made with their ancestors,
> on the day when I took them by the hand to lead them out of the land of Egypt;
> for they did not continue in my covenant,
> and so I had no concern for them, says the Lord.

> This is the covenant that I will make with the house of Israel
> after those days, says the Lord:
> I will put my laws in their minds,
> and write them on their hearts,
> and I will be their God,
> and they shall be my people.
> And they shall not teach one another
> or say to each other, 'Know the Lord,'
> for they shall all know me,
> from the least of them to the greatest.
> For I will be merciful toward their iniquities,
> and I will remember their sins no more."
>
> In speaking of "a new covenant," he has made the first one obsolete. And what is obsolete and growing old will soon disappear. (Heb 8:1–13, NRSV)

The vocabulary and dynamic in this section are derived from the singular mention of a New Covenant in the Old Testament, in the book of Jeremiah (31:31–34). The terminology of Hebrews has often been understood as derived from Platonism, suggesting that the "sketch" and "shadow" are simply replaced by "the true" and "the better", the shadow by reality.[8] However, this does not take into account the real problem with the "old", a problem fully recognized in the Old Testament. In fact, the vocabulary of old and new is derived from the Scriptures of Israel and not from Plato. The vocabulary is more one of continuity than substitution in making the comparative claim that the new is better than the old.[9] The key to this understanding is that the new is not yet manifest even after Christ but rather is placed on an eschatological horizon: "What is obsolete and growing old will soon disappear" (Heb 8:13, NRSV). The old is growing old, to disappear at some future time. This language of continuity and fulfillment is founded on the entire presentation of the priestly cult in the Old Testament, an essential backdrop to the vocabulary, syntax, grammar, and discourse of Hebrews. The horizon of the disappearance of the priestly cult in an eschatological future represents the teleology of Old Testament priestly worship.

In the conclusion to the central section of the epistle, the author again refers to the citation from Jeremiah, creating thereby an inclusion that encapsulates the center of the epistle:

Since the law has only a shadow of the good things to come and not the true form of these realities, it can never, by the same sacrifices that are continually offered year after year, make perfect those who approach. Otherwise, would they not have ceased being offered, since the worshipers, cleansed once for all, would no longer have any consciousness of sin? But in these sacrifices there is a reminder of sin year after year. For it is impossible for the blood of bulls and goats to take away sins. Consequently, when Christ came into the world, he said,

> "Sacrifices and offerings you have not desired,
> but a body you have prepared for me;
> in burnt offerings and sin offerings
> you have taken no pleasure.
> Then I said, 'See, God, I have come to do your will, O God'
> (in the scroll of the book it is written of me)."

When he said above, "You have neither desired nor taken pleasure in sacrifices and offerings and burnt offerings and sin offerings" (these are offered according to the law), then he added, "See, I have come to do your will." He abolishes the first in order to establish the second. And it is by God's will that we have been sanctified through the offering of the body of Jesus Christ once for all.

And every priest stands day after day at his service, offering again and again the same sacrifices that can never take away sins. But when Christ had offered for all time a single sacrifice for sins, "he sat down at the right hand of God," and since then has been waiting "until his enemies would be made a footstool for his feet." For by a single offering he has perfected for all time those who are sanctified. And the Holy Spirit also testifies to us, for after saying,

> "This is the covenant that I will make with them
> after those days, says the Lord:
> I will put my laws in their hearts,
> and I will write them on their minds,"

he also adds,

> "I will remember their sins and their lawless deeds no more."

Where there is forgiveness of these, there is no longer any offering for sin. (10:1–18, NRSV)

Again, the opposition between "shadow" and "true form", between what is "abolished" and what is established in its place, might lead one astray. However, it is significant that the "single sacrifice for sins" fulfilled in Christ's offering is described as a model for those who seek to follow him, a yet unrealized *telos*. The newness of Christ is his fulfillment of the Old Testament priestly cult rather than its replacement. The citation of Psalm 40:6–8 (according to the Greek) insists on this:

> Sacrifices and offerings you have not desired,
> but a body you have prepared for me;
> in burnt offerings and sin offerings
> you have taken no pleasure.
> Then I said, "See, God, I have come to do your will, O God."

The sacrifices and offerings represented by the gifts brought to the Temple have reached their fulfillment in the human body of Christ, a body that Christ offers in doing the will of the one commanding sacrifice. Sacrifice and priesthood are not abolished, but their locus is no longer primarily an exterior ritual in a Temple but rather existential, embodied life of the one being conformed to Christ. As Radner explains in his study of Leviticus, "Hebrews, in fact, locates the work of God depicted in Leviticus in the actual body of Christ."[10]

What is abolished by Christ doing God's will persists for all who are not yet conformed to the image of Christ, all who are yet to do God's will (that is, everyone). In similar fashion, Paul in his Epistle to the Romans exhorts the disciples to live as Christ lived: "I appeal to you therefore, brethren, by the mercies of God, to present your bodies as a living sacrifice, holy and acceptable to God, which is your spiritual worship. Do not be conformed to this world but be transformed by the renewal of your mind, that you may prove what is the will of God, what is good and acceptable and perfect" (12:1–2).

Believers in Christ are called into the priesthood of Christ, where they, like Christ, are priest and sacrifice, not restricted to a religious rite performed in a Temple but primarily an existential way of living, "good and acceptable and perfect" in the sight of God. Transfiguration is the purpose of priestly worship in the Old Testament and brought to fulfillment in Christ. God renders the covenant old by sending Jesus, for whom the covenant is not an external letter but defines his existential reality as the perfect Son of the Father. The newness of the covenant, the newness of the priesthood, is their fulfillment in the life of Christ, a goal on the eschatological horizon for all who follow him.

Christ's fulfillment of the Father's will is the way, as yet unfulfilled, for his disciples. By following him, the disciples strive to conform to his image and likeness. Jesus led the way, according to Hebrews, with great struggle: "Although he was a Son, he learned obedience through what he suffered; and having been made perfect he became the source of eternal salvation to all who obey him, being designated by God a high priest according to the order of Melchizedek" (5:8–10). What is rendered obsolete by Christ's sacrifice, his living according to the will of God, is a cult that does not lead the human person to a life lived according to that will, something repeatedly underlined by Israel's prophets.[11]

The awareness of the potential disconnect between cult, even if perfectly fulfilled, and covenant faithfulness is central to the concern of the writers of the Old Testament. Jeremiah points to the reality of a broken covenant. The people have been unfaithful to God's covenant, and the consequence is that God turns the divine face from them as described in the passage from chapter 31.[12] The deep prophetic frustration at the people's infidelity does not, however, prevent the prophet from understanding that God remains faithful nonetheless. After all, the primordial covenant with Abraham was an unconditional one—no breaking of it is possible—but the one at Sinai is conditional, so it can be broken by infringement of the Law (Torah). Jeremiah underlines this and points to an eschatological horizon implicit in the Old Covenant. For, as Albert Vanhoye points out, "The Old Testament as prophecy announces its own end as institution; the Old Testament as revelation manifests the provisional character of its legislation."[13] Reading carefully the figure of the priest in the Old Testament reveals its provisional character.

The Priest in the Old Testament

In the world of the Old Testament, the priest is one of four principal mediators between God and God's people. The four mediators, each defined by his role, are priest, king, sage, and prophet.[14] Each one has a particular role in mediating God's presence in the life of Israel, called to be priest, king, sage, and prophet in the service of the nations who do not yet know God. Whereas the king and the prophet are central characters in the often-dramatic events that mark the history of salvation, the priest and the sage are central in regular routine, worship, and day-to-day life in the world. In the Pentateuch, the Law focuses on the function of the priest in the life of a people called to be "a kingdom of priests" and "a holy nation" (Ex 19:6). It is the priest, specifically in offering a sacrifice for sin, who is first named "messiah", in the book of Leviticus.[15]

A Priestly Theology of Holiness

Key to understanding the role of the priest in the Old Testament is the refrain in Leviticus: "*You shall be holy for I the Lord your God am holy*" (see Lev 11:44–45; 19:2; 20:26, emphasis added). God is holy and the priest is "made holy" (consecrated) in service of the people: "Now this is what you shall do to them to consecrate [make holy] them, that they may serve me as priests" (Ex 29:1; cf. 40:13–15). The priest officiates in safeguarding God's holiness and making the people holy.

What is holiness? The word "holy" is not conceptually clear. Walter Brueggemann writes: "The term has such rich and varied usage precisely because it seeks to articulate what is most characteristic and therefore most hidden and inscrutable about God."[16] God is totally other in the priestly conception, wholly separate from the world that God has created and from the human person who seeks to worship God. Holiness is godliness, the quality that is consistent with who God is. However, it is this quality that the human person, although totally separate from God, is called to emulate. According to the priestly conception, holiness is incompatible not only with sin (intentional or unintentional contravention of God's commandments) but also with impurity (being bodily contaminated by various secretions or contact with objects) and with disorder (confusion of categories of holy and common). Categories of virtue, purity, and distinguishing between holy and common often seem to conflict with modern consciousness, which resists the seemingly arbitrary nature of dividing into categories of virtuous/sinful, pure/impure, and holy/ common. Yet the vocation of the Old Testament priest depends on precisely this discernment and separation.

In Leviticus, the priest's role is described when God speaks to Aaron, the proto-priest: "You are to separate between the holy and the common, and between the impure and the pure; and you are to teach the people of Israel all the statutes that the Lord has spoken to them through Moses" (Lev 10:10–11, adapted). As mediator of holiness, the priest has two main roles: separating and teaching. The two verbs used here are essential to understanding how the priests form a holy people for a holy God. Distinguishing between holy and common and pure and impure ensures order, and confusing them provokes disorder. Gordon Wenham explains: "Everything that is not holy is common. Common things divide into two groups, the clean (pure) and the unclean (impure). Clean (pure) things become holy when they are sanctified."[17] The role of the priest is to know what can become holy and what cannot, what can open up the channel of blessing that God seeks to impart and what cannot open up this channel. Furthermore, the priest must teach what obstructs holiness (sin and confusion). Impurity is not sinful in itself (it is not endowed with magical or demonic destructive power), but it is contagious and invades the space of holiness and, therefore, must be contained. Sin is incurred when impurity is disregarded, the danger deriving from confusing categories and not only from committing explicit sin.

In mediating between a holy God and a people constantly threatened by impurity, confusion, and sin, the priest has a central role in actualizing the communion between God and God's people. The priest is the safeguard and teacher of holiness. Ultimately, as a priestly vicar of God, the priest is authorized, according to the holy rites ordained by God, to make holy those things that can be made holy, to contain those that cannot, and to know the difference between the two. Firstly, the priest forms the people to be vessels of God's holiness, celebrating the rites of holiness and teaching them to distinguish between pure and impure and holy and common. However, secondly, the priest officiates at rites of "atonement",[18] ordained by God so that whatever impurity and confusion have been accumulated and whatever sins have been committed, they might be washed away and a new start can be made on the path to holiness. These two roles create an inherent tension between the ideal—the priest teaching what must be done—and the real—the people's (including the priest's) failure to live up to the standard of holiness, resulting in the need for atonement. This tension is at the heart of the priestly cult. The priestly texts are astonishing because they claim that in the priestly cult, God "has granted Israel a reliable, authorized device whereby Israel can be restored to full relationship with the Lord".[19]

Historical-critical research has outlined the characteristics of literature that are traditionally ascribed to a priestly school. Without entering into the complex question of authorship, the canonical center of the Pentateuch (probably redacted by this priestly school) is the book of Leviticus, supreme expression of a priestly perspective, and the texts that precede it in the book of Exodus (25–31 and 35–40) that describe the construction of the Tent of Meeting.[20] Research also insists on the priestly contours of the first text in the Bible (Gen 1:1—2:4). This initial and foundational text provides an important introduction to the priestly role in the Bible. In this creation narrative, the remarkable expression "image and likeness" is introduced: "Then God said, 'Let us make man in our image, after our likeness'.... So, God created man in his own image, in the image of God he created him; male and female he created them" (1:26–27). The expression is a strikingly visual representation of the priestly insistence that the human person is to be holy as God is holy. In creation, God is already forming "a kingdom of priests and a holy people", humanity, who are ordered to maintain creation in its holy state by filling the earth with God's image and likeness.[21]

The canonical narrative within the Pentateuch presents a series of receding circles of priesthood as the human creature confounds and obstructs God's insistence on holiness and order. Adam and his descendants constitute a first extensive circle that comprises all mankind with the mission to keep creation holy. The human person is separated from the rest of the creatures by being created in the image and likeness of the Creator. The first use of the verb "to make holy" is for time, the Sabbath. The Sabbath is a temple in time that precedes any temple in space.[22] The consecration of the Sabbath underlines the separation between holy and common. The six days of the week are not "sinful" or "unclean", but the Sabbath day is a conductor to God, a channel of blessing that facilitates God sharing life with the human person despite the abyss of otherness that separates them. Sabbath rest is profound communion across unbridgeable difference. In the book of Leviticus, the repeated admonition "to keep my Sabbaths" (19:3, 30; 26:2) is matched with the terrible consequences of descent into nothingness at the end of the book (26:34, 43). The Sabbath is the pinnacle of creation, when the human person is in the image and likeness of God, resting, and thus emulating God, becoming holy as God is holy.[23]

The sons of Adam are excluded from the "kingdom of priests" because of contravening God's word. The sins of Adam and Eve, Cain, and Noah on exiting the ark accumulate. Noah's priestly acts on entering the ark (separating among clean and unclean species, Gen 7:2) and on exiting the ark (building an altar and making sacrifice, 8:20) are countered by his drunkenness and its consequences. The culmination of sin is in the building of Babel, city and tower. The motivation for its construction is explicit: "Come, let us build ourselves a city, and a tower with its top in the heavens, and let us make a name for ourselves, lest we be scattered abroad upon the face of the whole earth" (11:4). They build the tower that is a city in order to make a name for themselves, rejecting that the Father names (see 5:1–3) and staying in one place, refusing to fill the earth. The refusal to fill the earth with God's image and likeness, the third and central commandment given to Adam (see 1:28), results in the unholiness of the children of Adam (mankind) and leads to the election of Abraham and his descendants, the children of Israel.

The priestly vocation of Israel is enunciated at Sinai: "You shall be to me a kingdom of priests and a holy nation" (Ex 19:6). The birth of Israel in the exodus-Sinai event does not stabilize the circle of priesthood, however. It recedes further when the people of Israel celebrate the Golden Calf in Moses' absence on the mountain at Sinai. Moses finds allies for the terrifying return of holiness in the tribe of Levi. The Levites wreak vengeance on idolatrous Israel, massacring the people as they go from gate to gate killing son, brother, friend, and neighbor. Moses says to them: "Today you have ordained yourselves for the service of the LORD, each one at the cost of his son and of his brother, that he may bestow a blessing upon you this day" (32:29). The circle of holiness recedes even further at Shittim, in the wilderness, when Israel worships the Baal of Peor in a festival of pagan orgiastic cult, seduced by the women of Moab/Midian. Phinehas, grandson of Aaron the priest, expresses God's vengeance, spearing together an idolatrous Israelite and a Moabite woman. God then says of him: "[He] has turned back my wrath from the sons of Israel, in that he was jealous with my jealousy among them ... therefore ... I give to him my covenant of peace ... the covenant of a perpetual priesthood, because he was jealous for his God, and made atonement for the sons of Israel" (Num 25:11–13).[24] The receding circle of holiness is directly correlated to the compromise of holiness by those called to be holy, a tragic reality in the story told in the Pentateuch. However, the priest, instituted to worship and instruct in holiness, is also instituted to make atonement for a sinful and disordered people.

A Priestly Theology of Order

The careful distinction between holy and common, pure and impure makes the priest the preeminent person of order. Order and nothingness are important themes in the Bible. The Creator has created an ordered world, the order of which guarantees its continued existence in harmony and peace. The Bible describes the seven days of God's creation of the world, focusing on the progressive domination of *tohu vavohu*,[25] a primordial nothingness, by divinely ordained order, initiated by God's word. The human person is to be custodian of this divine order. Nothingness threatens this world as a constant menace that surges out to engulf creation and reduce it again to *tohu vavohu*.

Whereas order guarantees life in a fertile land that knows peace, nothingness is a barren wasteland ravaged by war that is synonymous with death. Creation and de-creation are important moments in the life of God with human beings.[26] Creation is God-ordained order, and de-creation the consequence of the human choice of nothingness. Within the Bible, the priest is to serve as the legitimator, enactor, and guarantor[27] of God's order *par excellence*. The priest underlines the centrality of worship as the locus for an affirmation of divine order in the face of invasive nothingness in the life of the People of God. Just as the cosmos passed from nothingness to order by the command of the Creator, so Israel passes from nothingness to order as the people enter the space where the acts of worship are enacted. Just as God commanded order for creation, separating the elements, distinguishing one from another, so the priest within cultic worship engages in a series of actions whereby the faithful receive the assurance of an ordered life. A world that rages against God's order (not only darkness, sin, and death but a constant invasion of uncleanness) finds its counterpoint in the ordered and rhythmed moments of cultic worship. Brueggemann masterfully comments: "While the temptation to a dualism that divides 'life' from 'worship' is real, it is important to see that worship models and enacts an alternative world of sanity that prevents Israel from succumbing to the seductive insanities of a world raging against the holiness of (the Lord) the Creator. The priesthood is to protect and guarantee the maintenance of this alternative world wherein Israel could 'see' God and see itself differently in the world."[28]

The construction of the Tent, a subject that takes up most of the second part of the book of Exodus (25–31; 35–40), is a reflection of creation. In the preparatory acts for worship, the human person becomes co-creator with God, fulfilling the role as vicar of God on earth, constructing a space for the intimate encounter between God and the human person, what creation was supposed to be.[29] When the Tent is completed, it becomes God's dwelling place in the midst of the people: "Then the cloud covered the tent of meeting, and the glory of the LORD filled the tabernacle" (40:34). Israel had been brought out of slavery (*'avdut*) in order to engage in worship (*'avoda*)—these two words share a common root in Hebrew. The construction of the Tent concludes the struggle for liberation from Egypt, underlining the necessity of clearly distinguishing between an earthly tyrant, Pharaoh, who serves as a grotesque parody of the Divine,[30] and the God of Abraham, Isaac, and Jacob, the Creator of heaven and earth, who is enthroned in the Tent at the center of Israel's life at the end of Exodus.

The priest understands order and nothingness as two poles of existence. Whereas order is represented in holy worship and holy living as ordained by God, nothingness is represented by idolatry, resulting in the confusion of holy and common, pure and impure. The Old Testament is very concerned with the sin of idolatry. False worship threatens the very foundations of Israel's election as a holy nation as well as the principles of the created order. In the second part of

Exodus, in between the two sets of instructions to build the Tent (God instructs Moses in 25–31 and Moses instructs the people in 35–40), there is the narrative of the Golden Calf (32). The Tent prefigures Solomon's Temple in Jerusalem, and the Calf prefigures the two calves that Jeroboam set up for worship in the Northern Kingdom (see 1 Kings 12). The struggle against idolatry is the struggle to engage in true worship, the sacrifice that enables one to adhere to the will of God, ultimately sacrificing himself.

While Moses is receiving the instructions to build the Tent, the people pressure Aaron to build for them a god. What emerges is a calf, a parody of the Egyptian (or Canaanite) divine bull. The Calf is formed by a people that is still enslaved in Egypt, whereas divine worship seeks to form a free people as children of God. The battle for the heart of the people continues here between God and Pharaoh. Exegetes have pointed out the similarity between the Golden Calf and the contents of the Tent. These similarities are particularly noticeable with regard to the *kapporet*, of which God says: "There I will meet with you" (Ex 25:22). This term is derived from the verb "to atone for". The *kapporet* is at the center of the rite of atonement, performed once a year for the people (Lev 16:13–15). John Hartley comments: "It is at the *kapporet* that the most critical blood rites for achieving expiation were performed on the Day of Atonement, for the *kapporet* was the cultic line of demarcation between the Lord and his people, the place where God's people might find forgiveness from the transcendent God who manifested his presence in the cloud."[31]

The Calf is a parody of the *kapporet*, the locus of God's presence. Both Calf and *kapporet* are made of pure gold and are molded into visible forms (calf and cherubim). The gold, collected from the people, had been taken from the Egyptians on exiting Egypt. The narrative of the Calf is the counter priestly text. It poses the important question of the second half of the book of Exodus: What is the difference between the building of the Tent and the fashioning of the Calf, between worship of God and worship of idols—ultimately, between order and nothingness? The Tent is a space, not an object; it is an expanse in which to meet, but it is not God. Here the human prepares himself for the coming of God into his life. The priestly liturgy renders God present, but there is no ultimate guarantee apart from the fidelity of God to the promise to be present. It is the fear of absence that provokes the forming of the Calf. God is represented by a creature who is unable to be absent, controlled as it is by the human hands that have formed it. Worship, in the priestly consciousness, is the human person's affirmation of God as God. True worship in the Tent is a condition for holy living in creation.

A Priestly Theology of Presence

Ordered sacred cult, according to the priestly perception, culminates in the celebration of the presence of God in the midst of the people. The promise of God at the very beginning of the commandments to prepare a place for the sacred cult is unequivocal: "And let them make me a sanctuary, that I may dwell in their midst" (Ex 25:8). At the outset, the dwelling among the people is emphasized rather than God's dwelling in the Tent. The word "tabernacle" is used for the first time in the verse that follows: "According to all that I show you concerning the pattern of the tabernacle, and of all its furniture, so you shall make it" (25:9). This is the verse cited in chapter 8 of the Epistle to the Hebrews too. The peak is reached after the instructions to construct the Tent and how to practice the priestly cult, in Leviticus, when Aaron initiates the cult "on the eighth day" (9:1). The sacrifices and cultic acts culminate in blessing: "Aaron lifted up his hands toward the people and blessed them; and he came down from offering the sin offering and the burnt offering and the peace offering. And Moses and Aaron went into the tent of meeting; and when they came out they blessed the people, and the glory of the LORD appeared to all the people. And fire came forth from before the LORD and consumed the burnt offering and the fat on the altar; and when all the people saw it, they shouted, and fell on their faces" (9:22–24).

The appearance of the glory of God to all the people is the consequence of the initiation of the priestly cult.[32] Whereas the prophet is the person who renders God present in the conjunction of the word and the act of hearing, the priest renders God present in the visual of cultic ritual. This presence is promised by God in the rituals that are carried out in the Tent. The elaborate biblical sacrificial cult does not imprison God but renders the human person present (again) to God, who has promised to be present. God is rendered present through the rite of representation that God has ordained.

The struggle to conform to God's word in the worship of a God who is totally other is immediately doomed to failure in the dramatic story of Aaron's sons, who offer a "strange fire": "Now Nadab and Abihu, the sons of Aaron, each took his censer, and put fire in it, and laid incense on it, and they offered strange fire before the LORD, such as he had not commanded them. And fire came forth from the presence of the LORD and devoured them, and they died before the LORD" (10:1–2, adapted). This strange narrative of Nadab and Abihu is the contrast to the transformative moment of the initiation of the priestly cult. Strange fire is understood as fire not commanded by God, "unholy" fire. Nadab and Abihu's rebellion evokes the rebellion of Adam in the Garden. The reconstituted microcosm, the Tent, which replaces the macrocosm, Eden, has been sullied. It is in the light of this desecration of the holy place where a holy God can come to meet a holy people that the role of the priest to separate and teach is detailed (see 10:10–11).

The finale of the long chapters that detail the states of impurity resulting from bodily emissions, impure food, contact with corpses, and skin ailments (see 11–15) is in the sacrifices of the Day of Atonement, a day to restore order, purity, and ultimately holiness (see 16). The rites of purity include intricate and detailed sets of reparations that mend the oversights, errors, and unintentional malpractices of the people often through the spilling of blood. The Day of Atonement restores the holiness of the Tent, sullied by an unholy people. The priest works in blood. The blood of animals is sprinkled, poured, and splashed in various directions: on the *kapporet*, on the altar, and even on the people. Blood is life and represents a meeting between God and the human person: "If any man of the house of Israel or of the strangers who sojourn among them eats any blood, I will set my face against that person who eats blood, and will cut him off from among his people. *For the life of the flesh is in the blood; and I have given it for you upon the altar to make atonement for your souls*; for it is the blood that makes atonement" (17:10–11).[33]

Blood, which conveys the life of the flesh, is at the heart of the central atonement rite that the priest must undertake once a year in order to sanctify the people and the place of worship on the Day of Atonement.

The offerings made by the priest *re-present* the people to God. The offerings are cultic and not psychosocial: They restore the people to holiness when this holiness is impaired by unintentional acts or involuntary states that sully them. The offerings are cultic and not ethical in that they make the people holy again so that they can come into the divine presence. Sins of a social nature are not rectified by this cultic worship; the cult does not replace social action.[34] Atonement with God is renewal for a life of holiness in the world, as the person restored to holiness goes out into the world in order to live in justice and righteousness. Cult does not replace the world but prepares and renews one for life in the world. The entire elaborate cult is a rite of preparation and renewal, of drawing close to God,[35] and of rendering matter, space, and time holy so that the human can be with God. Ultimately, all creation must become holy space, all humanity holy beings, and all time holy Sabbath.

A Priestly Theology of Joy

The word "joy" is used in Leviticus in relation to the feast of Tabernacles when it is said: "You shall rejoice before the LORD your God seven days" (23:40). However, the experience of joy resounds in the texts that describe the living out of the cult, in Deuteronomy, the Books of Chronicles, Ezra, Nehemiah, and the Psalms, all concerned with priestly worship. In Deuteronomy, being in the presence of the Lord is cause for rejoicing (see 12:12, 18; 14:26; 16:11, 14, 15; 26:11; 27:7). In the book of 1 Chronicles, David is described as meticulously ordering the cult in the holy place, ordaining singers and musicians who accompany the cult and who are commanded "to raise sounds of joy" (15:16). The Ark is carried "with rejoicing" (15:25), as David ecstatically dances before the Ark (15:29; see also 2 Sam 6:16). The psalms commanded by David, within this context, are to invoke, to thank, and to praise the Lord: "Honor and majesty are before him; strength and joy are in his place" (1 Chron 16:27). As the gifts to build the Temple flow into the treasury, the Chronicler writes: "Then the people *rejoiced* because these had given willingly, for with a whole heart they had offered freely to the LORD; David the king also *rejoiced greatly*" (29:9). This joy is featured throughout the Chronicler's writings (see 1 Chron 29:17, 22; 2 Chron 7:10; 15:15; 23:21; 24:10; 30:23, 25–26) and continues through Ezra and Nehemiah too (Ezra 3:12–13; 6:22; Neh 8:12, 17, 27; 12:43–44).

Finally, the book of Psalms accompanies the priestly cult. Psalm 122 is exemplary: "I was glad when they said to me, 'Let us go to the house of the LORD!'" (122:1). The joy resounds in the psalm for Tabernacles: "This is the day which the LORD has made; let us rejoice and be glad in it" (Ps 118:24). Psalm 100 expresses this too: "Make a joyful noise to the LORD, all the land! Serve the LORD with gladness! Come into his presence with singing!" (1–2).

Conclusion: The Old Testament Priest and Christ

Priesthood in the Old Testament is instituted to bring atonement, at-one-ment with God, lost through sin. The vision presented in the Pentateuch is of a profound reparative system commanded by a loving God. As pointed out by the Pontifical Biblical Commission: "The cult is a vast symbolism of grace, an expression of God's 'condescension' (in the Patristic sense of beneficent adaptation) towards human beings, since he established it for pardon, purification, sanctification and preparation for direct contact with his presence (*kabod*, glory)."[36] The writer of the Epistle to the Hebrews knows this God and the profound goodness of the priesthood. However, the writer also knows that human failings impeded the priesthood's implementation, making of it a promise as yet imperfectly fulfilled. It was not to be abolished or replaced but to be fulfilled.

Priesthood can become "manipulative self-indulgence".[37] As man of the law, the priest can become legalistic and obsessive about formal categories, ignoring the social space in which he must function. The cult might take precedence over the dignity of the human person. The priest might overemphasize the boundaries between temple and creation, retreating into "sacred" space and ignoring that God's sacred space knows no boundaries. This kind of cult "substitutes self-referenced manipulation for trustful submissiveness".[38] Cult for cult's sake is idolatry. The cult's purpose is for the human person to return to the world as a priestly presence, making God visible in a life of holiness.

In the Old Testament, the prophets protest against a cult that is impervious to a living God and a sinful, suffering humanity. The priests cannot imprison God in cult but rather must prepare men for a living encounter with God. Isaiah's words ring out: "What to me is the multitude of your sacrifices? says the LORD; I have had enough of burnt offerings of rams and the fat of fed beasts; I do not delight in the blood of bulls, or of lambs, or of he-goats.... When you spread forth your hands, I will hide my eyes from you; even though you make many prayers, I will not listen; your hands are full of blood. Wash yourselves; make yourselves clean; remove the evil of your doings from before my eyes" (1:11–16). Priestly cult is preparation for holy living beyond cult in righteousness and justice.

The notable difference between Old Testament priesthood and Christ's priesthood in the Epistle to the Hebrews is that the old sacrifices had to be repeated over and over, but Jesus' sacrifice is once and for all (see 7:27; 9:12, 26–28; 10:2, 10). In the Eucharist, Jesus' disciples are enacting a memorial of his unique sacrifice until he comes again.[39] Hebrews speaks of Jesus in priestly terms but points out that Jesus is "the *pioneer and perfecter* of our faith, who for the joy that was set before him endured the cross" (12:2). The Cross has become the place of the supreme sacrifice—Christ offering himself as that ultimate sacrifice—and all those participating in this cult follow him. Their lives, like his, will be lived in holiness, existence transformed into sacrifice, remembered and actualized ever anew in the sacrament of the Eucharist, "the memorial of Christ's Passover, the making present and the sacramental offering of his unique sacrifice".[40]

Thomas Aquinas raises the question of whether it is fitting that Christ be conceived of as a priest.[41] Is not Christ far superior to an Old Testament priest? He resoundingly refutes the objections to Christ being seen as a priest, responding that it is most fitting that Christ indeed be a priest, as he is the mediator who reconciles humanity with God. This is what the Epistle to the Hebrews states at the outset: "Therefore he had to be made like his brethren in every respect, so that he might become a merciful and faithful high priest in the service of God, to make expiation for the sins of the people" (2:17). In reading the role of the priest in the Old Testament, it is clear that the priesthood of Christ is the fulfillment of Old Testament priesthood. At the center of the Epistle to the Hebrews, Christ's sacrifice on the Cross brings atonement with God. This atonement is the central purpose of the Old Testament priest, promised in the cult, imperfectly practiced in Israel, and achieved fully in Christ's priesthood on the Cross. Atonement achieved, life itself is holiness in God's presence.

Section 2

Tradition

5

Aquinas on the Jews and Judaism

Bruce D. Marshall

Like many medieval Christian theologians, especially from the thirteenth century and before, Thomas Aquinas offers a fundamentally ambiguous account of the Jewish people and Judaism. Succinctly stated, Aquinas is clearly committed to a belief in God's irrevocable election of the Jewish people and in the permanent presence and importance of the Jews in salvation history as Christians understand it. At the same time, he is clearly committed to a belief in the gravely sinful, indeed damnable, character of the Jewish religion and of the practices constitutive of Judaism after the coming of Christ. On each of these cardinal points he is quite unambiguous. The ambiguity arises when the two are set side by side, since, as we will explain, it is hard to see how they can be compatible. If he holds the first, it seems that he should not hold the second, and conversely.

Aquinas was hardly alone among medieval Christian theologians in writing extensively on the significance of the Jewish people and Jewish practices, both before and after the coming of Christ. The authors of the *Summa fratris Alexandri*, William of Auvergne, Robert Grosseteste, Albert the Great, and Robert Kilwardby, among others, did the same, with varying results but, on the whole, to a similarly ambiguous effect. In presenting an irreducibly ambiguous theological view of the Jews and Judaism, these medieval theologians follow a pattern well established long before them, especially by Augustine. The ambiguity they bring to light is, as we will see, not a medieval peculiarity, and still less a Western one, but emerges from deep-laid features of the Christian faith, which insists on both the finality and universal saving mission of Christ and his Church and the unfailing promises of God to the Jewish people.

The Election of Israel

Saint Thomas' insistence on the election of the Jewish people is not only clear but also highly ramified and detailed.[1] God has chosen the Jewish people to live in a unique intimacy with him and to that end has clearly distinguished Israel from all other nations, giving the Jewish people a complex array of gifts, privileges, and responsibilities unique to them.

The election of the Jewish people takes the form of a promise made to their forefathers, a divine pledge, made in love, to bestow great goods on the fleshly or carnal descendants of Abraham, Isaac, and Jacob. These benefits are not only temporal but also—indeed, primarily—spiritual, or, as we could say, religious. Aquinas numbers God's benefits to the Jewish people in various ways, but they are chiefly three, "goods that stood out among the Jews, and from which the gentiles were excluded" before the coming of Christ. These were the worship of the one true God according to his own commands, the privilege of being loved by that God (*privilegium dilectionis*), and freedom from original sin, conferred by the sacrament, as Aquinas understands it, of circumcision.[2]

God's promised blessing to the patriarchs and their descendants extends not only to the earthly present but also to the eschatological future, the end and consummation of all things. The election of Israel is ultimately a promise of salvation. In his electing love for Abraham, Isaac, and Jacob, God has promised salvation to their descendants according to the flesh, even to the end of time. Thomas sees this as the clear teaching of Paul. God showed an abundance of grace and mercy to the fathers of Israel "so that for the sake of the promises made to them [the fathers], their offspring too might be saved".[3] Especially in his commentary on Romans 11:25–32, Thomas attributes great soteriological weight to the election of Israel, in a fashion not unlike that of contemporary commentaries. "From eternity God freely elected both the fathers and the sons, but in this order, namely that the sons would obtain salvation for the sake of the fathers"—for the sake, that is, of God's fidelity to the promise of salvation he made to the patriarchs concerning their offspring, not because of any merit on the fathers' part.[4]

For Thomas, the biblically attested election of Israel belongs to the Jews of his own time, and not only to those of the scriptural past. He is especially clear about this when he considers the suggestion that the election of Israel has been made void by Jewish rejection of the gospel and so may be regarded as temporary. When Paul says that God's gifts are "without repentance" (*sine poenitentia*, Rom 11:29, D-R), someone might claim that while the Jews were formerly "most dear" (*charissimi*, 11:28, D-R) on account of their fathers, because they have rejected the gospel they are now no longer dear to God and have lost any possibility of final salvation. Aquinas thinks this is just wrong, since Paul teaches that God's gifts and call are without repentance: "The Apostle insists that this is false."[5] He instructs the Christians of his own time not to suppose that the present unbelief of the Jews nullifies their election by God, or that "because of the unbelief of some, there is nothing left for the Jew."[6] "Let no one despair of the future salvation of the Jews, because they do not seem to repent" of their unwillingness to believe in Christ.[7] Thomas therefore admonishes his own contemporaries to heed Paul's warning (see 11:25) about what will happen if they draw the wrong conclusions from the mystery of Israel's present unbelief: "Ignorance of this would be damnable for you."[8]

In thinking about the final salvation of the Jews, Aquinas avails himself of a complex eschatological scenario, originating primarily from Augustine, the details of which we cannot go into here. Briefly, in the saving plan of God, the Jews must, on the whole, wait for the conversion of the gentiles before themselves coming to faith in Christ and so to salvation. But in the end, the Jews will return to their native ardor for Israel's God, and this will be the harbinger of the final salvation of the gentiles and the resurrection to life eternal. Thus will be realized the Apostle's teaching that the restoration of the Jews will mean life from the dead (11:15).[9] At that time, as Paul also teaches, "all Israel will be saved" (11:26). That is, all the Jews (*universaliter omnes*) will then be saved, whereas now only some come to faith in Christ and attain salvation.[10]

By this Thomas seems not to mean simply that all the Jews who happen to be around at the end will be saved. His warning to Christians against despairing of the future salvation of presently unbelieving

Jews would be pointless if those Jews were irretrievably lost. As Aquinas reads Paul, the fall of the Jews in Romans 11 is neither "useless" nor "irreparable". More than that: "The Jew does not receive salvation from the gentile, but conversely."[11] The Jewish people are, as Paul teaches, the root that supports the gentiles in the saving plan of God (see 11:18). Therefore, the gentiles have no right to assume that the Jews, even those presently cut off by their unbelief, are forever excluded from the life that flows from the root. Inclusion remains natural for them, whereas even the most fervent gentile believer has been grafted in against nature. This excludes any boasting directed by gentile Christians against the Jews—not only against those who have converted to Christianity but also against those who have not.[12] The Jews are, indeed, the already existing "Church", the *Ecclesia Iudaeorum*, into which the gentiles are grafted by faith in Christ.[13]

The survival of the Jews to the end of time is not an accident, still less a punishment, but is for the sake of their eschatological salvation, in fulfillment of the unfailing promises God made to their forefathers according to the flesh. In all of this, to be sure, salvation is always in Christ, so the promised salvation of the Jews will be their incorporation into the New Covenant. They, too, will come to share fully in the grace of Christ, which was the source of their election and dignity all along, and in the salvation the gentiles now receive by being grafted into the *Ecclesia Iudaeorum*, the "Church of the Jews".

It is important to emphasize that Aquinas understands Jewish election in genuinely carnal or physical rather than strictly spiritual terms. To be a Jew, and so one of God's elect, is first of all simply to be descended (*progenitus*), according to the flesh, from Abraham and the other *patres* of Israel. In this, Thomas explicitly follows Deuteronomy 4:36–37, a passage that recurs frequently in his discussions of biblical Israel and her election. God loved the *patres* and chose (*elegit*) their "seed" or descendants to receive the Law and the benefits that come with it.[14] The special dignity of the Jews, Aquinas observes in comment on Romans 9:4–5, belongs to them in the first place simply on account of their origin (*ex origine*). They are the nation or people descended from Jacob, and precisely as such they enjoy a unique dignity among all the nations: "That is, because they are descended according to the flesh from these fathers, who were most highly acceptable to God."[15] To Israel, as Aquinas reads Scripture, belong not simply those who have Jewish faith but those who have Jewish flesh. To be a Jew, to have Jewish flesh, is already to be among God's chosen. As long as there are fleshly descendants of the fathers of Israel beloved of God, God's Chosen People will endure. And since Aquinas is confident that Jewish flesh will endure until the eschaton, God's election of Israel is in force not just for a time, but to the end of all things.

Israel's election means both that she must live apart from the nations, visibly distinct from them, and that she lives close to God, as the nations do not. To live apart from the nations requires publicly visible signs of her distinctiveness, manifold marks to show that she does not live as the gentiles do. Following a tradition that goes back to the Church Fathers, Aquinas sees circumcision as a privileged mark of the distinction of Jew from gentile. It was "the sign in their flesh" that the Jews accepted so that they would not forget their descent from Abraham, a visible declaration of their commitment to imitate him, who first believed in and followed the one true God.[16] But for Aquinas, God gives not simply circumcision but the whole of the "Old Law" in order to distinguish Jews from gentiles, and so to serve Israel's election. This applies not simply to the moral commandments, which the pagans fail to follow, but to Israel's whole religious and cultic practice, by which she gives herself over to the one true God in worship and daily life.[17] As a whole and in all its details, Israel's distinctive way of life, her *singularis conversatio*, is given by God as a testimony that she, alone among the nations, has been chosen by God.[18]

The Jewish people are chosen not only to live apart from the nations, but to live close to God. The immediate purpose of the Law is Israel's own sanctification, her intimacy with the holy God. Under the conditions of sin, this demands Israel's separation from the nations, lost in idolatry and the evils that follow upon it. Israel is thus set apart from the surrounding mass of gentiles for the sake of her proximity to God, his dwelling in her midst. This begins with the worship of the true God and the rejection of idolatry. "God was worshipped in this people alone, all other peoples having been corrupted by idolatry."[19] The Jews were the friends of God (*quasi amicis*), and God opened up to them, as friends do, the secrets of his own heart. For this reason, following Romans 3:2, God entrusted to them alone his *eloquia*, his teaching about himself and his purposes with humanity.[20]

This high estimate of Israel's election may seem incongruous at best, given the regularity with which Aquinas attributes all kinds of vices to the Jews. They were a people "inclined to idolatry" and to "pride", a "carnal and stiff-necked people" who were "prone to cruelty", and so forth.[21] In these passages, though, Aquinas is speaking about Israel as depicted in Scripture. When he attributes such failings to the Jews in the time of what he calls "the Old Law", Aquinas is for the most part simply following the lead of the Old Testament itself, which marvels at God's electing love for Israel in spite of her sin.[22] Aquinas takes even a harsh New Testament text like John 8:44 as an opportunity not to pause over any inherent wickedness of the Jews, still less to question their status as God's elect, but to make an argument against the Manichean idea that the Jews (or anybody else) are evil by nature.[23]

More disturbing is Thomas' endorsement of the view, by his time well established in both canon and civil law, that "the Jews, by reason of their guilt, are assigned to perpetual servitude."[24] This is not a point on which Aquinas dwells or that he often repeats, but it would be fatuous to suggest that he does not believe it. The claim concerns not biblically attested Israel but the Jews of his own time, and indeed until the end of time. The "guilt" to which this remark refers is that ascribed to the Jews in the suffering and death of Christ, on account of which the Jewish people as a whole must undergo penal servitude for all time. This attribution of perpetual guilt to the Jews for the Crucifixion is sometimes called the "deicide charge", to which we will return. For the moment, the question is whether Aquinas' manifest acceptance of various repressive measures against the Jews as requirements of a Christian society conflicts with his biblically rooted understanding, also plain, that the Jews have been chosen by God for a perpetual relationship of love with him.

Aquinas clearly does not think there is a problem here—not even an ambiguity, let alone an inconsistency. This comes to light when he considers the question, often discussed by medieval theologians and canonists, whether the children of Jews (and other non-Christians [*infideles*], he sometimes adds), can be baptized against the will of their parents. Thomas' opposition to the baptism of a child without the consent of the parents is sharp, even vehement, probably in part because toleration of this practice was on the rise in his own time. He embraces the traditional Western position that the baptism of a Jewish child *invitis parentibus*, even if necessary for the child's salvation, traduces the natural right of the parents over their children. In the process, he flatly rejects the argument that the legal servitude of the Jews, which effectively makes them the servants of their prince, without the freedoms accorded by law to Christians, makes this practice licit: "The Jews are servants of the princes by a civil servitude, which does not exclude"—that is, does not overrule—"the order of natural and divine law."[25] Natural and divine law, in his view, rule out baptism without parental consent. *A fortiori*, the election of the Jews, as we have seen, belongs to God's revealed will for the salvation of the world and is inseparable from God's gift of his own Law to the Jews. Their standing with God cannot, therefore, be judged from their present social state. We are, of course, repelled by Thomas' tolerance, and that of his age, for the legal repression of the Jews, but he does not think the civil servitude of the Jews can count as evidence against their election by God. These are two different matters, which have to be distinguished if we are rightly to understand either one.

Israel and Christ

Aquinas, then, offers a vigorous account of Jewish election, and with that of the soteriological importance of the distinction between Jew and gentile. On this score, his reading of the Epistle to the Romans is not far from that of recent historical critics (the so-called new interpretation of Paul). At the same time, Aquinas insists that the election of Israel is ultimately for the sake of Christ. God chooses this people as his own and bestows great gifts upon them so that the redeemer of all the nations may, in the fullness of time, be born among them: "God gave the law and other special benefits to this people for the sake of the promise he made to their fathers that Christ would be born from them." Christ's future advent is the primary reason for God's unique relationship with Abraham and his descendants, the reason why God "elected this people, and no other".[26]

Israel's whole being is ordered to Jesus Christ. God's electing love for Abraham and his fleshly descendants, the Law and every other good he bestows upon them as the fruit of this love, the holiness that the elect people realize through the Law—all are *propter Christum*, for the sake of Christ. The immediate purpose of the gift of the Law is Israel's sanctification, but this is not an end in itself. The *telos*, the ultimate purpose, of Israel's sanctification is that Christ come forth from this holy people: "It was fitting that the people from whom Christ was to be born be strengthened by a special kind of sanctification, according to Lev. 19."[27] Israel's cult, therefore, accomplishes more in the way of holiness than bringing Israel close to the one true God, essential though that is. Israel's rites—the complex network of temple, sacrifices, ornaments, feasts, purifications, properly vested Levitical priests, and much else—all teach faith in Christ. They look forward clearly to the redeemer who is to come from this elect people and elicit a saving reliance on him. This is already evident in the pre-Levitical sacrament of circumcision, which is a *protestatio* or profession not only "of faith in the one God" but "of faith in Christ" yet to come.[28] More than that: By circumcision and the Levitical cult, the Israelites are freed from original sin and come to possess saving righteousness. The Jews under the Law are already justified, by faith in Christ and union with him. It is essential for Aquinas that justification and salvation can happen in no other way, whether before or after Christ's coming in the flesh.

Another way of holding that Israel's election aims entirely at Christ is to say that Israel's existence is figural. In fact, for Aquinas "everything about the condition of this people is figural and prophetic", following Saint Paul, who teaches that "everything happened to this people as a figure" (1 Cor 10:11) of what was to come in Christ (Vulg.: "Omnia in figura contingebant illis").[29] This applies in particular to what Aquinas calls the ceremonial Law, as we have already observed in the case of circumcision. He insists that Israel's cultic regulations have a literal purpose or *ratio*. They enable God's elect people to worship him, while the nations worship their idols. But God gave the cultic Law chiefly for a second, figurative purpose: to join Israel with Christ, by teaching of his future advent and orienting Israel to his presence.[30]

It might be supposed (and nowadays often is supposed) that ascribing a Christological *telos* to the election of Israel voids any professed commitment to Jewish election, and especially to its permanence or irrevocability. Assigning the Jewish people and their election a place in the Christian story, in a Christ-centered understanding of God and

God's purposes, inevitably devalues the Jews and their election, making them theologically dispensable as far as Christians are concerned.

For Aquinas and the tradition to which he belongs, the opposite is the case. As he sees it, being ordered to Christ is being ordered to the highest good. The deeper and more complex its tie to Christ and his Cross, the more significant any created reality is in the divine work of salvation. Nothing in all creation before the coming of Christ is more closely tied to him than God's elect people and their religion. Mary of Nazareth, the faithful Jew full of grace who gives to God incarnate his human flesh, is not an exception to this generalization, but its fullest realization.

As Thomas understands it, to have Christ as final end is not to devalue the Jewish people, or Jewish existence in its particularity. For him, everything, the whole of the actually existing order of creation and salvation, is ordered around Jesus Christ. Created realities do not lose value from being ordered to Christ; they *get* value from being ordered to Christ. Precisely on account of their ordering to Jesus Christ—their election, seen in light of its final purpose—the Israelites have, as Saint Paul teaches, great advantage over the gentiles (Rom 3:1–2; 9:4–5). They "cling to God and are instructed by him", which is "the greatest human good".[31]

The lengths to which Aquinas goes to give a Christological account of Israel do not attest to a low estimate of the Jewish people, but rather—as with his Christological accounts of the Blessed Virgin and the sacraments—indicate how significant a reality of saving history he takes Israel to be. This is not, of course, the way Jewish faith understands the place of the Jewish people in the designs of God, but it is not on that account a place of dishonor. That depends on what *sort* of Christological account Aquinas gives. That God elects the Jewish people as the needed means to the end of his supreme and saving purpose for all creation gives the election of Israel, he argues, a gravity it could have in no other way. That gravity extends, as we have seen, to the permanence of Jewish election.

As the saving history willed by God actually comes to pass, the Jewish people are so closely tied to God's purposes that God himself could not become flesh without them, without the holiness that sets them apart from the nations. The Incarnation of the Word requires flesh that is holy in itself, flesh on which God has set his heart in love on account of the fathers of Israel whom he chose (see Deut 10:15). More than that, though, the Incarnation of the Word requires the holiness of Israel's worship, her service of the one true God. In a world corrupted by sin, beginning with the worship of idols forbidden by the very first commandment, God could not become incarnate as a gentile; he could not have his human flesh from a gentile mother.[32] His coming into the world could be celebrated not by pagan rites, but only by the circumcision that marks him as a member of God's covenant people.[33] He could not worship in the sanctuaries of the gentiles, but only in the temple of the Lord, and among the people who know and serve the true God, by the laws God has given and the words of the prayers Israel's holy ones have taught. In sum: "Just as the source of health must be healthy, so the source of salvation, which comes through true knowledge of God and true worship, must have the true knowledge of God." Precisely because Jesus Christ is "the source and cause of salvation", he "must come forth from them" among whom God is known.[34]

The necessity that binds the Incarnation of the Word to Jewish flesh and Jewish sanctity is, to be clear, conditional rather than absolute. It is the kind of necessity that links the appropriate means (Israel's election) to a freely willed end (God's Incarnation), rather than the necessity that belongs to what could not possibly be otherwise. As in most patristic and medieval theology, Aquinas holds that God could have saved humanity from sin otherwise than by becoming incarnate, and otherwise than by the Passion and Cross of the incarnate Son, though these together are the most suitable and fitting way for God to deliver us from the evil we have done.[35] The election of Israel is the necessary preparation for the saving work of the Word incarnate. This is what it means to say that the Jewish people exist "for the sake of Christ".

So far as I can see, Aquinas is not explicit about whether, given God's decision for his own redemptive Incarnation in Christ, Jewish election is strictly necessary for reaching that end (as eating is necessary for preserving life) or is the best and most reliable way to reach the end, but not the only way (as, in Aquinas' world, riding a horse, as opposed to going on foot, was the best way to travel from Ravenna to Rome). He at least strongly suggests that having willed the redemptive Passion and Cross of the incarnate Son, their "prefiguration in the practices of the Old Testament" is strictly necessary for that end, a condition without which the end cannot come to pass.[36] Even if Aquinas is not clearly committed to going quite this far, he holds that God in fact wills the election of Israel, including the whole religious and social existence of the elect people, and the redemption of the world by Jesus Christ together. The two are related as promise and fulfillment, needed means and final end. God wills them as a unit; they are distinct but inseparable and intended by God as such.

Following the logic of ancient conciliar Christology, to which he is emphatically committed, Aquinas recognizes the human nature assumed by the eternal Word as fully God's own, as much as your humanity or mine is our own. On account of the Incarnation of the Word, God is a human being, in just the same sense that Socrates is a human being.[37] The flesh—the Jewish flesh—the Word becomes (see Jn 1:14) is nothing less than the *caro Dei*, the flesh of God, and as such has not simply supreme, but infinite, dignity or worth.[38] This means, on the one hand, that God himself, in the person of the Word, is not simply a human being but a Jew, born of a Jewish woman who is, on this account, the Mother of God. With the Jewish flesh of Mary's Son, God has entered into the most intimate relationship he can possibly have with a creature, that of personal or hypostatic union. On the other hand, this basic Christological point is essential to understanding the notorious "deicide charge", which Aquinas clearly makes, and to grasping what is, and is not, involved in rejecting it.

The Christological rule, basic for Aquinas, that whatever belongs to the human being Jesus belongs to God entails that if Jesus is killed by other human beings, God (in the person of the Son or Word) is killed by them—by killing this human being they have committed deicide, the killing of God. Aquinas does not use the term "deicide". But he clearly sees it as an essential commitment of Christian faith in the Incarnation, that as God has a human mother, just because Jesus does, so God dies a human death, just because Jesus does. If we believe in the Incarnation—as we do, for example, in calling upon Mary as *Mater Dei* and *sancta Dei Genetrix*—then we believe that on the Cross, God himself suffered death at the hands of violent men.[39]

This Christological background is essential to understanding how Aquinas can make the remark, naturally disturbing to us, that the Jews are "the crucifiers not only of Christ a human being, but of God".[40]

Following the New Testament, Thomas allots responsibility for Jesus' Passion to gentiles as well as Jews and indeed finds figurative significance in the fact that his Passion was begun by Jews and finished by gentiles, who alone had the actual legal authority to kill him.[41] Since the gentiles, too, are responsible for the slaying of Jesus, they, too, have committed deicide; they have crucified and killed God in the flesh, no less than the Jews have.

But the consequences of their shared deicide are quite different. Thomas maintains that the Jews sin more gravely than the gentiles in the killing of God incarnate. This goes especially for the leading priests, the *maiores* or *principes* among the Jews, who knew the Law well enough to grasp its clear figurative significance and so recognized that Jesus was Israel's promised Messiah, but still rejected him. The *minores*, the ordinary Jews of the time, did not fully grasp the figurative import of the Law and so sinned less than the *maiores*, while the gentiles, who knew nothing at all of the Law, sinned least of all, though of course still gravely.[42] Yet even the leading priests did not knowingly "crucify God", a suggestion Thomas takes to be ruled out by 1 Corinthians 2:8 ("If they had known, they would not have crucified the Lord of glory"): "They were ignorant of the mystery of his divinity."[43]

There are mitigations, then, of the responsibility even of the Jews of Jesus' own time and place for his violent death. In this, Aquinas follows a well-established pattern of Christian teaching. At the same time, he does not contest the claim, also traditional, that the Jews have been punished with unparalleled severity for their role in the Crucifixion, even if he does not dwell on the point. "The Jews have been punished for the sin of killing Christ, the murder of God himself, which the magnitude of their penalty shows"—an apparent, though not wholly explicit, reference to an ongoing punishment of the Jews.[44]

When it comes to the Jews of Christ's own time, Aquinas' position bears some resemblance to what would later be said at Vatican II, in its paragraph repudiating the "deicide charge" against the Jews: "What happened in [Christ's] passion cannot be charged against all the Jews, without distinction, then alive."[45] When it comes to the Jews of *his* own time, however, Aquinas accepts the idea of a present and continuing punishment, which *Nostra aetate* no. 4 rejects (what happened in Christ's Passion cannot be charged "against the Jews of today"). *Nostra aetate* no. 4 also rejects, emphatically, any presentation of the Jews as rejected (*reprobati*) or cursed (*maledicti*) by God. Aquinas, though, makes no such presentation; he never speaks of the Jews as rejected or cursed, and as we have seen, he does not think Christians have license to take the present punishment of the Jews as warrant for claiming that they are no longer God's elect. Aquinas' position on these very difficult issues does not fit the disjunctive categories of postconciliar theology: either guilty of deicide without qualification or innocent of deicide without qualification.

Mortifera: Jewish Existence After Christ

Aquinas holds that with the coming of Christ, and more precisely with the completion of his saving Passion, the entire "ceremonial" Law of the Old Testament need no longer be practiced, and soon must not be practiced. The fullness of time has come, and the purposes for which God gave to Israel the Law that comprises the whole of her worship and ritual have been accomplished. These purposes, to recall, are two: the holiness of the Chosen People and the prefiguration of Christ to come, especially of his redemptive work.

To continue observing the cultic and ritual laws given by God to prepare for the coming of Christ after Christ has actually come in the flesh is no longer to draw close to him and the God who sent him but to act as though he is still yet to come. And this is to deny that he has already come and accomplished his saving work. Once the Incarnation and the saving Passion of the incarnate Word have been made known to the world, keeping the ceremonial laws of the Old Testament (and the judicial laws too, though that is less important here) is, as Aquinas is well known for saying, *mortifera*—now death-dealing rather than, as it once was, life-giving: "The ceremonial laws have been voided (*evacuata*) to such an extent that they are not only 'dead' (*mortua*) but also 'deadly' (*mortifera*) for those who observe them after Christ, especially after the promulgation of the gospel."[46] Thomas is consistent about this throughout his writings, including the *Lectura* on Romans, notwithstanding the high view of Jewish election we have seen there: "The [ceremonial] laws are not only dead but deadly, so that anyone who observes them sins mortally."[47]

In the thirteenth century, Western Christians were beginning to become acquainted with the content of the Talmud and the practices of post-biblical Judaism (a development that was not, on the whole, helpful to Jews in the late Middle Ages), but Thomas knows practically nothing of this. He is aware that the Jews continue to practice circumcision, and he takes this as emblematic of the status of Jewish religious life after the whole of the cultic Law God gave them should have been put to rest: "To be circumcised, and to observe the rest of the ceremonial Law, after the passion of Christ is mortal sin" (with reference, characteristically, to Galatians 5:2).[48]

Thomas thus regards the practice of the Jewish religion as grave sin once the gospel has been proclaimed. He does so not out of contempt for Jewish belief and practice but for a religious and theological reason he takes to be of the greatest possible importance. The chief matter in all of Christian doctrine, he holds, "is the salvation accomplished by the cross of Christ".[49] The whole saving work of God, and in fact the whole of creation, is ordered in one way or another to the Cross. As we have seen, God's elect people and their divinely given religion are ordered to Jesus Christ in an especially intimate and significant way. Among the manifold ways this ordering holds good, the cultic or "ceremonial" Law of Israel is of special importance, as it gives precise and detailed shape to the redemption Christ will accomplish. His redemptive work, we could say, is precisely to realize in all its richness the full figurative potency of the Law God gave to Israel, and thus to perfect and fulfill the Law as a whole. "The salvation accomplished by the cross of Christ" is inseparable from the full cultic life of God's elect people, providing the pattern of redemption that he will live out to the full. But likewise, the biblical religion of the Jews is inseparable from the Cross, being without remainder its prefigurative preparation and anticipation. To practice the biblical religion of the Jews after Christ has accomplished salvation by his Cross is, precisely because of this intimate relation between the two, inevitably a denial of Christ, a rejection of the salvation-historical purpose for which God gave the Chosen People their religion in the first place.

Despite the massive importance of Aquinas for Catholic theology since the sixteenth century, his highly detailed treatment of "the Old Law" in *Summa theologiae* I-II, qq. 98–105 for a long time drew little attention from commentators. Understandably concerned with Thomas' classification of Jewish religious practice after Christ as a deadly rejection of saving faith in him, readers of Thomas now look for strategies to argue that Aquinas' teaching is not what it appears to be; the Law God gave to Israel is not truly *mortifera* after the coming of Christ.

One is to observe, rightly, that Thomas thinks circumcision and the rest of the Old Law does not become *mortifera* immediately upon the death of Christ. The Old Law only becomes deadly to those who practice it after the promulgation (*divulgatio*) of the Gospel to the nations, which takes a certain amount of time. Here Aquinas agrees with Augustine, who argued against Jerome that there is a "middle period" (*tempus medium*) between Israel's obedient worship prefiguring Christ to come and the adequate proclamation of his accomplished saving work to the world. With the Passion of Christ, the ceremonies lost their earlier capacity to mediate salvation to those who practice them, but during this middle period, they were not yet fatal. They were "dead" but not yet "deadly". Like Augustine, Aquinas takes this view in order to accommodate the biblical indications (Acts 16:3; 21:17–26) that even the apostles kept the Old Law for a time after Christ.[50] The mitigating strategy is to argue that Thomas thinks we are still in the "middle period" between Christ's Passion and the adequate public promulgation of the Gospel. In that case, Jewish rites, even in Aquinas' own time, would not be *mortifera*, mortal sins.

Whatever the merits of this idea, it is not Thomas' own. The period prior to the *divulgatio* of the Gospel, in the sense in which he uses the term, was only "a short time" (*modico tempore*), apparently equivalent to "the outset of the time of the apostles" (*sicut tempus Apostolorum in principio*)."[51] He evidently thinks this period had already passed by the time Paul wrote to the Galatians, since they made the deadly error of supposing that circumcision was necessary for salvation "after grace had been promulgated".[52] Or more succinctly, "Someone who now [when Aquinas is writing this] bears witness to his faith by saying that Christ is still to be born sins mortally, even though the ancients [Israel before the coming of Christ] said this piously and correctly." By their very nature, circumcision and the other practices of the Mosaic Law are just such a witness (*protestatio*) to belief that the Christ promised by God has not yet come, a belief now gravely mistaken.[53]

A second mitigation strategy focuses on this last point and argues that whether the Law of Moses is sinful in the way Aquinas describes depends on the intention of the person who practices it. Jews do not follow the requirements of Torah with the intention of denying that Christ has come but in order to worship the God of Israel in obedience to his own commands. On this reading, it might be sinful for Christians to continue with the practices of the ceremonial Law, since they accept it as a prefiguration of Jesus Christ not yet come in the flesh, but this practice is not sinful for Jews.

Aquinas' intricate analysis of morally responsible acts certainly includes a role for the agent's intention in determining the moral quality of an act. Whether an act is good or evil depends chiefly, however, on what is done—on the outcome of the act. It is thus possible to have a good intention and nonetheless to act with an evil will—that is, to sin.[54] As a result, there are many acts that are evil and sinful in themselves, regardless of the intention with which one undertakes them—acts that no good intention, and no ignorance of the nature of the act, can make good.

So it is, on Thomas' account, in this case. The temporal prefigurative character of the ceremonial Law is inherent, willed as such by God. The outcome of observing the ceremonial Law is the prefiguration of Christ still to come, regardless of the intention of the one observing it. To observe circumcision and the rest of the ceremonial laws in their proper time was good, but "observed in a time not their own they are evil, and therefore they cannot be made good by a good intention."[55] Whether keeping the ritual laws of the Old Testament is sin depends not on the person who keeps them (whether he is a Jew or a Christian, for example), but on the time in which they are kept—before or after the coming of Christ. For this reason, Thomas says that the ceremonial laws are now deadly for "anyone (*quisquis*) who observes them", not deadly for some but salutary for others.[56]

In one tantalizing passage, Thomas suggests that circumcision and the rest of Jewish worship might not be ruled out as mortal sin after the coming of Christ. The rites of the Jews ought to be permitted in a Christian society, Aquinas argues, because Jewish worship "formerly prefigured the truth of the faith which we hold", and by observing their rites in our own time, "they make present to us in a figure, as it were, what we believe."[57] Since what Christians believe cannot, one presumes, be figuratively present in rites that are gravely sinful, this would imply that observance of the ceremonial Law after Christ is not inherently *mortifera* after all. This is the only place, however, where Aquinas says this or anything close to it. What it attests to, I think, is that even when it comes to the status of Jewish cultic practice after Christ, a matter about which he is on the whole painfully clear, ambiguity finds its way into Thomas' teaching.[58]

Ambiguity and the Refusal of Replacement

Since Vatican II, the idea has taken hold that for its whole history, Christianity has been committed without reserve to a "replacement theology" (or "supersessionism"). This supposed "replacement theology" claims that God rejected the Jews at the coming of Christ, ending their election and replacing them with the Christians as his elect people—an outlook both theologically groundless and morally odious.

Writers who assume a long-standing replacement theology in the Christian tradition do not usually try to offer convincing examples of people who actually held this view, but in any case, it is clear that Aquinas did not. All creatures are ordered to Christ, and for Aquinas the way they are ordered to Christ depends, in a basic and irrevocable way, on whether they are Jews or gentiles. As Aquinas sees it, the distinction God has made between Jews and gentiles belongs to the deep structure of God's saving purposes in Christ and is evidently permanent. It is an elementary principle of salvation history, a soteriological prime number, and will abide until the last day, even though the role of Israel in saving history changes dramatically after Christ. Israel's election, and the promise of eschatological salvation that comes with it, is irrevocable. The Jews are not replaced as God's elect.

At the same time, the way creatures are ordered to Christ depends on their temporal location. Jesus Christ is the axis of all matters human and the absolute center of human history. His coming, above all his Passion and Cross, changes everything. God has provided created means by which human beings can be united to Christ's saving work before his Passion, and not only after it—the whole existence, especially the religious existence, of the elect people from whom he will be born. But the Cross makes all things new. The kind of saving significance any created reality can have depends on whether it is shaped by what has yet to happen in Christ or by what has already happened in Christ, by a salvation yet to be accomplished or a salvation already accomplished. There are sacraments under the Old Law, and also under the New. Both bring about salvation through union with Christ crucified. But the sacraments themselves are—and must be—irreducibly different, depending on whether they come before or after "the salvation accomplished by the cross of Christ". The religion God gave the Jews, beginning with the sign of circumcision, has not been replaced by Christianity, as though it were annihilated and something else took its place. It has, however, been fulfilled by the Cross and thereby profoundly transformed into the sacramental life of the Church. There is nothing needful left for the old religion to do.

If we were to think only of Aquinas' commitment to the irrevocable election of the Jewish people, we might infer that he accepts the practice of Judaism. How, after all, will the Jewish people abide until the end of time, as Aquinas clearly thinks they must, without their religion? Yet he thinks the rites of the Jews, while Christians should not seek to hinder them, are death-dealing. If we were to think only of Aquinas' commitment to the transformation of Israel's cultic existence into the sacramental life of the Church by the Passion of Christ, we might infer that he does not believe that God's election of the Jews is permanent. But quite clearly, he does.

Today there are communities of Catholics who intend to remain visible as Jews within the Church—to be the *Ecclesia Iudaeorum* in our own time. This was not true in Aquinas' day and indeed has not been true in any consistent way since the earliest days of Christianity. By this form of life perhaps these Hebrew Catholics can, in time, help the whole Church understand how we can all believe, beyond compromise and ambiguity, in both the irrevocable gifts and call of God to the Jewish people and the magnitude of the difference that Christ makes.

6

Jewish Practices: The Council of Florence and Benedict XIV's 1756 Encyclical *Ex Quo Primum*

Robert Fastiggi

Introduction

This chapter examines the Catholic Church's attitude toward Jewish practices as expressed by the Council of Florence (1439–1445) and by Pope Benedict XIV in his 1756 encyclical *Ex quo primum*. As a prelude to the examination of these two documents, the chapter begins with an overview of Christian attitudes toward the Jewish ritual Law in the New Testament. The chapter continues with an overview of Catholic attitudes and teachings on Jews and Jewish practices before the fifteenth century in order to better understand the decisions of Florence. The essay then turns to the Council of Florence itself, which is sometimes referred to as the Council of Basel–Ferrara–Florence–Rome of 1431–1445 because the council began in Basel before moving to Ferrara and then to Florence before concluding in Rome. Two documents on Jewish practices from the Basel phase of the council will be examined before looking at the bull, *Cantate Domino*, of 1442. As will be seen, this bull teaches that Christians who observe Jewish practices risk the loss of eternal salvation. The chapter then examines two encyclical letters of Pope Benedict XIV (r. 1740–1758) that touch on Judaism. The first is *A quo primum* of 1751, which expresses concern about growing Jewish influence in Poland. The second is *Ex quo primum* of 1756, which manifests a more positive attitude toward Jews and the use of

Jewish practices by Christians. The chapter ends with some observations about the development of the Catholic Church's attitude toward Jews and Jewish practices.

Christians and the Jewish Law in the New Testament

One of the central teachings of the Catholic faith is that Christ's death on the Cross is the "meritorious cause" of our justification.[1] In Romans 3:28, Saint Paul states that "we consider that a person is justified by faith apart from works of the law."[2] The "works of the law" would include the Jewish laws of worship, ritual purity, and diet.[3] Even the covenantal sign of circumcision is regarded by Paul as unnecessary: "For in Christ Jesus, neither circumcision nor uncircumcision counts for anything but only faith working through love" (Gal 5:6). For Saint Paul, the Cross of Christ "broke down the dividing wall ... abolishing the law with its commandments and legal claims" (Eph 2:14–15).[4]

The early Church, though, needed to come to grips with the tensions between Jewish converts, who still felt attached to the Jewish ritual laws, and gentile converts, who never practiced the Jewish "works of the law". The apostles and the presbyters resolved the controversy at the Council of Jerusalem described in Acts 15. After much discussion and interventions by Peter (15:7–11) and James (15:13–21), a letter was written that reflected the consensus of the apostles, the presbyters, and the whole Church. This letter contained these instructions to the Christian brethren of gentile origin in Antioch, Syria, and Cilicia: "It is the decision of the Holy Spirit and of us not to place on you any burden beyond these necessities, namely to abstain from meat sacrificed to idols, from blood, from meats of strangled animals, and from unlawful marriage. If you keep free of these, you will be doing what is right" (15:28–29).[5]

This letter was intended for Christians of gentile origin (15:23), and the gentile Christians were "delighted" by its contents (15:31).

In theory, the abolition of the law "with its commandments and legal claims" (Eph 2:15) would apply to all Christians. It seems, though, that many Christians of Jewish background continued to observe Old Covenant laws of ritual purity and worship. Out of respect for Jews of the region of Lystra and Iconium, Paul had Timothy circumcised because he had a Jewish mother—though his father was Greek (see Acts 16:1–3). Paul himself still seemed to follow Jewish traditions. At Cenchreae, "he had his hair cut because he had taken a vow" (18:18). This was presumably the Nazarite vow described in Numbers 6:1–21 and taken by the judge, Samson (Judg 16:17). When the Jewish high priest, Ananias, brings charges against him to the governor, Paul declares: "I worship the God of our ancestors and I believe everything that is in accordance with the law and written in the prophets" (Acts 24:14). He states that he has come to Jerusalem "to bring alms for my nation and offerings" (24:17). When he is brought before the Roman procurator, Festus, in Caesarea, Paul defends himself by saying: "I have committed no crime either against the Jewish law or against Caesar" (25:8). Commenting on Acts 24:11–13, William S. Kurz, S.J., notes that "Paul does not consider his conversion to Christ a departure from Judaism; rather, he has continued his Jewish devotional practices."[6]

Although the gentile Christians were exempt from the Jewish cultic laws—except those specified in Acts 15:29—the question of how Jewish Christians were to interact with gentile Christians in table fellowship took time to resolve. Paul's rebuke of Peter's inconsistency in Galatians 2:11–14 shows that there were Christians of Jewish origin who still believed they should not have table fellowship with gentiles—even those who had become Christian.[7] Acts 10:28–29 indicates that Peter, based on a supernatural revelation, had no problem with eating with gentiles. As he says: "God has shown me that I should not call any person profane or unclean" (10:28).[8] When Peter is challenged by the circumcised believers in Jerusalem, he relates the vision he had in Joppa, which revealed to him that "what God has made clean, you are not to call profane" (11:9).

In light of this revelation, Peter eats with the gentiles when he first comes to Antioch (Gal 2:12). When, however, "some people came from James ... he began to draw back because he was afraid of the circumcised. And the rest of the Jews [also] acted hypocritically with him, with the result that even Barnabas was carried away by their hypocrisy" (2:12–13). When Paul sees what is going on, he confronts Peter and says to him: "If you, though a Jew, are living like a Gentile and not like a Jew, how can you compel the Gentiles to live like Jews?" (2:14).

Much has been written about Paul's rebuke of Peter. The incident clearly shows that there were some Christians of Jewish origin in the early Church who believed that Jewish traditions—such as not eating with gentiles—were still to be followed. Peter had rejected this belief, and he had eaten with gentile Christians in Antioch before becoming afraid of "the circumcised". The "circumcised" in this context were part of a faction of Jewish Christians who still insisted on observing Jewish laws of purity.[9] Paul rebukes Peter (Cephas) for his hypocrisy and inconsistent behavior. He does not, however, challenge his doctrinal authority or primacy. Moreover, we know about the incident only from Paul's perspective. It could be that Peter did not want to upset the circumcision party and cause an unnecessary confrontation. Paul might also have been overstating the matter because Peter was not trying to make gentiles become Jewish. Peter's conduct, though, could give the impression that he "considered Gentile Christians unclean".[10] Paul's rebuke of Peter is, therefore, justified. It reveals that "Christians are not called to accept circumcision or other 'works of the law.'"[11]

Paul's correction of Peter, however, should not be used as a reason for rejecting the Catholic doctrine of Petrine primacy or the divine assistance enjoyed by the successors of Peter in their teaching ministry. Paul, in fact, was reminding Peter that "he used to eat with the Gentiles" when he first came to Antioch (Gal 2:12). Peter, in fact, was contradicting his own doctrine. Paul's rebuke of Peter serves as a reminder that even holy popes can make mistakes in their prudential judgments. This is why we should pray for them.[12]

From the New Testament, it is clear that gentile Christians were not required to follow the Jewish cultic Law. Although Christians of Jewish origin such as Paul continued to observe Jewish practices, the example of Peter in Acts 10–11 shows that all Christians, including those of Jewish origin, were not bound to observe Jewish traditions and ceremonial laws.

Catholic Teachings on Jews and Jewish Practices up to the Council of Florence (1439–1445)

The focus of this essay is the Council of Florence and the 1756 encyclical letter *Ex quo primum* of Pope Benedict XIV. It is important, though, to provide a brief overview of Catholic attitudes and teachings on Jews and Jewish practices before the fifteenth century to help put the decisions of Florence into historical context.

Before the Edict of Milan of 313, Christianity was not recognized as a legal religion within the Roman Empire. Christians endured periodic persecutions, which were sometimes violent. In the fourth century—apart from the reign of Julian the Apostate (361–363)—Christianity gradually assumed prominence in the Roman Empire. By the end of the century, Emperor Theodosius (r. 392–395) and his sons began to issue decrees outlawing pagan worship. Before Christianity became the religion of the Roman Empire, both Jews and Christians had to survive under pagan Roman rule. Once Christianity became the religion of the Empire, the question of how to treat the Jews emerged. Because, as John K. Roth writes, "Jewish belief and practice persisted as counter-testimony to Christianity's most basic claims," some Church Fathers such as Justin Martyr (c. 100–165), Tertullian (c. 160–225), and John Chrysostom (c. 347–407) wrote works seeking to refute Jewish arguments against the Christian faith. According to some scholars, these *Adversus Judaeos* writings represented a "teaching of contempt" toward Judaism.[13]

A more positive view of Judaism was taken by Augustine (354–430). According to the bishop of Hippo, the ongoing presence of Jews and their Scriptures demonstrated that the Christians had not forged the prophecies about Christ.[14] According to Father Lawrence E. Frizzell, Augustine saw the role of the Jews as "witness people".[15] If pagan opponents of Christianity "questioned the antiquity of biblical prophecies, the Christian teacher could point to the Jews"[16] to show that the prophetic books were both ancient and authentic. Augustine also believed that God willed a portion of the Jews to remain Jewish until Christ's return. This would fulfill the prophecy of Zechariah 12:9–10: "On that day I will seek the destruction of all nations that come upon Jerusalem. I will pour out on the house of David and on the inhabitants of Jerusalem a spirit of grace and petition, and they shall look on him whom they thrust through, and they shall mourn for him as one mourns for an only son, and they shall grieve over him as one grieves over a firstborn."

Augustine was convinced that this Scripture plainly refers to "the crucifixion of Christ".[17] When Christ returns, "the Jews shall believe,"[18] at least "those that receive the spirit of mercy and grace".[19]

The Jews who are saved at the time of the Parousia will recognize Christ as the one who was condemned and crucified at the time of their ancestors. As Roy H. Schoeman notes,[20] this teaching of Augustine is affirmed by the *Catechism of the Catholic Church* when it says: "The glorious Messiah's coming is suspended until the recognition by 'all Israel', for a 'hardening has come upon part of Israel' in their 'unbelief' towards Jesus' (Rom 11:20–26; cf. Mt 23:39)."[21]

Augustine believed that the Church should preach the Gospel to the Jews, but he understood that some of them would remain Jews until Christ's Second Coming. He also believed that, according to divine providence, the Jews would be "dispersed among all nations, wherever the Church of Christ is spread abroad".[22] According to Willehad Paul Eckert, Augustine "put forward the theory, which long remained part of Christian theology, that it was the will of God to keep a remnant of the Jews alive in a degraded state as living witnesses of the Christian truth".[23]

When the Roman Empire became Christian, the question emerged whether Jews should be allowed to practice their faith openly. There is no doubt that many Jews living in Catholic countries suffered from various forms of prejudice and discrimination.[24] There were also cases of open hostility and acts of violence committed by both Christians and Jews.[25] The Catholic Church, in her official teachings, upheld the right of Jews to practice their faith, but certain restrictions were sometimes imposed. For example, local Catholic synods at Elvira (c. 305), Vannes (465), and Orleans III (538) prohibited Christians from sharing meals with Jews—which repeated a Jewish tradition but from a Christian perspective.[26] Other locals councils—such as those at Orleans II (533) and Clermont (535)—prohibited mixed marriages between Christians and Jews.[27] The local councils of Orleans II (533), Mâcon (583), and Rome (734)—as well as others—forbade Jews from owning Christian slaves and from converting them to Judaism.[28]

In spite of these restrictions placed on Jews living in Catholic countries, forced baptisms and conversions were prohibited. During the reign of Emperor Theodosius II (402–450), the *Codex Theodosianus* was composed as "a compilation of all laws enacted since the reign of Constantine".[29] Completed in 438, the *Codex* recognized Judaism as a lawful religion (*religio licita*), and it upheld basic rights and freedoms for Jews.[30] It also imposed various restrictions. Jewish proselytism, for example, was prohibited, as were conversions to Judaism and marriages between Jews and Christians.[31] Jews were also "excluded from all public offices".[32] Under the Code of Emperor Justinian I (r. 527–565), more restrictions were added. Jews, for example, could not practice law or testify against a Christian.[33] The *Codex Theodosianus* and the Justinian Code applied in theory to the entire Roman-Byzantine Empire, but, as Father Edward H. Flannery notes: "Jewish fortunes from East to West, from Gaul to Spain, Persia to Arabia" often depended as much on the local authority in charge as on the law.[34]

Pope Gregory I (r. 590–604) solidified the prohibition against forced conversions, and he upheld the right of Jews to worship and celebrate their feasts openly. According to the Jewish historian Jules Isaac (1877–1963), Pope Gregory I inaugurated "a policy of humanity, equity, and relative protection, which does him honor, and will do honor to popes after him; for a tradition was thus established from which many—but not all—would have the goodness of mind and heart to find their inspiration".[35] Gregory I wrote letters to the bishops of Terracina, Palermo, and Cagliari ordering that synagogues seized from the Jews be returned or restored.[36] In 602, he received complaints from the Jews of Naples that they were being prevented from celebrating their solemn feast days in public. In November 602, he sent a letter to Bishop Paschasius of Naples defending the religious freedom of the Jews:

> For the Jews who live in Naples complained to Us that some people have unreasonably sought to prevent them from celebrating some of their solemn feast days, so that they were not permitted to celebrate their solemn festivals, as they, up to the present, and their ancestors for a long time previously, were allowed to observe or honor.... This, then, is the agendum: by being encouraged by reason and gentleness, they are to wish to follow not flee from us, so that by showing them what we affirm from their Scriptures, we may be able, with God's help, to convert them to the bosom of Mother Church.... But they should have the complete freedom (*liberam*) to observe and celebrate all of their feasts and holy days as up till now ... they have possessed.[37]

As can be seen, Gregory I wanted Jews to convert to the Christian faith, but they should never be coerced. Rather, they should be encouraged "by reason and gentleness" and arguments taken from their own Scriptures.[38] If Jews were baptized against their express will, their baptisms were considered invalid. Medieval canonists, though, debated whether the baptisms of Jews were valid if they agreed to be baptized under duress or in bad faith.[39] Pope Innocent III tried to address this question in his 1201 letter, *Maiores Ecclesiae causas*, to Archbishop Humbert of Arles:

> It is contrary to the Christian religion to force others into accepting and practicing Christianity if they are always unwilling and totally opposed. Wherefore, some, not without reason, distinguish between unwilling and unwilling, forced and forced. For whoever are violently drawn by fear of punishments and receive the sacrament of baptism to avoid harm to themselves, such persons just like those who come to baptism in bad faith, receive the imprint of the Christian character; and, since they gave their consent conditionally though not absolutely, they are to be held to the observance of the Christian faith.
>
> But the one who never consents and is absolutely unwilling receives neither the reality nor the character of the sacrament because express dissent is something more than not consenting at all; just as one does not incur the mark of any culpability who, totally contradicting and protesting, is violently forced to offer incense to idols.[40]

The response of Innocent III forbids the baptism of Jews who are completely unwilling and opposed to being baptized. His response, though, reveals a problem that emerged due to the separation of Jews and Christians into two separate communities and the restrictions placed upon Jews living within Catholic realms. Because of these restrictions and other forms of oppression, some Jews were willing to be baptized and become Christians for social advantages while still secretly practicing the Jewish faith. The reality of insincere conversions was a problem noted centuries earlier in canon 8 of the Second Council of Nicaea of 787:

> Since some of those who come from the religion of the Hebrews mistakenly think to make a mockery of Christ who is God, pretending to become Christians, but denying Christ in private by both secretly continuing to observe the Sabbath and maintaining other Jewish practices, we decree that they shall not be received to communion or at prayer or into the church, but rather let them openly be Hebrews

> according to their own religion; they should not baptize their children or buy, or enter into possession of, a slave. But if one of them makes his conversion with a sincere faith and heart, and pronounces his confession wholeheartedly, disclosing their practices and objects in the hope that others may be refuted and corrected, such a person should be welcomed and baptized along with his children, and care should be taken that they abandon Hebrew practices. However if they are not of this sort, they should certainly not be welcomed.[41]

Canon 8 of Nicaea II reaffirms Gregory I's prohibition against forced conversions, but it also insists that Jewish converts to the Catholic faith abandon Jewish practices. The desire to separate the Christian faith from Jewish rituals was already evident at the First Council of Nicaea (325) in its demand that the brethren in the East follow the Roman custom rather than the Jewish custom regarding the date of Easter.[42] The local Synod of Antioch (341) forbade Christians from celebrating the Passover with Jews.[43] The Council of Chalcedon (451) and the Council of Trullo (691) warned Catholics about being too intimate with Jews.[44]

Why, though, were these councils so opposed to the celebration of Jewish practices? Various reasons could be offered, both cultural and religious. One possible reason was the fear of Jewish efforts to influence or convert Catholics. Father Edward H. Flannery offers this description of the Catholic attitude toward the Jews up through the Middle Ages: "Jews were not opposed as persons or as a people, and indeed heretics still fared worse than they. The Church still had reason to worry about Jewish influence in social and religious life. The Talmudic withdrawal of Judaism was never complete. Many Jews, especially those who reached posts of influence in civic or economic spheres kept the doors to and from the Christian world open. The legislation of both church and state must, in effect, be seen, above all as a defense against Jewish proselytism."[45]

The theological reasons for Catholic resistance to Jewish practices have already been examined. Because salvation is through the saving death of Jesus, reliance on the "works of the law" reflects the error of the Judaizers who were so strongly opposed by Saint Paul. The Church during the Middle Ages reaffirmed the need for Jewish converts to abandon Jewish practices. Canon 70 of Lateran IV (1215) specified that "converts to the faith among the Jews may not retain their old rite."[46] The fear was that "in keeping remnants of their former rite, they upset the decorum of the Christian religion by such a mixing."[47]

For Saint Thomas Aquinas, the precepts of the Old Law needed to be distinguished as moral, judicial, or ceremonial.[48] The moral law as expressed by the Decalogue continues in the New Law and is perfected by it. The judicial laws were time-bound ordinances for the ancient Israelites, and, therefore, they do not bind forever.[49] With regard to the ceremonial laws—which would include laws of worship, circumcision, and ritual purity—Aquinas maintained that the apostles continued to observe the legal ceremonies after the Passion because they did not wish to scandalize the Jews and prevent their conversion.[50] Jewish converts were able to observe the ceremonial laws without sin during the period between the Passion of Christ and the promulgation of the Gospel "provided they did not put their trust in them so as to hold them to be necessary unto salvation, as though faith in Christ could not justify without the legal observances".[51] Aquinas allowed for this temporary observance of Jewish rituals because, unlike pagan rituals, they were not unlawful in themselves. They simply ceased being lawful after they were fulfilled through Christ's Passion.[52] As we will see, the views of Aquinas are reflected in the Council of Florence (1439–1445).

The Council of Florence on Jewish Practices

The Council of Florence (February 26, 1439–August 1445) is considered the seventeenth ecumenical council by the Catholic Church. Some historians, knowing that it was the continuation of the Council of Basel (begun in 1431), which was moved to Ferrara, then to Florence, and finally to Rome, believe it should be called the Council of Basel–Ferrara–Florence–Rome. They also give the dates of the council as 1431–1445.[53] When Pope Eugene IV, on September 18, 1437, announced that he was moving the Council to Ferrara, the majority of the bishops in Basel refused to accept this transfer, and they continued the council in Basel until 1449. The bishops who remained at Basel deposed Eugene IV as pope and elected Felix V[54] (who was later declared an antipope[55]). The first twenty-five sessions of Basel are believed to have ecumenical value, but the decrees of Basel after the transfer to Ferrara (and then to Florence) are considered to be those of a schismatic assembly.[56] Because the three main bulls of union—with the Greeks, the Armenians, and the Copts, Jacobites, and Ethiopians—took place in Florence between 1439 and 1442, the council is usually called simply the Council of Florence, and its dates are given as 1439–1445.[57]

There are three documents of the Council of Florence that concern the Jews and Jewish practices. The first is from session 19 (September 7, 1434) of the Basel phase of the council, and it is entitled *Decree on Jews and Neophytes* (*Decretum de Judaeis et neophytis*).[58] This decree instructs bishops to train preachers who can help bring the Jews to conversion by giving them the appropriate linguistic skills (for example, Hebrew, Arabic, Greek, and Chaldean). The decree repeats the restrictions of previous councils: Jews are not allowed to hold public office, and they are "to wear some garment whereby they can be clearly distinguished from Christians".[59] Finally, Jews are to live apart from Christians, and on Sundays and other solemn festivals, "they should not dare to have their shops open or work in public."[60]

The second decree is also from session 19 of September 1434. It is entitled *About Those Who Desire Conversion to the Faith* (*De his qui volunt ad fidem converti*).[61] This decree exhorts the faithful to welcome converts and assist them financially if needed. It also says that "bishops should strive that, at least for a long time, they [the newly converted] do not mingle much with Jews or infidels."[62] Then this severe warning is given: "Converts should be forbidden, under pain of severe penalties, to bury the dead according to Jewish custom or to observe in any way the Sabbath and other rites and solemnities."[63] The newly converted should frequent sermons and churches "like other Catholics, and conform themselves in everything to Christian customs".[64]

The third document from the Council of Florence that deals with Jews and Jewish practices is from the February 4, 1442, Bull of Union with the Copts, *Cantate Domino*, which is also called the Bull of Union with the Copts and the Ethiopians and the *Decree for the Jacobites*.[65] The bull teaches that the legal prescriptions of the Old Testament—divided into ceremonies, holy sacrifices, and sacraments—"were instituted to signify something in the future".[66]

They were "adequate for the divine cult of that age",[67] but they came to an end with the coming of Jesus Christ and the beginning of the Christian sacraments. The bull goes on to make this declaration: "Whoever, even after the Passion, places his hope in the legal prescriptions and submits himself to them as necessary for salvation, as if faith in Christ without them could not save, sins mortally."[68] The bull then reaffirms the position of Aquinas when it says that the Church "does not deny that from Christ's Passion until the promulgation of the gospel they [Jewish practices] could have been retained provided they were in no way believed to be necessary for salvation. But she asserts that after the promulgation of the gospel they cannot be observed without the loss of eternal salvation."[69] The bull then makes this strong denunciation: "Therefore, she denounces all who after that time observe circumcision, the Sabbath, and other legal prescriptions as strangers to the faith of Christ and unable to share in eternal salvation, unless they recoil at some time from these errors. Therefore, she strictly orders all who glory in the name of Christian not to practice circumcision either before or after baptism, since whether or not they place their hope in it, it cannot possibly be observed without the loss of eternal salvation."[70]

How is this stern warning to be understood? Some have tried to moderate its force by claiming that only the Bull of Union with Greeks, *Laetentur caeli* (July 6, 1439), is infallible at Florence.[71] Others have noted that what is said about Jewish practices in *Cantate Domino* must be understood "in the light of later Magisterial teaching, such as Benedict XIV, *Ex quo primum*", which implies that what *Cantate Domino* teaches "should be considered to be a particular disciplinary measure binding only in those circumstances, as was the ruling of the Council of Jerusalem".[72] Such an understanding seems plausible when we consider that Florence's 1439 *Decree for the Armenians*, *Exsultate Deo*, teaches that the matter of the sacrament of holy orders is the handing over of the instruments corresponding to the order conferred.[73] Pius XII, however, did not consider this ruling to be definitive because in his 1947 constitution, *Sacramentum ordinis* (November 30, 1947), he specified that the matter of the sacrament of holy orders is the imposition of the bishop's hands, and "the handing over of the instruments is not necessary for the validity of the holy orders of the diaconate, the priesthood, and the episcopate."[74] Pius XII also noted that the Council of Florence did not ask the Greeks to change their rite of ordination and include the handing over of the instruments.[75] Even if the Council of Florence at one time required ordinations in the Latin Rite to have the handing over of the instruments for validity, "all know the Church can also change and abrogate what she has established."[76] Following this principle of Pius XII, we need to see whether Benedict XIV, in his March 1, 1756, encyclical letter *Ex quo primum* changed, abrogated, or qualified what the Council of Florence taught about Christians and Jewish practices.

Benedict XIV and His Encyclical Letter *Ex Quo Primum* of 1756

Benedict XIV (1675–1758) was pope from August 17, 1740, until May 3, 1758. Even before becoming pope, he was recognized as a scholar and historian. His treatise *De servorum Dei beatificatione et beatorum canonizatione* (1734–1738), on the beatification of the servants of God and the canonization of the blessed, "remains an indispensable study".[77] With regard to the Jews, his record is mixed. He intervened to counter the "blood libel" accusation against the Jews in Poland,[78] but he also "reinstituted rigorous measures against Hebrew literature, and in 1747, he ruled that a Jewish child once baptized, even against Church law, had to be brought up a Christian".[79]

Benedict XIV wrote two encyclical letters that touch on Jewish matters. The first is his June 14, 1751, encyclical, *A quo primum*, on Judaism in Poland.[80] In this letter, he manifests concern for "the influence of Jewish faithlessness (*Judaicam perfidiam*)" in Poland (no. 1). He reaffirms the prohibition of Jews in public office (no. 5), and he manifests his wish that Jews and Christians live apart (no. 6).

Benedict XIV's encyclical letter *Ex quo primum* of March 1, 1756, is more positive toward Jews, even though its focus is on the Greek *Euchologion* (liturgical book) and not Judaism.[81] The letter is addressed to the archbishops, bishops, and other clerics of the Greek Rite "who enjoy favor and communion with the Apostolic See". It is divided into seventy-five sections, and numbers 60–74 touch on questions related to elements of the Old Law retained in the Greek liturgical life. In no. 60, he raises the question whether in the Greek

Euchologion "the observance of legal ceremonies of the old Law was being added to or retained alongside the new law and the Gospel". In no. 61, Benedict XIV recalls the decision of Acts 15 to prohibit food "sacrificed to idols ... from the meat of strangled animals, and from blood". He says that this prohibition "was suitable at that time to remove cause for disagreement between Jew and Gentile", but once the reason for this prohibition came to an end, "the prohibition too has come to an end."

In no. 62, Benedict XIV recalls prior teachings, including those of Urban VIII (1642), Thomas Aquinas (*ST* I-II, q. 103, a. 4, ad 3), and Florence's *Decree for the Jacobites*. These sources note that no foods should be avoided as unclean. For health reasons, though, they can be avoided. In no. 63, he reinforces the truth that "the ceremonial precepts of the old Law came to an end with the promulgation of the Gospel." In no. 64, he recalls the calumny of the pagans that Christians eat the flesh of infants and human blood, and this is why some Christians abstained from the blood of animals and the flesh of strangled animals. He mentions, though, that in some areas abstinence from these types of food was continued out of custom but not because such foods were absolutely forbidden.

In no. 65, Benedict XIV cites the French Benedictine Antoine Augustin Calmet (1672–1757), who pointed out that some Latin churches distinguished between clean and unclean foods and continued abstinence from blood and the meat of strangled animals into the tenth and eleventh centuries. He then cites other authorities who have supported Calmet's findings. In no. 66, he notes that both Calmet and the great Scripture scholar Cornelius a Lapide (1567–1637) testify to the widespread abstinence from blood and strangled meat in the Greek Church. The Armenians, though, who entered into communion with Rome, abandoned this practice. Some authors, however, point out that when the Greeks abstain from blood and the meat of strangled animals, they are abiding by traditions of the Church, not the Old Law.

In no. 67, Benedict XIV appeals to the Greek convert to the Catholic faith Leo Allatius (1586–1669), who argues that it is wrong to claim that someone Judaizes when he, like the Jews, abstains from blood and does not eat flesh of strangled animals. Pope Benedict cites the words of Allatius:

> It cannot be absolutely asserted that that man Judaizes who does something in the Church which corresponds to the ceremonies of the old Law. If a man should perform acts for a different end and purpose (even with the intention of worship and as religious ceremonies), not in the spirit of that Law nor on the basis of it, but either from personal decision, from human custom, or on the instruction of the Church, he would not sin, nor could he be said to Judaize. So when a man does something in the Church which resembles the ceremonies of the old Law, he must not always be said to Judaize.

In no. 69, Benedict XIV mentions Leviticus 12 and the ritual need for the purification of women after childbirth. In no. 70, he cites several authors who testify to women in the early Church who continued the ritual purifications of Leviticus 12. He notes that the medieval canonist Gratian (d. c. 1159) believed there was no sin on the part of a woman who observed this ritual purification. Even the Blessed Virgin Mary observed the ritual purification of Leviticus 12. In no. 71, Benedict XIV points out that the Greek Church still observes the need for purification of women after childbirth. While some believe this practice should be censured, Benedict XIV quotes Pope Saint Gregory the Great (r. 590–604), who states: "The excess of nature cannot be counted as a sin, and it is not just to prevent a woman from entering the church because of what she endures against her will." In no. 72, Benedict XIV cites the French Dominican Jacobus Goarius, who said that the Greeks require the ritual purification of women as a duty, but Latin women do it only out of reverence. In no. 74, Benedict XIV affirms the counsel that "the ceremonial rites of the old Law could be observed under the new Law if only they were not done as obligations of the old Law, which was abrogated, but as a custom, or a lawful tradition, or as a new precept issued by one enjoying the recognized and competent authority to make laws and enforce them", as the Jesuit Gabriel Vasquez (1549–1604) says.

In no. 74, Benedict XIV states that he decided that no change was needed in the section of the *Euchologion* dealing with the rite of ritual purity for women in the Greek Church. He notes that the Greeks do not invoke prayers in the way Jews of old did. Instead, they invoke the patronage of the Blessed Virgin Mary. In no. 75, he tells the Greek Catholic archbishops, bishops, and clerics that in their *Euchologion* "everything was kept which could possibly be kept, and some benevolent interpretation was employed to save your Rite from any appearance of attack."

The importance of Benedict XIV's 1756 encyclical *Ex quo primum* is that it recognizes that the Greek *Euchologion* has preserved many practices that derive from Judaism (or at least resemble those of Judaism). The recognition of the continuation of Jewish practices by the Greek Church led to a more benevolent attitude of the Catholic Church toward the Christian use of Jewish practices. Benedict XIV affirms the legitimacy of these Greek practices as lawful customs. Even though these customs derive from those of the Old Law, they do not imply the continuing obligation of the Old Law for Christians.

Conclusion

We have seen how justification through the saving death of Christ and not "works of the law" led Christians to abandon Jewish ritual practices. Although the Church prohibited forced conversions of Jews to the Catholic faith, the multiple restrictions on the Jews led to greater resentment and sometimes feigned conversions. Opposition to the practice of any Jewish rites—including circumcision—led the Catholic Church to require Jewish converts to abandon all Jewish practices and to make a complete break from Judaism. What was required in canon 8 of the Second Council of Nicaea was made even more manifest in the Bull of Union with the Copts and the Ethiopians—also called the *Decree for the Jacobites*—at the Council of Florence. Benedict XIV's 1756 encyclical *Ex quo primum* led to the acceptance of Jewish rituals still practiced by the Greeks. As Lawrence Feingold observes: "Although in the encyclical Benedict XIV was not considering the situation or practice of Hebrew Catholics, the principle he lays down is significant with regard to the practice of celebrating the Passover Seder and other elements of Jewish prayer, to which many Catholics are rightly attracted. They are legitimate as long as one recognizes the primacy of Christ and the Church, and defers to her judgment."[82]

During the early centuries of the Church and throughout the Middle Ages, Jews were often looked upon with suspicion and fear. The Church wanted them to convert, but conversion meant a complete repudiation of the Jewish "works of the law". Through missionary experience and efforts to inculturate the Gospel, the Church has gradually learned that conversion does not mean a repudiation of anything that is good or holy in one's culture.[83] The Jewish culture is the culture of Jesus, the Virgin Mary, and the apostles. It is a culture that was formed by a covenant with God, a culture that is good and holy. There is no reason the practices that nourish the Jewish way of life should not be preserved by Jews who have embraced Christ and his Church. These Jewish traditions can be celebrated as part of their religious and cultural patrimony, but not as means of salvation.

Section 3

The Church in the Modern World

7

Jewish Identity Within the Church—Two Jews, Three Opinions

Roy Schoeman

The relationship between Jew[1] and gentile[2] in the Church has been the subject of theological discussion since the very first days of the Church. In fact, Saint Paul and Saint Peter's disagreement about it required the calling of the first Church council, the Council of Jerusalem, around A.D. 50 (see Acts 15). Most of the theological issues have long since been resolved,[3] but to this day, Jewish identity in the Church is an intensely personal issue for Jews who enter the Catholic Church, and it has important pastoral implications.

Perhaps because it is intensely personal, it is unrealistic to expect widespread agreement on the issue among Catholic Jews—hence the chapter title. This chapter is intended as a discussion of the range of views prevalent among Jewish converts,[4] rather than an evaluation of the relative legitimacy of those views. A number of concerns underlie the divergence in views:

- Theological—What does God desire or require from Jews after they enter the Catholic Church? What behavior and what self-identity?
- Evangelistic—What form of Jewish identity in the Church best facilitates the conversion of Jews, and is such conversion what God wants?
- Ecclesiastical—What understanding of Jewish identity in the Church conforms best to Catholic doctrine and ecclesiology? What is best for the Church as a whole?

- Personal—What allowance should be made for the personal preferences of Jews in the Church, reflecting broad differences in their liturgical backgrounds, personal spiritualities, and practical situations?

The Church, and her relationship with the Jewish community, has passed through dramatically different phases over the two thousand years of her existence. As a result, the Church has, at different times, held very different postures with respect to the Jewish community and very different policies and proscriptions with respect both to Jews and to Jewish converts. Before addressing the current situation, some discussion of the past is necessary in order to understand the attitudes of both the Church and the Jewish convert today, since both are heavily influenced by what has gone before.

The initial period following the death of Jesus and the birth of the Church saw widespread confusion about the respective roles of Jew and gentile in the Church, including whether gentiles (non-Jews) qualified for entry into the Church at all. As mentioned, the disagreement on this issue between Saints Peter and Paul necessitated the calling of the first Church council.[5]

During the subsequent first few centuries of Christianity, a steady stream of conflicts permeated the relationships between the Jewish community and the Church, between Christian and non-Christian Jews, and between Jewish and gentile Christians.[6] From the very start, the emergence of Christianity from the bosom of Judaism presented the danger, in the eyes of the Jewish leaders, that Jews might leave traditional Old Testament Judaism. This fear was already expressed by the Jewish leaders during the life of Jesus (see Mt 12) and began to be fulfilled at the first Pentecost when three thousand Jews and proselytes were baptized (see Acts 2). The Jewish community's hostility toward early Christian evangelization is amply testified to in the New Testament accounts that follow the Crucifixion, beginning with Saint Peter's imprisonment (see Acts 5) and Saint Stephen's stoning (see Acts 6) and continuing throughout the letters of Saint Paul. Any possibility of Jewish Christians continuing to participate in the life of the synagogue ended definitively around the time of the second Jewish revolt, circa A.D. 132. The leader of that revolt, Bar Kochba, claimed to be the Messiah, and the leading rabbi of the day, Rabbi Akiba, supported the claim, making participating in the revolt a religious obligation. The Christian Jews refused, since to do so would be to deny Jesus, thus branding them as traitors. It was around this time that the *Birkhat Ha-Minim*, or curse against the *minim*, was inserted into the daily synagogue prayers. The word *minim* ("apostates") originally referred to Jewish followers of Christ and had the effect of preventing any Jewish followers of Jesus (secret or otherwise) from participating in the synagogue. Over time, it came to be understood to mean all Christians, with the unfortunate consequence of fueling Jewish-Christian hostility for centuries.[7]

Political factors also played a role. At the time of the birth of the Church, the Jewish community in the Roman Empire enjoyed the special privilege, unique in the Empire, of being exempt from the obligation to honor pagan gods. The Church, as an offshoot from Judaism, wished to be included in this favored treatment. The Jewish community was strongly opposed to this, in part because it did not want to be included in the hostility generated toward the Church due to its perceived threat to the social order,[8] and also perhaps, as Saint Clement suggests,[9] out of simple envy.

As the Jewish community felt the need to resist the encroachment of Christianity, the early Church also felt a need to respond to the danger of communities of Jewish Christians "backsliding" into Judaism or introducing Judaizing heresies into the Church.[10] There was at times an overreaction to this danger, as evidenced in Saint John Chrysostom's invective against Jews in his *Adversus Judaeos* homilies,[11] which were frequently cited by the Nazis in defense of their actions against the Jews.[12] Thus the conflicts, heresies, and polemics of this early period left permanent remnants that have continued into our time.

As Christianity spread and Christian states emerged, the issue arose of what the policy of a confessional Christian state should be with respect to nonbelievers, particularly Jews, residing in the state.[13] Since the well-being of the citizenry is a primary responsibility of government, and the salvation of souls is the ultimate well-being, Christian rulers saw it as their responsibility to protect the citizenry from morally or theologically corrupting influences. Since the Jewish community, by definition, denied Christ, this resulted in no small amount of conflict and persecution, further increased by differences in mores and values between the two communities.

The understanding that a primary responsibility of Christian sovereigns was to protect Christians from the pernicious influence of Jews was reflected in a host of Church edicts, sometimes coming from local authorities, sometimes from Rome.[14] Restrictions imposed on the Jewish population in these edicts included banning Jews from most trades, limiting permissible Jewish interaction with Christians, and prohibiting them from living outside small walled-off areas of the city (the original "ghettos") into which they were locked at night, and so on. Worse, Jews were subject to periodic expulsions from various Christian kingdoms.[15] The desire to avoid such persecution resulted in widespread false conversions of Jews to the Church,[16] which in turn, required a severe response by Church authorities to stop insincere Jewish converts from sacrilegiously participating in the sacraments. For instance, effective evangelization combined with periodic persecution of the Jewish communities in Portugal and Spain in the fourteenth and fifteenth centuries resulted in a large number of Jews entering the Church—some as genuine converts, others still secretly following Judaism (the Marranos). The Spanish Inquisition, which was unfortunately guilty of extreme abuses, was in large part introduced in order to root out these false converts.[17]

After centuries of conflict between Jewish communities and the confessional states of Christendom, the emancipation of the Jews finally came about through the overthrow of Christian monarchies, beginning with the French Revolution in 1789. The Jewish communities were typically on the side of the revolutions, since in them lay the Jews' only hope for equality and civil rights. It was only with the French Revolution that "for the first time in Europe, Jews were granted equal citizenship.... The civic equality they attained became a model for other European Jews during much of the 19th century."[18] The Jewish communities' support for the overthrow of Christian monarchies unsurprisingly resulted in intense animosity between the Catholic Church and the Jews. At times, their financial support, or lack thereof, was instrumental in the outcome.[19] Once again, the collision between the Church fulfilling its mission and the Jewish communities fighting for their emancipation and survival resulted in conflict between the two.[20]

What does the consideration of this sordid history have to do with how Jews today view their identity in the Church? A lot. Most Jews have grown up against the backdrop of this history. It is a reality that must be dealt with by Jewish converts in reconciling themselves with their identities as Catholics. It is also not just an internal matter to many Jewish converts. The broader Jewish community, to which the convert formerly belonged, sees entry into the Church, especially the Catholic Church, not simply as leaving Judaism but as going over to the historical persecutor of the Jews—the "enemy". The response is far more hostile than when, for instance, a Jew becomes an atheist or a Buddhist. Thus, understanding the dynamics of Jewish conversion to the Catholic Church is impossible without being aware of this historical backdrop.

This history not only affects the Jew entering the Church but is also partly responsible for the Catholic Church's attitude toward the evangelization of Jews. In the aftermath of this history, and then the Holocaust's attempt to exterminate the Jews, which took place in Christian, often Catholic, Europe, the Church has bent over backward to be conciliatory to the Jewish community. Since nothing antagonizes the Jewish community more than the threat of evangelization, the Church has backed off from the evangelization of the Jews, and even from praying for the conversion of the Jews. The extreme of this position, commonly expressed even by Church authorities (although never with the force of dogma), is the "dual-covenant" theory, which claims that "the Church believes that Judaism, i.e. the faithful response of the Jewish people to God's irrevocable covenant, is salvific for them",[21] in the words of Cardinal Kasper, at the time the president of the Pontifical Commission for Religious Relations with the Jews, later repeated in a USCCB document. Thus, many Church leaders, in their desire to be positive and conciliatory (or should I say postconciliar) to the Jewish community, have gone to the point of denying the need for or even the appropriateness of the evangelization of Jews.[22] This has resulted in a lack of proper guidance for Jewish converts by Church authorities.

With this background to the current situation, we will turn to specific issues in Jewish conversion and some of the prevalent responses.

Should There Be a Separate, Visible Community of Jews in the Church? If So, of What Form?

A Separate, Canonical Rite?

A number of considerations lie behind the view that there should be a visibly separate Jewish community within the Church. The strongest institutional form for such a separate community would be a separate rite in the Church, which was the goal of Jewish convert and Carmelite priest and monk Father Elias Friedman, who founded the Association of Hebrew Catholics specifically to promote such a rite. He argued that without such a rite, future generations of the descendants of Jewish converts would lose their Jewish identity, whereas Jews maintaining their Jewish identity through the generations is an irrevocable part of their unique vocation. Thus, he wrote in the founding manifesto of the Association of Hebrew Catholics: "The Association aims eventually at petitioning the Holy See to approve the erection of a Hebrew Catholic Community, into which Jewish converts would be integrated at baptism and to which their descendants would belong."[23]

Ronda Chervin's introduction to Father Friedman's book, *Jewish Identity*, summarizes well a key point of Friedman's thesis:

> Many Hebrew Catholics are assimilated in such a way that they and their children no longer think of themselves as Hebrews. The result of such loss of identity ... constitutes a failure to respond to the irrevocable vocation of the Hebrew to be part of the people of the election. It also impedes any large-scale conversion of Jews to the Catholic religion since assimilation, if unchecked, would eventually lead to the annihilation of the people. [Being] born an Israelite ... "results in an innate quality [the origin of which is] a transcendental relation between the person and the divine will.... The 'election factor' is irrevocable for the person so born." [Father Elias draws the conclusion that] If there is no way of preserving the Jewish identity of the convert ... and his descendants, then it is wrong to actively proselytize Israelites.[24]

In short, Father Friedman's argument is that absent a visible community of Jews within the Church, widespread conversion of Jews would lead to the disappearance of the Jewish people, which would be contrary to God's will.

It is true that Scripture explicitly prophesies that an identifiable Jewish community will remain until the time of the Second Coming. This is clearly stated in the *Catechism of the Catholic Church*: "The glorious Messiah's coming is suspended at every moment of history until his recognition by 'all Israel'."[25] But Father Friedman's proscription assumes that divine providence would not alone control the rate of conversion of Jews to ensure that a visible Jewish community remains until the Second Coming.

Other Jewish Catholics do not share Father Friedman's concern. Given the primary importance of the Great Commission ("Go therefore and make disciples of all nations" [Mt 28:19]), Jesus' own sorrow at the failure of so many of his own people to follow him ("Jerusalem, Jerusalem ..." [23:37]), and the fact that, of course, Jesus pretty much evangelized only Jews ("It is not fair to take the children's bread ..." [15:26]; "Go nowhere among the Gentiles ..." [10:5]), they feel that the Church should do everything possible to encourage Jews to enter the Catholic Church.[26]

Practical considerations also dictate against attempting to create a new Jewish rite in the Church. Additional rites are typically introduced into the Church when communities that have their own distinct Christian rite enter the Catholic Church. However, there is no such existing rite among Jews—it would have to be created from scratch, which to my knowledge would be unprecedented.[27] Who would develop such a rite, and how could consensus be achieved about what it should be? Which Jewish liturgical tradition would it reflect (Ashkenazi, Sephardic, and so on)? Which of the Catholic rites would it be modeled on (Roman, Byzantine, and so on)?

A Visible Community but Not a Rite?

A visible Jewish community in the Church short of a rite would still be very valuable. The existence of such a community would be both a great aid in bringing more Jews into the Church and invaluable for catechizing the Church at large on the Jewish roots of Christianity and the continuing significance of Jews in salvation until the Second Coming.[28]

Such a community could be simply a fraternal organization. There is in fact already such a one—it is what, de facto, Father Friedman's Association of Hebrew Catholics has turned into. No longer committed to the formation of a separate Jewish rite in the Church, the Association itself constitutes a visible community of Jews in the Church, where they can meet, support one another, and address a wide range of theological and liturgical issues of special interest to Catholic Jews. It is also a valuable resource for Jews who are interested in the Catholic Church, enabling them to be in contact with others who have trodden the path before them.

Since many Jews feel that their Jewish identity is an intrinsic part of their being, the presence of such a visible Jewish community in the Church lowers the threshold for prospective converts. It enables them to see that many Jews in the Catholic Church still consider themselves to be Jews—Jews in the Church, not gentiles.

A stronger visible Jewish presence would be created by a Jewish-Catholic worship community composed of Jews in the Church. In Israel, Jewish converts occasionally gather for Catholic Mass, sometimes celebrated by a Jewish convert priest in Hebrew, taking advantage of inculturation to give the Catholic liturgy a more "Jewish" feel.[29] The recent past has seen a new emphasis on facilitating inculturation in the Church—the policy of allowing different peoples and cultures to retain elements of their culture or aesthetics in their practice of the Catholic religion. The International Theological Commission of the Catholic Church's document *Faith and Inculturation* reads, "The process of inculturation may be defined as the Church's efforts to make the message of Christ penetrate a given sociocultural milieu.... Inculturation [is] the incarnation of the Gospel in native cultures and also the introduction of these cultures into the life of the Church."[30]

Religion is not just disembodied belief; along with one's religion comes a manner and environment of worship, a culture, perhaps a sacred language, even a norm of music, architecture, body position, and so forth. The Catholic Church in the West has historically been characterized by the use of Latin, kneeling, a certain type of music and architecture, and so on. In order to enable those from other cultures to feel at home in the Church, the Church makes allowance for, and even encourages, inculturation. Allowing for a distinctively Jewish style of worship for Jews in the Church would allow Jews to feel more at home in the Church, as well as facilitate conversion. It is worth noting that the success of the Messianic Jewish[31] movement around the world is in large part due to this phenomenon, for it allows Jews who have come to faith in Jesus as the Jewish Messiah to worship him together with other Jews, in a liturgical style in which they feel at home.

Should Jews in the Church Maintain Their Jewish Identity?

There is a wide range of views among Jews in the Church as to whether it is normative for them to maintain their Jewish identity and, if they do, with what practices.

Some Jewish converts wish to have nothing to do with their Jewish identity at all, but rather to have, so to speak, the waters of baptism wash them clean of it. Yet the explosive growth in Messianic Jewish congregations (from a few hundred participants in the early 1960s in the United States to over five hundred thousand today), as well as organizations such as the Association of Hebrew Catholics, suggest that many, if not most, Jewish converts still retain their sense of Jewish identity, a love of Jewish practices, and even perhaps a predilection for the Jewish community. Often their love for their fellow Jews expresses itself in a desire to share with their coreligionists the treasure they have found in the Jewish Messiah and the Church he founded. And often, their conversion results in an even much greater appreciation for their Jewishness, since the convert is able for the first time to make sense of and recognize the fulfillment of all the promises of Judaism. For it is difficult to reconcile the promises in the Old Testament with almost two thousand years of no Temple, no animal sacrifice, no sacramental priesthood, no homeland, and no Messiah. As the Lemann brothers, two very notable Jewish converts,[32] expressed the problem: "If the Messiah has already come, it's Jesus Christ, and we must become Christians. If he has not yet come, we must nevertheless no longer remain Jews, because the time of the promise has passed and our books have lied."[33] Later they wrote: "A Jew in becoming Catholic does not change his religion, but fulfils his religion, completes it, crowns it. The Jew become Catholic ... has grown into his fullness, as the seed grows into the flower."[34]

This sense—that entry into the Church makes a Jew more, not less, a Jew—is an almost universal[35] one among Jewish converts:

Rabbi Israel Zolli: "I have not given [the Synagogue] up [for the Church]. Christianity is the integration (completion or crown) of the Synagogue."[36]

Cardinal Lustiger, archbishop of Paris: "I explained [to my father] that baptism would not make me abandon my Jewish condition—quite the contrary, it would lead me to find it, to receive the fullness of its meaning. I did not have the feeling that I was betraying my heritage, or camouflaging myself or abandoning anything whatsoever. Just the opposite: I felt that I was going to find the import, the meaning of what I had received at birth.... There was never for one instant a question of disowning my Jewish identity."[37] On his tomb in Notre Dame Cathedral in Paris, he had written: "I was born a Jew. I received the name of my paternal grandfather Aaron. Christian by faith and by baptism, I remained a Jew, as did the Apostles."[38]

Religious foundress Mother Miriam of the Lamb of God [formerly Rosalind Moss]: "In the fullness of Judaism, which is the Catholic Church, I have all that God has given us.... The most Jewish thing a Jew can do is to become Catholic."[39]

What Jewish Practices Should/Can Be Maintained by Jews in the Church?

In the attempt to maintain Jewish identity after entry into the Church, some converts maintain these Jewish practices:

- keeping the Jewish dietary laws
- observing the laws for the Jewish Sabbath
- observing the laws regarding Jewish head covering and ritual fringes
- celebrating Jewish holidays, for example, Passover, Yom Kippur, and Hanukkah

Some continue these practices out of subjective motivations—they enjoy them, it feels right to them, it feels like a way of honoring God. Some believe that the religious obligation to observe these prescriptions of the Old Testament is still incumbent on them and on all Jewish Catholics.

These questions arise:

- Is the obligation for such ritual observance still binding?
- Is such ritual observance permissible?
- Is such ritual observance prohibited?

To hold that it remains incumbent on Jews in the Church to maintain the observance of Jewish ritual laws seems to this author to be contradicted by numerous passages of the New Testament as well as by traditional Church teaching, although one does find Jewish Catholics who argue that it does.[40] Passages that suggest otherwise include Jesus saying, "To eat with unwashed hands does not defile a man" (Mt 15:20) and "There is nothing outside a man which by going into him can defile him; but the things which come out of a man are what defile him" (Mk 7:15); a voice from heaven saying to Peter, "What God has cleansed, you must not call common" (Acts 10:15); the Epistle to the Hebrews saying, "When there is a change in the priesthood, there is necessarily a change in the law as well" (7:12) and "If that first covenant had been faultless, there would have been no occasion for a second" (8:7); as well as other passages (for example, Mt 12:2–12; Jn 5:9–18; 9:14–16).

Throughout much of Church history, any observance of Jewish ritual law was held to be forbidden. Some of the early Church Fathers were concerned that such observance could blur the distinction between Judaism and Christianity and might draw Catholics, both Jewish and gentile, into Judaism.[41] Others simply dismissed Jewish ritual law as either invalid from the outset or entirely abrogated.[42] Saint Thomas Aquinas held that observing Jewish practices was mortal sin, for it was tantamount to denying Christ: "As a man would sin mortally who, in professing his faith, were to say that Christ was to be born, which the ancient fathers said devoutly and truthfully, so one would sin mortally who observed the ceremonies which those of old kept with devotion and fidelity."[43]

More recently, some Church authorities have suggested that such condemnations apply only if the observance of Jewish ritual law takes place in the context of denying the fullness of faith in Jesus, whereas if, on the other hand, it is done in the context of acknowledging Christ, it can serve as a valuable catechetical tool to illustrate the hidden Christology in Judaism and the transformation of Judaism into the Catholic Church.[44]

Today there is a somewhat different objection to Jews in the Church observing Jewish practices—that it should be avoided lest it offend the sensibilities of the Jewish community, which bridles at the idea that one can be both Jewish and Christian. Naturally any suggestion that the Catholic Church is in fact the natural—even more, the divinely ordained—continuation of Judaism after the coming of the Jewish Messiah is going to grate on Jewish sensibilities, yet it is an inescapable conclusion if the Catholic faith is true.

However, it is not uncommon for Jewish converts today, out of their own sense of Jewish identity and fidelity to God, to maintain some observance of the Jewish liturgical calendar, such as the Jewish

Sabbath, the Passover Seder, or the Yom Kippur fast. On occasion, such observance has had the explicit approval of Church authorities.[45] One is reminded of Saint Paul's prescription: "So, whether you eat or drink, or whatever you do, do all to the glory of God" (1 Cor 10:31).

Is There a Theological Significance to Jewish Identity in the Church?

The preceding discussion has addressed how Jewish converts deal with their subjective sense of Jewish identity after they enter the Church and the implications of such Jewish identity for evangelization and liturgical practice.

However, there remains the broader question of whether there is any objective theological significance to Jewish identity in the Church. Are Jew and gentile identical in the eyes of God once they are united in the Church? On this question, there are apparently conflicting Scripture passages, and here, too, the Church teaching (not dogmatic teaching) has changed through the centuries.

A number of passages in the epistles make it clear that Jew and gentile are equal in the eyes of God: for instance, "There is neither Jew nor Greek, there is neither slave nor free, there is neither male nor female; for you are all one in Christ Jesus" (Gal 3:28).

Such statements stress that all are equal in the eyes of God. In the eyes of God, a man is not superior to a woman, a free man to a slave, or a Jew to a gentile. All are equal in being "one in Christ Jesus". However, even once a Catholic, a slave is still a slave, not a free man; a male is still male and not female; and by extension, a Jew is still a Jew, not a Greek, which in this context means gentile.

Saint Paul's metaphor of the olive tree in Romans 11, in which the Jews are the original cultivated branches and the gentiles wild olive branches, makes clear that despite the equality between Jew and gentile in the Church, an enduring difference remains: "For if you have been cut from what is by nature a wild olive tree, and grafted, contrary to nature, into a cultivated olive tree, how much more will these natural branches be grafted back into their own olive tree ... as regards election they are beloved for the sake of their forefathers. For the gifts and the call of God are irrevocable" (Rom 11:24, 28–29).

In a number of writings, the future Pope Benedict XVI has suggested that the extension of the promise to Abraham to the gentiles did not abrogate the special mission of the Jewish nation:

> Abraham's sonship is to be extended to the "many".... This means that all nations, without the abolishment of the special mission of Israel, become brothers and receivers of the promises of the Chosen People.[46]

> The people of Israel, to whom belong "the adoption as sons, the glory, the covenants, the giving of the law, the worship, and the promises; theirs are the patriarchs, and from them comes Christ according to the flesh, he who is over all, God, blessed forever. Amen" (Romans 9:4–5), and this not only in the past, but still today, "for the gifts and the call of God are irrevocable."[47]

It is, of course, necessary to reconcile the fact that Judaism has been replaced by—or better said, transformed into—Christianity, with these assertions that the election of the Jews and the special mission of Israel continue. This requires distinguishing between the *sacramental system* provided by God for the Jews in the Old Testament and the *election of the Jews*. The sacramental system for the remission of sin, as given by God to the Jewish people in the Old Testament, was abrogated—or, if you prefer, transformed into the sacraments of the Catholic Church—at the time of the Crucifixion, as demonstrated by the miraculous tearing of the veil in the Temple. However, the end of the sacramental system does not necessarily imply the end of the election of the Jews—that is, of God's predilection for them as the seed of Abraham in fulfillment of his promise in Genesis. According to Romans 11, this election remains: "As regards the gospel they are enemies of God, for your sake; but as regards election they are beloved for the sake of their forefathers" (Rom 11:28). The sacramental system given to the Jews by God in the Old Testament required animal sacrifice and hence has not been possible since the destruction of the Temple. In the aftermath of the Jews' exile from Jerusalem, the Jewish authorities developed the current form of Judaism—often called Talmudic Judaism—in order to enable the continuation of Judaism without animal sacrifice.[48] Talmudic Judaism's substitution of prayers, fasting, and almsgiving for the remission of sin, whether or not it is honored by God, is in any case not the sacramental system given to the Jews in the Old Testament.

Conclusion

It would have been imprudent to expect that a chapter with the title "Two Jews—Three Opinions" would resolve definitively the complex theological issues raised by Jewish identity in the Church. I hope, however, to have exposed some of those issues and broadly traced out the lines of reasoning used by those in the Jewish-Catholic community in arriving at their own, sometimes subjective, resolutions.

8

Hebrew Catholics and the Nature of the Fullness of the Catholic Church

Gavin D'Costa*

Introduction

I will advance two arguments in this chapter.

First, I will trace the slow recognition of the importance of the visible elements of the Jewish ecclesia that constitutes the nature of the Church beginning with the documents of the Second Vatican Council. This was not a new ecclesiology but the recognition of a more literal element in what had often been seen as figurative in the past: The Church of "Jews and gentiles" began to have new implications. This recognition continues and develops until today. This process in the magisterial teachings of the Church and through the organs of the Magisterium is the central focus of this chapter. Gentile Catholics (I am one) should understand that this is not an issue just for those Catholics who are Jewish or for those Catholics involved in dialogue with the Jewish people. It is an internal matter of ecclesiological doctrine about the nature of the Church.

Second, I argue that this visibility has varying functions. I will focus on how it recovers the Pauline view that the covenant God makes with his people, Israel, is irrevocable—and this is signified by the existence of the Jewish people today who do not become Christian and those who do become Christian. Israel encompasses both groups. It comes to encompass gentiles only after these two groups. Hence, it is impossible to separate the Jewish-Catholic dialogue and the internal Catholic doctrinal ecclesiology emerging, in part, through such discussions. This is a very sensitive issue to many Jews who see in the "church of the circumcision" the valorization of Jewish apostates and suspect new missionary strategies designed to destroy the covenant people; and it is sensitive to some Catholics who see this question as an obstacle to good relations with Jews, while other Catholics see it as a Judaizing of the Church that has been condemned in the Tradition and by the Magisterium.[1]

Some terminology will help negotiate the terrain ahead. In this essay, "biblical Judaism" denotes Judaism until the time of Jesus; "Rabbinic Judaism" denotes the form of Judaism beginning in the second century and slowly emerging as Judaism(s) today; "Hebrew Catholics" denotes Jewish followers of Jesus who unite themselves to the Roman Catholic Church and have various levels of practice regarding written and oral Torah; and "Messianic Jews" denotes Jewish followers of Jesus who operate with various senses of unity (if not formal union) with gentile churches and have different levels of practice regarding written and oral Torah. "Catholics" denote those in visible unity with the bishop of Rome, the pope.

The Second Vatican Council and the Nature of the Church[2]

The Dogmatic Constitution on the Church *Lumen gentium* (1964) is often referred to regarding its treatment of the Jewish people in no. 16, along with the Declaration of the Church's Relationship with Non-Christian Religions *Nostra aetate* (1965), no. 4, which also deals with the Jewish people. In both documents, it is not entirely clear that Rabbinic Judaism is being addressed. Biblical Judaism is unambiguously addressed. Inasmuch as biblical Judaism is addressed, there are interesting elements that will later help the Church realize its relation to both Hebrew Catholics within its own body and Rabbinic Judaism outside it and in a *sui generis* relationship to the Church.

The Council fathers did not have Hebrew Catholics in mind. I want to show that the ecclesiological architecture that would later accommodate Hebrew Catholics, and indeed show their centrality to the concept of Church, was slowly emerging.[3] The Council fathers did have in mind a number of issues that help this trail emerge: a desire to return to biblical imagery and patterns; a desire to see the

Church's positive relation to all mankind, both before and after the time of Christ; and a return to a more historical sensibility.[4]

Regarding the status of the Hebrew Catholic Church as a doctrinal element, it should be noted that a doctrine can take hundreds or even thousands of years to develop. For example, Mary's divine motherhood (Ephesus, 431) took more than two hundred years to flower into and generate the organically related doctrine of the perpetual virginity of Mary (Lateran, 649). It then took another thousand years for the organically related Immaculate Conception to be promulgated (1854). Fifty years is a very short time for the emergence of what I would call in this case a doctrinal enfleshing—that is, to see that the "figurative" elements in a doctrine may contain "literal" elements whose significance has not been previously fully registered. The Church of "Jews and gentiles" might really mean preserving the difference between Jews and gentiles in unity in Christ, just as it has with preserving the difference between male and female.

In *Lumen gentium*, there are three references to "Jews", six to "Israel", one to Jesus as "Messiah", and two to the Church as "messianic".[5] All references point to an increasing understanding of the Church emerging as a Jewish Messianic community that invited gentile followers into the Jewish covenantal relationship with God. The primary Jewish element of the ecclesia is sometimes used figuratively, sometimes literally in the document, but the latter is not given any sustained attention—nor is it ruled out. The references relate to three separate chapters of the Constitution: chapter I on the "mystery of the Church" (no. 2); chapter II on the "People of God" (nos. 9, 16); and chapter IV on "the laity" (no. 32).

The first reference (no. 2) is central in the architecture of God's initiative and founding of his people. God desired to share the "divine life", and even after Adam's fall (representative of mankind) has provided humans "with the means of salvation" (*semper eis auxilia ad salutem praebens*) in the history of Israel, always "having in view Christ the redeemer". This tension, that the "means of salvation" were present before Christ but always in "view of Christ", is important because the history of salvation extends to all mankind, from "Abel the just right to the last of the elect" (no. 2). The *telos* of all God's dealings with mankind first (through creation), and then biblical Israel specifically (through the history of revelation), led eventually to their fulfillment in Christ. This means, as Aquinas had argued, that Jewish rites had an efficacy, as they were teleologically oriented to Christ, the Messiah, to whom these rites pointed. While Aquinas probably viewed these rites as losing their efficacy after the coming of Christ, the Council (no. 16) seems to think otherwise.[6] These rites belonged to "the people of Israel and in the ancient covenant", and they prefigure/foreshadow (*praefigurata*) and prepare (*praeparata*) for the event of Jesus Christ and the outpouring of the Spirit. However, "prefigures" and "prepares" are not presented in the document as making biblical Judaism redundant, and in the light of no. 16, that covenant is said still to be valid, as God does not take back his promises and gifts.

This theme is picked up in no. 9, in part II, which turns to the "People of God". Part II also includes how other Christians are "joined" (*coniuncitam*) (no. 15) and how the Jewish people are "related" (*ordinantur*) (no. 16) to the Church.

In no. 9, we should note that the theme of preparation continues. There is no sense that biblical Israel is somehow redundant, but through Christ and the Spirit, biblical Israel now grasps a "fuller revelation" that confirms or "ratifies" Israel's history.[7] Through this process, the covenant that had been made with biblical Israel is now opened to gentiles. This is fully in keeping with the expectations of biblical Judaism, for example found in Jeremiah 31:4. Many strands of biblical Judaism affirm the entry of the nations into the covenant through the coming of the Messiah. Most significantly, this new community is made up of Jews and gentiles, united in Christ. The Jewish element of the ecclesia is central in no. 9:

> He therefore chose the race of Israel as a people unto Himself. With it He set up a covenant. Step by step He taught and prepared this people, making known in its history both Himself and the decree of His will and making it holy unto Himself. All these things, however, were done by way of preparation and as a figure [*praeparationem et figuram*] of that new and perfect covenant, which was to be ratified [*feriendi*] in Christ, and of that fuller revelation [*plenioris revelationis*] which was to be given through the Word of God Himself made flesh [here, Jeremiah 31:4 is cited in full] .... Christ instituted this new covenant, the new testament, that is to say, in His Blood, [1 Cor 11:25] calling together a people made up of Jew and gentile [*Iudaeis ac gentibus*], making them one, not according to the flesh but in the Spirit. This was to be the new People of God.

Significantly, no. 9 continues to address the Church in strictly Jewish terms as a "messianic [*messianicus*] people", who act as a "sure seed of unity, hope and salvation for the whole human race". It is equally clear that this is a deepening of Israel's vocation, because now it is right to call the messianic community not only the "Church of God", as was biblical Israel's name, but also, more precisely, the "Church of Christ" (or one might say the "messianic Church", for the Greek word "Christ" (*chrīstós*) translated the Hebrew "Messiah" (*mesiach*). While these passages are not addressing biblical Israel or Rabbinic Judaism, no. 16 will clarify that on the latter, it clearly includes Jews who followed Jesus—the Church of "Jews and gentiles" that began no. 9: Israel according to the flesh (*carnem*), which wandered as an exile in the desert, was already called the Church of God (*Dei ecclesia*) (see Neh 13:1; Num 20:4; Deut 23:1–6). So likewise the new Israel, which, while living in this present age goes in search of a future and abiding city (see Heb 13:14), is called the Church of Christ (*etiam ecclesia Christi*) (see Mt 16:18).

We see a clear structuring of the messianic Church as inclusive of the carnal Israel, literally Jews, and the Church as continuing that identity in the church of "Jews and gentiles". This phrase from Paul is indicative of an empirical reality of the early Church community, where the Council of Jerusalem in Acts 15 determines not only that Jews can continue their Jewish practices but also that the gentiles entering this Messianic Jewish community should be bound by the minimal Jewish requirements laid upon gentiles.[8]

I will not dwell on no. 16, which treats Judaism (biblical and Rabbinic?) as part of those who "have not yet accepted the gospel" but are "related" to the Church.[9] The Pauline insight of an irrevocable covenant with God, "for God does not repent of the gifts He makes nor of the calls He issues",[10] characterizes these people. This was developed in the postconciliar Church by Saint Pope John Paul II to apply to Rabbinic Judaism, and in 2015, allowed the Commission for Religious Relations with the Jews to say there can be no question that rabbinic Jewish rites participate in God's salvation (and they could have used *Lumen gentium*'s "in view of Christ"): "That the Jews are participants in God's salvation is theologically unquestionable, but how that can be possible without confessing Christ explicitly, is and remains an unfathomable divine mystery."[11] The implication of no. 16 for our focus is that Rabbinic Judaism's rites came to be seen as efficacious (assuming invincible ignorance) by 2015. One might thus ask, What of those Jews who follow Jesus as Messiah? Would their use of Jewish rites be appropriate? It could be argued that Jews using Jewish rites in their following of Christ is legitimate, as long as the use of these rites in no way obscures or denies the salvific efficacy of Christ's Cross or causes scandal.[12]

The last reference to the Jewish ecclesia in *Lumen gentium* is found in no. 32, in chapter IV, which deals with the laity. This part is to be read in the context of preserving different roles and diversity within the Church, primarily between laity and clergy, but also between genders (without discrimination) and races (without racism). This diversity is not part of a liberal social agenda but is grounded in God's will, and within that will it includes the difference between "Jews and gentiles", as in no. 9, so now in no. 32: By divine institution (*divina institutione*), Holy Church is ordered and governed with a wonderful diversity. "For just as in one body we have many members, yet all the members have not the same function, so we, the many, are one body in Christ, but severally members one of another" (Rom 12:45). There is, therefore, in Christ and in the Church no inequality on the basis of race or nationality, social condition or sex, because "there is neither Jew nor Greek: there is neither bond nor free: there is neither male nor female. For you are all 'one' in Christ Jesus" (Gal 3:28; Col 3:11).

The Catholic Church has been at the forefront of holding that there is a difference between male and female, even as they are one in Christ. Sexual difference is not eradicated by this profound "unity". Many readings of Paul indicate the same regarding Jew and Greek. One cannot erase that difference, although these two groups now find a unity in the messianic community that brings Jews and Greeks together. This divinely willed difference is to be celebrated, not eradicated.[13]

One final passage from *Nostra aetate*, no. 4, helps to flesh out, by implication, the importance of the Jewish ecclesia. Since *Nostra aetate* was published after *Lumen gentium*, *Nostra aetate* refers to no. 16 regarding Romans 11:28–29. In *Nostra aetate*, there is almost a summary of the materials I have covered above, keeping open the same avenues that will be developed after the Council: that the Jewish ecclesia, as a visible element, is part of the nature of the Church. This point is made in the opening sentences of *Nostra aetate*. "As the sacred synod searches into the mystery of the Church [*mysterium ecclesia*], it remembers the bond that spiritually ties the people of the New Covenant to Abraham's stock."[14]

Thus, the Church of Christ acknowledges that, according to God's saving design, the beginnings of her faith and her election are found already among the patriarchs, Moses and the prophets. She professes that all who believe in Christ—Abraham's sons according to faith (see Gal 3:7)—are included in the same patriarch's call, and likewise that the salvation of the Church is mysteriously foreshadowed (*praesignari*) by the Chosen People's exodus from the land of bondage. The Church, therefore, cannot forget that she received the revelation of the Old Testament through the people with whom God in his inexpressible mercy entered into an ancient covenant. Nor can she forget that she draws sustenance from the root of that well-cultivated olive tree onto which have been grafted the wild shoots, the gentiles (see Rom 11:17–24). Indeed, the Church believes that by his Cross, Christ, our Peace, reconciled Jews and gentiles (*Iudaeos et gentes*), making both one in himself (see Eph 2:14–16). She also recalls that the apostles, the Church's mainstay and pillars, as well as most of the early disciples who proclaimed Christ's gospel to the world, sprang from the Jewish people. Later, the Church would say that all these mainstays and pillars were practicing Jews (see below).

The conclusion from this brief analysis is that the Council, in seeking a more biblically based ecclesiology (not questioning previous types advanced), retrieves one that delineates (a) that biblical Jewish rites and practices were "means" to salvation because of their Christological orientation; (b) that the Messianic Jewish community integrates gentiles in Christ through the coming of the Spirit but does not lose its identity as primarily a Jewish messianic community; and (c) that the Church is made up of "Jew and Greek", the Chosen People and the nations, as is the biblical manner of viewing the distinction. The significance of this architecture is developed after the Council.

Further Landmarks After the Council: 1974–2015

A more comprehensive analysis would require attention to papal writings that carried the Council's momentum forward. Here, I will instead focus on the writings of the Commission for Religious

Relations with the Jews (CRRJ), which wrestle with the mystery of the Church in thinking through the relation with the Jews.

The Commission's 1974 document, its first in the year of its inauguration after the Council, raises the question of the Jewish church in recognizing the liturgical connections between Christians and Jews. It inchoately but implicitly registers that the earliest liturgies were Messianic Jewish liturgies. The messianic character of the early Church was already introducing novelty and discontinuity into biblical Judaism, with an underlying continuity present. However, these liturgies were quickly developed by an almost exclusively gentile church, which became locked into a form of mutual antagonism with the emerging Rabbinic Jews, so that the idea of practicing Jewish Christians had probably virtually disappeared by the fourth century. The 1974 CRRJ document holds:

> The existing links between the Christian liturgy and the Jewish liturgy will be borne in mind. The idea of a living community in the service of God, and in the service of men for the love of God, such as it is realized in the liturgy, is just as characteristic of the Jewish liturgy as it is of the Christian one. To improve Jewish-Christian relations, it is important to take cognizance of those common elements of the liturgical life (formulas, feasts, rites, etc.) in which the Bible holds an essential place.
>
> An effort will be made to acquire a better understanding of whatever in the Old Testament retains its own perpetual value (cf. *Dei Verbum*, 14–15), since that has not been canceled by the later interpretation of the New Testament....
>
> When commenting on biblical texts, emphasis will be laid on the continuity of our faith with that of the earlier Covenant, in the perspective of the promises, without minimizing those elements of Christianity which are original.[15]

This double movement, of exploring the mystery of the Church while being engaged with the relations between Jews, also characterizes the turning-point speech of John Paul II later in 1980, when addressing a Jewish audience in Mainz, Germany.[16] The pope recognizes Rabbinic Judaism as inheriting the biblical covenant (biblical Judaism in my terminology). Interestingly, before the pope makes this link, he speaks of the inner mystery of the Jewish ecclesia, making clear the dangers of eradicating this Jewish identity at the heart of the Church:

> In the *Declaration on the Relationship of the Church with Judaism* in April of this year, the bishops of the Federal Republic of Germany put this sentence at the beginning: "Whoever meets Jesus Christ, meets Judaism." I would like to make these words mine, too. The faith of the Jesus Christ, the son of David and the son of Abraham actually contains what the bishops call in that declaration "the total heritage of Israel for the Church", a *living heritage which must be understood and preserved in its depth and richness by us Catholic Christians.*[17]

The heritage of (biblical) Israel should be preserved in its depth and richness by Catholics, because whoever meets Jesus meets biblical Judaism. The importance of preservation becomes a return to the Jewish Messiah and his followers, an element within the Church that has been long forgotten.

The pope then turns to the Holocaust and anti-Jewishness. While condemning all forms of anti-Semitism, he chooses to name a victim of anti-Semitism, a contemporary Jewish Catholic, Edith Stein. Her canonization caused upset to many Jews who claimed that the Church seemed to be appropriating murdered Jews as Catholic martyrs. By naming Saint Edith Stein, who had been beatified by this same pope two years earlier, the pope is suggesting that one can be both a Jew and a Catholic: "And also to those people who, as Christians, affirming they belonged to the Jewish people, traveled along the *via crucis* of their brothers and sisters to the end—like the great Edith Stein, called in her religious institute Teresa Benedicta of the Cross, whose memory is rightly held in great honor."[18]

The pope is interestingly honoring a Jewish apostate in the company of Rabbinic Jews. He can perhaps do no other if Messianic Judaism forms the Church—as the Council had already acknowledged—so citing Stein is entirely appropriate. The heart of the Church is constituted by Jewish Scripture, which was Jesus' Scripture and constitutes the mystery of both the Incarnation and the Church. Here are his words:

> The first dimension of this dialogue, that is, the meeting between the people of God of the Old Covenant, never revoked by God [cf. Rom. 11:29], and that of the New Covenant, is at the same time a dialogue *within our Church*, that is to say, between the first and the second part of her Bible. In this connection, the directives for the application of

> the conciliar declaration *Nostra Aetate* say: "The effort must be made to understand *better everything in the Old Testament that has its own, permanent value ... since this value is not wiped out by the later interpretation of the New Testament, which, on the contrary, gave the Old Testament its full meaning*, so that it is a question rather of reciprocal enlightenment and explanation."[19]

This is a long way from endorsing Hebrew Catholicism, but it is also giving that concept its theological authority and grounding, which had already emerged in 1970 through the Association of Hebrew Catholics and through Jews who had become Catholics and wished to affirm their Jewish identity.

The 1982 document from the CRRJ, entitled "Notes on the Correct Way to Present the Jews and Judaism in Preaching and Catechesis in the Roman Catholic Church", is momentous. Once the pope affirmed the active covenantal status of Rabbinic Judaism, the Commission was able to explore new areas proposed by the pope. It turns to the implicit significance of Hebrew Catholicism in recognizing (a) that Jesus was Jewish, operating within religious Judaism as part of that complex tradition, and thus a practicing Jew; (b) that Paul should also be viewed as within Judaism rather than representing a break from it; and (c) that the phrase "the Church of Jews and Gentiles" has more than a purely figurative meaning; it encompasses a literal dimension. This particular treatment merits full citation:

> Jewish Roots of Christianity
>
> 1. Jesus was and always remained a Jew, his ministry was deliberately limited "to the lost sheep of the house of Israel" (*Mt* 15:24). Jesus is fully a man of his time, and of his environment—the Jewish Palestinian one of the first century, the anxieties and hopes of which he shared. This cannot but underline both the reality of the Incarnation and the very meaning of the history of salvation, as it has been revealed in the Bible (cf. *Rom* 1:3–4; *Gal* 4:4–5).
> 2. [Jesus'] relations with biblical law and its more or less traditional interpretations are undoubtedly complex and he showed great liberty towards it (cf. the "antitheses" of the Sermon on the Mount: *Mt* 5:21–48, bearing in mind the exegetical difficulties; his attitude to rigorous observance of the Sabbath: *Mk* 3:1–6, etc.).

But there is no doubt that he wished to submit himself to the law (cf. *Gal* 4:4), that he was circumcised and presented in the Temple like any Jew of his time (cf. *Lk* 2:21, 22–24), that he was trained in the law's observance. He extolled respect for it (cf. *Mt* 5:17–20) and invited obedience to it (cf. *Mt* 8:4). The rhythm of his life was marked by observance of pilgrimages on great feasts, even from his infancy (cf. *Lk* 2:41–50; *Jn* 2:13; 7:10 etc.). The importance of the cycle of the Jewish feasts has been frequently underlined in the Gospel of John (cf. 2:13; 5:1: 7:2, 10, 37; 10:22; 12:1; 18:28; 19:42; etc.).

3. It should be noted also that Jesus often taught in the Synagogues (cf. *Mt* 4:23: 9:35; *Lk* 4:15–18; *Jn* 18:20 etc.) and in the Temple (cf. *Jn* 18:20 etc.), which he frequented as did the disciples even after the Resurrection (cf. e.g., *Acts* 2:46; 3:1: 21:26 etc.). He wished to [put in] the context of synagogue worship the proclamation of his Messiahship (cf. *Lk* 4:16–21). But above all he wished to achieve the supreme act of the gift of himself in the setting of the domestic liturgy of the Passover or at least of the paschal festivity (cf. *Mk* 14:1, 12 and parallels; *Jn* 18:28). This also allows of a better understanding of the "memorial" character of the Eucharist.
4. Thus the Son of God is incarnate in a people and a human family (cf. *Gal* 4:4; *Rom* 9:5). This takes away nothing, quite the contrary, from the fact that he was born for all men (Jewish shepherds and pagan wise men are found at his crib: *Lk* 2:80–20; *Mt* 2:1–12) and died for all men (at the foot of the cross there are Jews, among them Mary and John: *Jn* 19:25–27, and pagans like the centurion: *Mk* 15:39 and parallels). Thus he made two peoples one in his flesh (cf. *Eph* 2:14–17). This explains why with the *Ecclesia ac gentibus* we have, in Palestine and elsewhere, an *Ecclesia ex circumcisione*, of which *Eusebius* for example speaks (H.E. IV, 5).
5. His relations with the Pharisees were not always or wholly polemical....
6. Jesus shares, with the majority of Palestinian Jews of that time, some pharisaic doctrines: the resurrection of the body; forms of piety, like alms-giving, prayer, fasting (cf. *Mt* 6:1–18) and the liturgical practice of addressing God as Father; the priority of the commandment to love God and our neighbour (cf. *Mk* 12:28–34) [there follow three paragraphs on Paul in the same vein]....
9. All this should help up to understand better what St Paul says (*Rom* 11:16 ff) about the "root" and the "branches". The Church

> and Christianity, for all their novelty, find their origin in the Jewish milieu of the first century of our era, and more deeply still in the "design of God" (*Nostra Aetate* 4), realised in the Patriarchs, Moses and the Prophets (ibid.), down to its consummation in Christ Jesus.[20]

The document clearly establishes the historical reality and theological significance of the Church of Jews and gentiles, now called the *Ecclesia ac gentibus* and *Ecclesia ex circumcisione*. Jesus and Paul both belonged to the latter according to the document. The next document, "We Remember: A Reflection on the Shoah" in 1998, would include Mary and other pillars of the Church in this Jewish practicing context.[21]

If this was true of Jesus, Paul, and Mary, the question of the practices of Jewish Catholics in the contemporary Catholic Church is highlighted. If Jewish practices were transformed through the coming of the Messiah, they were no less Jewish. If today, Jewish Catholics wish to return to or develop such practices to make visible the church of the circumcision, surely there is a very strong case for this. And after the Shoah, the visible emergence of such Catholics who had more confidence to claim their Jewish identity increased.[22]

In 2015, the CRRJ celebrated the fiftieth anniversary of *Nostra aetate* with another document, titled " 'The Gifts and the Calling of God Are Irrevocable' (Rom 11:29): A Reflection on Theological Questions Pertaining to Catholic-Jewish Relations on the Occasion of the 50th Anniversary of '*Nostra ætate*' (No. 4)".[23] Here we find the key concept of the *Ecclesia ex circumcisione* or "Jewish Christians" (nos. 14, 43) with two new features in addition to what we have established above. First, the document claims that the matter is not just about numbers, for there are very few Hebrew Catholics; but that this Jewish ecclesia is constitutive of ecclesial identity, along with the church of the gentiles. Second, it includes a reference to the church of the circumcision where we would least expect it. Recall this is a document about relations with Rabbinic Jews, and we find this reference in no. 6: "The Church's mandate to evangelize in relation to Judaism".

Philip A. Cunningham cites one source for the two references to the Jewish ecclesia. Regarding no. 43, Cunningham cites an interview with Cardinal Koch, prefect of the CRRJ, responding to the question:

"May Messianic Jews, who recognize Christ as a Messiah and fulfiller of their Judaism, be a bridge between Christianity and Judaism?"

> They could be a bridge, and they are a reality which it is impossible to ignore. For very many Jews, however, the messianic communities represent a major challenge. This question therefore has to be considered very sensitively so as not to jeopardize the official dialogues with Judaism.[24]

It is clear that there is an awareness that non-Catholic messianic communities have an important significance, but it is one that may easily jeopardize Catholic dialogue with Jews. At the same time, this intrinsic Jewish element in the Church raises the same problem. It is clearly difficult to raise all the implications of what is going on internally in the Church in the context of this special dialogue. Earlier, in no. 15 in the section "The special theological status of Jewish-Catholic dialogue", it is said that dialogue with Jews is unlike interreligious dialogue because of the intrinsic Jewish nature of the Church. It picks up the threads we saw initially in *Nostra aetate*, that the Old Testament, biblical Judaism, is the source of Christianity—and Rabbinic Judaism. In that sense, there is a triangulated picture that emerges: Biblical Judaism is present in the heart of Christianity and also in the heart of Rabbinic Judaism. Biblical Judaism facilitates a deep closeness to Rabbinic Judaism—like two siblings who have one mother, which could also explain the dark depths of sibling rivalry of the younger child. I cite the entire passage because it goes a long way to untangle hidden and implicit elements in the Jewish-Catholic dialogue showing that at the same time, it generates a conversation that must go on within the Church:

> Dialogue between Jews and Christians then can only be termed "interreligious dialogue" by analogy, that is, dialogue between two intrinsically separate and different religions. It is not the case that two fundamentally diverse religions confront one another after having developed independently of one another or without mutual influence. The soil that nurtured both Jews and Christians is the Judaism of Jesus' time, which not only brought forth Christianity but also, after the destruction of the temple in the year 70, post-biblical rabbinical

> Judaism which then had to do without the sacrificial cult and, in its further development, had to depend exclusively on prayer and the interpretation of both written and oral divine revelation. Thus Jews and Christians have the same mother and can be seen, as it were, as two siblings who—as is the normal course of events for siblings—have developed in different directions. The Scriptures of ancient Israel constitute an integral part of the Scriptures of both Judaism and Christianity, understood by both as the word of God, revelation, and salvation history. The first Christians were Jews; as a matter of course they gathered as part of the community in the Synagogue, they observed the dietary laws, the Sabbath and the requirement of circumcision, while at the same time confessing Jesus as the Christ, the Messiah sent by God for the salvation of Israel and the entire human race. With Paul the "Jewish Jesus movement" definitively opens up other horizons and transcends its purely Jewish origins. Gradually his concept came to prevail, that is, that a non-Jew did not have to become first a Jew in order to confess Christ. In the early years of the Church, therefore, there were the so-called Jewish Christians and the Gentile Christians, the *ecclesia ex circumcisione* and the *ecclesia ex gentibus*, one Church originating from Judaism, the other from the Gentiles, who however together constituted the one and only Church of Jesus Christ.[25]

The final lines are important in registering two distinct communities, with differing origins, gentile and Jewish, that together "constituted" the one and only Church of Jesus Christ. "Constituted" has a historical aspect but also speaks about the very nature of the Church. The statement supports the reading of Acts 15 that allows for a legitimate practice of Jewish forms of ecclesia that constitutes the Church. The statement generates the question: What then of Jews today in the Church?

No. 43 responds to both these questions quite unequivocally. The context of no. 43 comes in section 6, "The Church's mandate to evangelize in relation to Judaism". The logic of no. 15 is now outworking itself as the Catholic Church no longer condemns either Judaism or Jewish practices or neglects the recognition of the Jewish dimension of the Church. No. 15 is unequivocal in its assertion that the disciples "gathered as part of the community in the Synagogue, they observed the dietary laws, the Sabbath and the requirement of circumcision, while at the same time confessing Jesus as the Christ, the Messiah".

Now, no. 43 makes clear that Jewishness is not just a matter of "spirituality" but is embodied within Jewish bodies that are part of the Church of Jesus Christ. The Jewish ecclesia made up of carnal Jews is given a constitutive and qualitative status within the Church:

> It is and remains a *qualitative definition of the Church of the New Covenant that it consists of Jews and Gentiles*, even if the *quantitative* proportions of Jewish and Gentile Christians may initially give a different impression. Just as after the death and resurrection of Jesus Christ there were not two unrelated covenants, so too the people of the covenant of Israel are not disconnected from "the people of God drawn from the Gentiles." Rather, the enduring role of the covenant people of Israel in God's plan of salvation is to relate dynamically to the "people of God of Jews and Gentiles, united in Christ," he whom the Church confesses as the universal mediator of creation and salvation.[26]

That this dual community of Jews and gentiles "is and remains" a qualitative definition transforms no. 15 from a historical observation of the New Testament community into an ecclesiological datum: that the Jewish church is actually required for the definition of Church, no. 43. This insight coheres with the emerging Hebrew Catholic reality in the Catholic Church. It does not give elaboration to the form of this ecclesia, but since it is using the early Christian community as its model—and we know from Acts 15 that Jews were allowed to continue many of their Jewish religious practices, messianically configured—it keeps wide open the extent to which Torah practice might be legitimate for Jewish Catholics.

The rest of the paragraph is vital to understanding the full significance of this ecclesiology. It contains a citation of *Lumen gentium* no. 16, which I have commented on elsewhere.[27] It reads:

> In the context of God's universal will of salvation, all people who have not yet received the gospel are aligned with the people of God of the New Covenant. "In the first place there is the people to whom the covenants and promises were given and from whom Christ was born according to the flesh (cf. Rom 9:4–5). On account of their fathers this people remains most dear to God, for he does not repent of the gifts he makes nor of the calls he issues (cf. Rom 11:28–29)" (*Lumen gentium*, 16).[28]

It is clear by the positioning of this paragraph at the end of the section on the controversial question of mission and evangelization that the existence of the Jewish ecclesia—the church of the circumcision—plays two roles. First, it seems to be a response to the rightful Jewish criticism that conversion to Catholicism/Christianity is an eradication of Jewish identity and thus against the Jewish covenant. No. 40 has already stated this difficulty very clearly, especially in the light of the Shoah:

> It is easy to understand that the so-called "mission to the Jews" is a very delicate and sensitive matter for Jews because, in their eyes, it involves the very existence of the Jewish people.... Christians are nonetheless called to bear witness to their faith in Jesus Christ also to Jews, although they should do so in a humble and sensitive manner, acknowledging that Jews are bearers of God's Word, and particularly in view of the great tragedy of the Shoah.[29]

The Jewish ecclesia shows the possibility of retaining Jewish identity while being part of the Church of gentiles, a position never made explicitly clear within Catholicism. Clearly, this Jewish identity is not that of Rabbinic Judaism but of Hebrew Catholicism. And the shape of this community of the circumcised is as yet a shadowy reality. Whether Jews would think this an "answer" to the problem of Jewish existence if they were to enter the Church is entirely another matter.[30]

One final observation: The Catholic Church seems to have followed the logic through, recovering its Jewish roots and denouncing anti-Jewishness and anti-Semitism: It is now free to accept the Jewish part of itself, to come to embrace the nature of the Church more fully and completely; and that, in turn, entails a new positive relationship with Rabbinic Judaism.

To complete this essay, I want to turn to one vision of what this Jewish ecclesia might look like. It is the most complete and sustained exposition on this matter in English that I know.

Antoine Levy and Hebrew Catholics: the "Jewish Church"

There have been important Hebrew Catholics in the twentieth century: Saint Teresa Benedicta of the Cross (Edith Stein), Cardinal Aaron

Lustiger (former chief rabbi of Rome), Israel Zolli, Elias Friedman, Daniel Rufeisen, and Marie-Théodor Ratisbonne (founder of the Sisters of Zion).[31] They have varied in adherence to Jewish religious practices, but all were proudly Jewish. Today's prominent Hebrew Catholic thinker is Antoine Levy. His important book *Jewish Church: A Catholic Approach to Messianic Judaism* (2021) will help to explicate the possible communal shape and theological rationale for Hebrew Catholics. Levy is a Dominican priest, born into a Jewish nonreligious Zionist home.[32] His work stands in continuity with Elias Friedman's vision[33] and is developed in conversation with Mark Kinzer's Messianic Judaism.[34]

Levy argues that there is an irreducible difference between Rabbinic Judaism and Messianic Judaism, or what I am calling Hebrew Catholicism, because for the former, the Torah (written and oral) is the mediator of God's will.[35] For the latter, it is Yeshua, the Messiah, through whom the written and oral Torah are understood and practiced. However, within Christ's Body, the Torah is practiced differently by Jews and gentiles. The practices of Hebrew Catholics are different from those of Rabbinic Jews in terms of intentionality, explicit *telos*, and actual rituals. For example, some prayers and rituals may remain the same as those of Rabbinic Jews, but their meaning is different because the Messiah has come. Levy argues that Kinzer's founding premise that Messianic Jewish communities are to be identified within Rabbinic Judaism's authority is thus not plausible.

He also rejects Kinzer's view that Messianic communities are a bridge and witness to both gentile Christianity and Rabbinic Judaism because of Kinzer's Messianic communities' false self-understanding. Messianic communities can properly witness to Rabbinic Judaism only by being united to the gentiles through a visible sign of unity, properly displaying the nature of the extension of the Jewish covenant to all the nations. "Properly" here means under the rules of Catholic ecclesiology.[36] For Levy, in comparison to Kinzer, practicing the Torah for Jewish followers of Jesus is not a strict obligation or a matter of religious vows. In Catholic terminology, it is not an intrinsically necessary means of salvation.

Second, Levy says the notion of Hebrew Catholicism requires explication. He suggests four characteristics for it to be "authentically Catholic", to properly express its universal nature. It must be corporate, "since this is about the presence of Israel *qua* Israel in the Church, in contrast to the limited existential options of private individuals". It will be distinct, "since it must give Jewish disciples the possibility to express the uniqueness of their calling as Sons and Daughters of Israel". It must be in "communion" with gentile brethren, "since such communion is at the foundation of a truly Catholic Church". This requires shared table fellowship and acceptance of the pope as the visible sign of unity. The Jewish church would also have its own bishops. It would be in unity in the same way as the Eastern Catholic churches, with their very different rites, are in communion with Rome. Levy prefers to think of the Jewish church as an "ordinariate", in order to preserve its vital role in the definition of the Church, constituting part of its DNA, so to speak. Finally, it must endure, "since it must contribute to God's project of preserving the existence of Israel as a corporate reality".[37]

These characteristics are the source of an important claim that closes Levy's book: The recovery of the Jewish church is central to a wider ecumenism. This allows us to gain an insight on how Hebrew Catholics might be regarded as the remedy of a particular lack that makes up what the Church is. Levy argues that the relationship of the subsistence of the Church of Christ in the Roman Catholic Church, claimed in *Lumen gentium* no. 8 (and a sequence of Vatican documents that follow it), expresses a tension. While the Church founded by God is the Catholic Church, it also always moves toward the fullness that makes it this true Church. The true Church, included in its form, constitutes the unity of the Jewish church and gentile church of Christ in visible unity. This is part of the DNA of the true Church of Christ. When this unity was broken by the slow rejection of the Jewish church by the emerging gentile church, partly due to its enmity over the Jewish rejection of Jesus,[38] the most "primal schism" began in the Body of Christ. Levy argues that this primal schism should not be attributed, as it often is, to the division between non-Messianic Jews and the gentile church, for here we do not have a unity that breaks into schism but a fundamental difference of belief. Rather, the primal schism is attributable to the Jewish church and the destruction of it by the gentile church, even if the motivation of the latter was related to its growing dispute with non-Messianic Judaism. Hence, Levy claims that the "authentic nature" of the Church is at stake. He writes:

> Reviving a Jewish *ekklesia* would mean renewing the communion that gave its most pristine—but also most fragile and short-lived—configuration to the Church of Christ.... The Church that truly corresponds to the First Council of Jerusalem could not endure due to the absence of a *structure* that would have guaranteed the survival of the Jewish nation, of Israel *qua* Israel within her visible boundaries. In our days, almost 2,000 years after the Council of Jerusalem, the Church is offered the opportunity to manifest her faithfulness to her most authentic nature through the establishment of a Jewish *ekklesia*.[39]

This would be one step in the longer journey required for Catholic ecumenism, that is the unity of all those who profess that Jesus is the Messiah of Israel. In Jesus, Israel's promises continue and are now extended to the gentiles. It would be the restoration of a unity that was primary, well before the denominational schisms developed in later Christianity. To heal the primal schism is the first step before later schisms can be addressed, because the truth of the Catholic Church in this healing becomes what it was destined to be: a Church for the Jews and the gentiles. Further, to accommodate the Jewish church means that we return to a model of "church" that allows for differences to be kept intact within a common confession in Yeshua under the visible sign of unity that is the pope. This restoration of the "authentic nature" of the Church is the presupposition to Christian ecumenism.[40]

Third, Levy argues that in preserving messianically transformed Jewish commandments (*mitzvot*) deriving from the Torah, Hebrew Catholic communities would create the true witness that Kinzer seeks to build. This witnessing is a byproduct, not the goal of such Hebrew Catholic communities. Levy is realistic in suggesting that rather than being a successful witness, this would more likely antagonize Rabbinic Jews. This Jewish church is thus a challenge to both communities, Jews and gentiles. To Rabbinic Jews, it is a witness to the reality that the Messiah has come and that he does not abolish Jewish identity but transforms it, as was always the expectation in both biblical and Rabbinic Judaism. To gentile Catholics, it is a witness to the Jewish covenant and how that covenant has been widened to now include the gentile nations and can never be revoked. To gentile Catholics, it is a witness to the living Jewish covenant that is enjoyed by Rabbinic Jews in their living from the Torah. To move toward the fullness of being, such an ecclesia demands a deep conversion to the charism and gifts of this Hebrew Catholic ecclesial reality, outlined by Levy in his work in extensive detail, without which the Church lacks the "marks" that make it true to its calling.[41]

Levy challenges gentile Catholics to become attuned to fostering such an ecclesia, and the 2015 CRRJ document has gone some way toward welcoming it, even without yet knowing what the shape of such a reality might be. Levy's important book offers a glimpse of what it might look like and its profound significance. Nurturing this ecclesial reality will entail difficult conversations with Jewish dialogue partners who see this phenomenon as both apostasy and encouragement of the extinction of the Jewish people as a nation. However, this difficult path cannot be avoided if the Church is to remain true to her ecclesial identity as a Messianic Jewish community through whom the gentiles enter into the Jewish covenant. This ecclesial identity, which the Church has perceived only dimly since the Council, has now entered more fully into the bloodstream of the Church.

9

The Great Commission and Jesus' Messianic Secret: A Hebrew Catholic Perspective on the Challenge of the *Missio ad Ludaeos* in Contemporary Israel

Antoine Levy

One evening, an old Dominican friar knocked at my door. I was still a freshman in the Dominican Order at the time, immersed in my initial theological training. The sight of this kind but austere brother standing on the threshold caught me off guard. As it turned out, this venerable brother merely wanted to show me what he cherished as a small treasure. Having spent many years working as a missionary in Iraq, he had heard about the life of another Dominican, Jean-Baptiste Levy, who was sent to Mossul in the nineteenth century and died there trying to cure his brothers and ordinary people of typhoid. My evening visitor possessed a copy of the first religious vows signed by brother Jean-Baptiste Levy, O.P., in 1858. He gave it to me, with a short account of Jean-Baptiste's life and his conversion to Christianity. As far as I can recall the story, Jean-Baptiste, who still went by the name Gustave at the time, was traveling from Strasbourg to Paris, where he was planning to study law. On a seat in his stagecoach, he discovered a copy of the New Testament left by a previous passenger and began to read it out of boredom. Having left Strasbourg as a "regular" Jew, he was already some manner of Christian by the time he got off the stagecoach in Paris. As it happened, Jean-Baptiste was among the first brothers to join the Dominican Order recently reestablished in France by Henri

Dominique Lacordaire. The Dominican brother who gave me these documents thought that I might be related to this Jean-Baptiste Levy. This could be the case, since my ancestors on my father's side settled in Alsace in the seventeenth century.

The reason I am bringing up the forgotten memory of Jean-Baptiste Levy has nothing to do with genealogical considerations though. The story of Jean-Baptiste's conversion strikes me as perfectly genuine for a Jew. It would be hard to find any trace of entangled motives or human influences therein. One can claim that the passenger who left a copy of the New Testament on the seat of Jean-Baptiste's stagecoach acted as an involuntary—more likely than voluntary—Christian missionary: "How are men to call upon him in whom they have not believed? And how are they to believe in him of whom they have never heard? And how are they to hear without a preacher?" (Rom 10:14). Still, Jean-Baptiste would have dismissed the reading with a wave of the hand had he not discovered in it *content* that turned his worldview immediately upside down. That was it: Because of who he was and the way the text read, Jean-Baptiste embraced its content and probably felt taken up into a new spiritual dimension. This experience has a name: It is what Christians call faith.

My own conversion process was slightly more complex. It involved conversations with Christian academics and the witness of unsophisticated but genuinely holy believers. Still, just as with my possible relative Jean-Baptiste Levy, no conversation or witness would have been sufficient to convince me of the truth of Christianity had immediate, unbiased access to the text of the New Testament not led me to this entirely unexpected—and far from wished-for—conclusion. A foreign human interference that I would have suspected of enticing me to join a specific group of people would have turned me away from considering the Christian faith as a possibility. But any human interference is excluded when what is decisive is the encounter between a reader and a book, a hearer and a message purportedly from God. It is left to the depth of one's conscience to determine whether this message comes from God indeed.

Freedom is a supreme value for any Jew. It is as free individuals that Jews become "sons and daughters of the commandments" as they take their place in *Klal Israel*, in the religious body formed of their Torah-observant kin. It is in the name of freedom again that a Jew can withdraw from this body, as he "goes out with a question", according to the Hebrew expression (*latzet b'sheela*). Finally, it is in the name of this same freedom that a small number of Jews have embraced, in the course of the centuries and especially during the most recent ones, a religious tradition that is different from the rabbinic one in so many fundamental ways. Sincere conversion that is independent of external pressure pertains to the inalienable human right to exercise religious freedom. The gospel *can* be presented to Jews. No conversion is possible when acquaintance with the gospel, even through a copy of the New Testament forgotten in a coach, is denied. However, it is *exclusively* as a fully free and conscious individual that a Jew ought to take the vertiginous step of embracing the faith of Christians.

One might think that the political and religious freedom that all Jews enjoy in the state of Israel would create the ideal, almost "eschatological" possibility of unbiased, unhampered access to the content of the gospel. However, one should not forget that the "freedom for" that Israel as a sovereign political state has enabled is inseparable from a "freedom from". There has always been a danger for the Jews of Western and Eastern Europe that is far worse than political marginalization and economic restrictions. I mean the threat of conversion, which carried with it the possibility of the extinction of the whole nation. Once made a Christian, a Jew would merge with the gentile masses, thus compromising the chances of survival of a people that would continue to be integrally Jewish. In the Christian world, the task of promoting Jewish conversion, whether by sheer coercion or on a more voluntary basis, has often been entrusted to dedicated individuals or organizations, something that defined the *missio ad Iudaeos* as a specific type of Christian ministry. One is therefore led to wonder whether one can conceive a type of *missio* in the contemporary state of Israel that would not be immediately perceived as the continuation of a bimillennial strategy to dismantle the Jewish nation—a *missio* that would provide Jews with the opportunity to acquaint themselves with the content of the Gospels without being suspected of preying upon Jews in order to gentilize them—a *missio* that would simply create a space for some mysterious encounter to take place (or not) in the depth of one's both irreducibly personal and irreducibly Jewish conscience. To summarize, the question is what type—if any—of *missio ad Iudaeos* corresponds to the providential or eschatological situation associated with establishing a state where all Jews are free citizens and responsible for their own religious convictions as individuals?

First, I will scrutinize the Great Commission as the scriptural and theological principle that underpins the *missio ad Iudaeos*. In what way can it be said that the *missio ad Iudaeos* derives from the very essence of Christian faith? I will then schematically retrace how this *missio* has been implemented throughout the centuries until the present era, both in the Catholic and the Protestant worlds. Finally, I will try to show how the contemporary challenges of the *missio* lead us to an interpretation of the Great Commission that might be respectful of the Jewish nation's newly and dearly acquired freedom.

The Great Commission as Cornerstone of the *Missio ad Iudaeos*

Hudson Taylor, the legendary Protestant missionary of China, popularized the theme of the Great Commission, an idea that the Baron von Welz had already expounded at length in the seventeenth century: It is the duty of all Christians to communicate their faith to those to whom it is foreign. Taylor buttressed his teaching by referring to the ultimate words of Jesus to his disciples before his Ascension into heaven, as reported in Matthew 28:19–20: "Go therefore and make disciples of all nations, baptizing them in the name of the Father and of the Son and of the Holy Spirit, teaching them to observe all that I have commanded you; and behold, I am with you always, to the close of the age."

Since Taylor, Christians of all denominations have found in the Great Commission the most fundamental argument in favor of the *missio ad Iudaeos*. Jews do not know Jesus; therefore, they should be evangelized, just like all nations who do not know him. Of course, Jews cannot be said to ignore Jesus in the sense in which nations or tribes that have evolved without contact with Christian tradition do. What is implied is that Jews do not know who Jesus truly is, "true knowledge" being tantamount to believing in him. Since Christians generally view this "knowledge" as the only doorway to salvation, they consider the task of spreading it to be priceless and to be a priority over other types of ministries.

However, the first question that needs to be asked is whether—or to what extent—the words of Christ in Matthew 28:19–20 apply to the Jewish nation.

The fact of the matter is that there is a remarkable absence of unity regarding this exact point among contemporary exegetes. A number of them (Douglas Hare, Daniel J. Harrington, Stephen Hre Kio) translate "all nations" (*panta ta ethnē*) as *goyim*—the "nations" as traditionally contrasted with the people of Israel. They suggest that the author of the Gospel might have given up the idea of preaching the good news to Jews by the time he wrote the conclusion of his book. Meanwhile, other scholars (Walter Grundmann, William F. Albright, Rudolph Schnackenburg, and many others) maintain that the "nations" include Israel. Several among them (John P. Meier, Aelred Cody, and Theo de Kruijf) argue that the distinction between Israel as *laos* and the heathens as *ethnē* is far from systematic in Matthew's Gospel.

What can be agreed upon is that Matthew does not *explicitly* exclude Israel from the proclamation of the gospel. Actually, the parallel passage in the Gospel of Luke (24:47) indicates that Jews are among the nations to whom the gospel should be preached. Exposing the ultimate meaning of Scriptures to his disciples, Jesus commands that "in his name, repentance for the forgiveness of sins would be preached *to all nations, beginning from Jerusalem arxamenoi apo Ierousalēm*."[1] At the same time, the fact that preaching to Jerusalem is specified here, together with the manner in which it is specified, is quite remarkable. The command to begin from Jerusalem is reminiscent of the kerygmatic speech of Peter to "the men of Israel" after the healing of the invalid at the gate of the Temple: "God, having raised up his servant, sent him to you first [ὑμῖν πρῶτον], to bless you" (Acts 3:26). It also echoes what Paul writes in his Epistle to the Romans: "I am not ashamed of the gospel: it is the power of God for salvation to every one who has faith, to the Jew first and also to the Greek [*tō pisteuonti, Ioudaiō te kai hEllēni*] (1:16; see also 2:9–10). If Jews are included among the addressees of the apostolic kerygma, they are so, it seems, in a manner that is distinct from the other nations—the "Greeks" or the non-Jews. This distinction is far from being contingent since it emphasizes a "priority" of the Jews over the non-Jews. One can discuss whether one should attach an axiological value to this priority ("the most important"). Still, there is undoubtedly a temporal aspect to it: The Jews ought to be the first to whom the gospel is preached because they are the first chronologically to whom the Word was sent. Accordingly, it is the whole ministry of Jesus that is ultimately hinted at: "He came to his own home, and his own people received him not" (Jn 1:11). The good news was announced to Jews before the Church was born and a kerygma proclaimed. That the apostles should continue to preach it to Jews after the death and Resurrection of Christ is but a natural consequence of this state of affairs. The distinction between the ministry of Peter and that of Paul in the early Church (see Gal 2:18) speaks to the fact that Jews fell into a particular category when it came to spreading the good news.

Naturally, the "special character" that distinguishes Jews from non-Jews does not mean that the reason the gospel should be preached to them is different from the reason it should be proclaimed among pagan nations. In the apostolic Church, the notion that faith in Christ, as a condition for the forgiveness of sins and—correlatively but not identically—salvation, was equally vital for Jews and non-Jews seems to reflect a consensus: "God has consigned all men to disobedience, that he may have mercy upon all" (Rom 11:32). For Paul, Jews are certainly much closer to the true God than heathens since "to them belong the sonship, the glory, the covenants, the giving of the law, the worship, and the promises" (9:4). Still, this is an additional reason that kindles his zeal toward his people, together with a motive for lament due to the latter's resistance to the gospel: "For I could wish that I myself were accursed and cut off from Christ for the sake of my brethren, my kinsmen according to the flesh" (9:3). As close to the true God as they are, Jews are not justified without the knowledge of Christ: "My heart's desire and prayer to God for them is that they may be saved [*hē deēsis pros ton theon huper autōn eis sōtērian*]. I bear them witness that they have a zeal for God, but it is not enlightened [*ou kat'epignōsin*]. For, being ignorant of the righteousness that comes from God [*dikaiosunē*], and seeking to establish their own, they did not submit to God's righteousness. For Christ is the end of the law, that every one who has faith may be justified" (10:1–4). A little further in the same epistle, Paul explains that Jews and non-Jews are on the same footing when it comes to the necessity of acknowledging Christ: "There is no distinction [*ou gar estin diastole*] between Jew and Greek; the same Lord is Lord of all and bestows his riches upon all who call upon him. For, 'every one who calls upon the name of the Lord will be saved'" (10:12–13). This vital necessity, equally shared by Jews and non-Jews, of coming to the knowledge of the word of salvation is what justifies and legitimates *mission* according to its most original—literally "apostolic"—meaning: "How are men to call upon him in whom they have not believed? And how are they to believe in him of whom they have never heard? And how are they to hear without a preacher? And how can men preach unless they are sent [*ean mē apostalōsin*]?" (10:14–15).

There is little doubt that, for the authorities of the very early Church, the word of salvation had to be "sent out" to Jews, and sent out *in priority* (*proton*), to the Jews. After all, at the most primitive stage of her formation, the Church was a strictly Jewish undertaking: She was established by Jews in order to spread the teachings of a Jew that were originally addressed to Jews. After deciding to welcome gentiles as gentiles (see Acts 15), the apostolic Church extended the preaching of salvation far beyond the boundaries of Israel to "all nations of the earth" (Mt 28:18–19). Still, obedient to what came to be called the Great Commission many centuries later, the apostolic Church did not lose sight of the command that this mission should "begin from Jerusalem". The *missio ad Iudaeos* is truly rooted in the teaching of Jesus and the awareness of the apostolic Church. It carried the most decisive task that can be conceived, that of renewing the ministry of Christ by communicating the word of salvation to whom it was originally destined. There is no way the Church could be faithful to her apostolic foundations without taking up this kerygmatic mission and carrying it further. Accordingly, if the legitimacy of a *missio ad Iudaeos* can be questioned, it is in relation not to its doctrinal or scriptural basis but to its mode of implementation.

The Implementation of the Great Commission Until the Contemporary Era: History at a Glance

Understood *stricto sensu*, as a technical term, the notion of *missio ad Iudaeos* is a modern invention. From a Roman Catholic perspective, the term "mission" indicates ministry among peoples and nations where a functional Church with a clergy is not yet extant. Still, a concerted and systematic effort to convert Jews is anything but foreign to the policy of the Catholic Church during the Middle Ages. This policy targeted Jews who were established within the boundaries of Christendom. It is not rare to find sincere, if often overly zealous, expressions of concern about the salvation of Jews during the medieval and early Renaissance periods. Saint Vincent Ferrier's (d. 1419) notorious "campaigns of conversion" witness to this fact. At the same time, these expressions were always linked to the desire to safeguard innocent Christian faithful against the pernicious influence of those whose denial of Christ's divine Messiahship held them apart from the rest of the population.

With the advent of the modern age, from the sixteenth to the eighteenth centuries, Christian—Catholic, but also Protestant—missions aimed primarily at evangelizing peoples and nations who hitherto had had little or no contact with the biblical revelation, such as the Japanese, the Chinese, the Indians, native Americans, and so on. The idea that some missionary work should be directed at Jews started to surface in Germany in the seventeenth century, as Protestant Hebrew scholarship and chiliastic philo-Semitism joined forces.[2] At the time, this inspiration was still mingled with the desire to contain the influence of Jews on harmless Christians. Still, compassion for the fate of those who, being so close to the Christian revelation, were kept in the ignorance of it soon became an independent source of missionary activity. By the middle of the nineteenth century, this trend eventually reached the Catholic Church. The foundation of the Congregation of Our Lady of Zion (1842 for the sisters, 1852 for the priests and brothers) under the impulse of two biological brothers, Alphonse and Theodore of Ratisbonne, who were Jewish converts, is part of this general context.

The notion that by evangelizing Jews, Christian churches were somehow coming back to the origin, to "Jerusalem" where it all began, was coextensive to the nineteenth-century *missio ad Iudaeos*. What was generally missing, however, was the awareness of the fundamental rift between the Church of the origin and the Church in her current state. After two millennia, the original Jewish church had turned into an exclusively gentile church. In the beginning, gentiles were invited to embrace their salvation by grafting themselves onto the Jewish wild olive tree. In the nineteenth century, Christian missionaries were asking Jews to relinquish their Jewish identity and tradition to welcome their salvation. Accordingly, the *missio ad*

Iudaeos was undermining the very uniqueness—that of the Jewish nation among all nations of the earth—that justified its existence in the first place.

Logically, it is the relative success of this missionary revival that brought the problem to the surface. Preeminent Jewish converts like the anonymous "One of the Second Tribe" writing in the *Jewish Expositor* (1817–1818), Ridley H. Herschell, Moses Margoliouth, Stanislaus Hoga, Carl A.F. Schwartz, Aaron A. Saphir, and Paul Levertoff, were not the only ones to denounce the endemic process of both active de-Judaization and tacit ostracization that they and their peers had to go through after joining traditional Christian churches. This is also the way learned and/or generous gentile philo-Semites (for example, John Priestley, Thomas Witherby, Michael C. Tonna, and John Oxlee) assessed the situation. Christian F. Frey (Joseph S. Levy) was the first Jewish missionary to establish a place of worship designed for Jewish converts (the Chapel at Bishopsgate, 1808). The Philo-Judean Society was created in 1826 with "unto the Jews as Jews as they might gain the Jews" as a motto to give some room to the observance of Jewish traditions among converts. The Hebrew Christian Alliance (Carl A. F. Schwartz, 1866) and the Hebrew Guild of Intercession (Michael Rosenthal, 1887) continued to work along more or less the same lines. Numerous journals made room for independent Jewish-Christian voices.

Throughout this period, however, the London Society for Promoting Christianity Amongst the Jews (LSPCJ), which was founded in 1809 and was an offshoot of the London Missionary Society, showed considerable reluctance to develop autonomous forms of "Jewish-Christian" religious life. The Society never endorsed teachings and liturgical practices that would depart from those observed in the Church of England. It upheld supersessionist ideas—Christ had abolished the precepts of the Old Covenant through his words and deeds—and adamantly stuck to the view that Jewish converts should join established churches, any other option being either impossible in practice or not in line with the structure of the apostolic Church. Clearly, as much as Jews ran this official "mission" at a concrete level, it still played into the hands of an ecclesiastical and political establishment that viewed it as a convenient means to solve—or at least alleviate—the burden of the "Jewish issue" within English society. This stance, which was advocated by both gentile and Jewish converts in leadership positions, created considerable tension with those who called themselves "Hebrew Christians" at the time. It was also the antipode of what Joseph Rabinowitz was endeavoring to establish in Kishinev, with his *Bnei Israel*, and what Paul Levertoff was doing in his parish of London's East End.[3] In the Catholic world, the benevolence of the Ratisbonne brothers toward Jewish customs and religious legacy never translated into the constitution of an autonomous Jewish-Christian entity. Ideally, baptized Jews individually supported by the Congregation, or coming from boarding schools associated with the Congregation, would gradually integrate into the life of standard Catholic parishes.

Among Protestants, the inner contradiction between a declared—if not always sincere—empathy toward the Jewish nation and an activity that would inevitably lead to the de-Judaization of converts became especially manifest whenever chiliastic conceptions inspired the *missio ad Iudaeos*. How could the notion that Jews were corporately called to play a crucial role in the realization of God's plan of salvation be reconciled with an activity whose effect was the concrete dismantling of the Jewish nation? From a few spiritualist circles of seventeenth- and eighteenth-century Germany, premillenarianism migrated to nineteenth-century England, where it underwent a thorough theological re-elaboration, giving birth to John Nelson Darby's (1800–1882) "dispensationalism"—and hither to the United States becoming a major reference of twentieth-century so-called Christian Zionism.

In the course of its peregrinations and inner evolution, premillenarians addressed this contradiction in two mutually exclusive ways. A number of them assigned the final conversion to the miraculous agency of God alone, which boiled down to voiding missionary activity of its purpose. Others claimed that the mission was meant to win over only a limited number of Jews—"the holy remnant"—who would spearhead the final conversion of the Jewish nation. As much as the last option implied an enduring sense of Jewish identity among converted Jews, it did not bridge the deep theological hiatus between the logic of mission and that of chiliasm. Indeed, was the unconverted Jewish nation a positive factor in God's design of salvation or a *massa damnata* calling for the preachers of the gospel to avert them from the wrong path?

It goes without saying that, from a traditional Jewish point of view, the *missio ad Iudaeos* was perceived as the continuation of the medieval effort to disintegrate the Jewish nation by other—softer, but also more cunning—means. The establishment of working places, schools, shelters, and medical facilities destined to provide crucial assistance to impoverished and socially marginalized Jewish neighborhoods not only witnessed to the good heart of missionaries but were in themselves a demonstration of a sense of charity that was supposed to be far superior to the mean pragmatism of Jews and could only be attributed to the influence of a faith more authentic than that of the rabbis. In brief, those whom the words of Christ had not persuaded would eventually be convinced by the works carried out in his name (see Jn 10:38).[4] To many Jews, religious-minded or not, the idea that missionaries would exploit the social or psychological weaknesses of Jewish minorities to implement a project that inevitably led to the disintegration of the Jewish nation was unbearable. Still, from the point of view of Christian missionaries, these were considerations of little importance when what was fundamentally at stake was the salvation of souls from eternal damnation.

One needs to wait until the tragedy of the Shoah to see the configuration of the *missio ad Iudaeos* change radically, both on the theological level and the practical one.

Twentieth-Century *Missio ad Iudaeos*: The Theological Lessons of a Crisis

If there is one good lesson one can learn from the Holocaust, it is that the life of the Jewish nation is precious. Any attempt to endanger it, even stemming from the best intentions, has a share in a project of destruction, the pure evil of which was unfurled during the time of Nazi Germany and World War II.[5] In the aftermath of the Shoah, the Christian world's new sensitivity to the Jewish struggle for survival could not help but affect Church attitudes and policies that had hitherto ignored or minimized the theological significance of Israel's ongoing existence. The increasing awareness of the negative consequences of traditional Christian proselytism toward Jews led Christian churches to see the *missio ad Iudaeos* in an entirely new light. As a result of this process, two fairly distinct approaches to this issue seem to have emerged, one that characterizes the Catholic Church and the other large sectors of the Protestant world.

The Catholic Church: Dialogue Versus Mission

The "*affaire* Finaly" in the 1950s served as a painful wake-up call for the Catholic Church. The Congregation of the Sisters of Our Lady of Sion had been involved in hiding two baptized Jewish brothers who were reclaimed by their biological family after World War II. They did not desist, in the face of public outrage or a French court of Justice's decision, until they were finally forced to yield. The examination of conscience that ensued in the congregation led to some sort of self-conversion of an organization that had itself been founded to convert others and Jews especially. In March 1964, Mother Laurice, the superior of the congregation, circulated a letter among the sisters that read: "The Church ... acknowledges the faith of Jews in a special way.... This faith can lead to salvation as long as God does not grant another light. Therefore, we will henceforth refrain from praying for the 'conversion' of Jews. To this effect, all leaflets, pamphlets, tracts connected with the API [Brotherhood of Prayer for Israel] are to be suppressed."[6] After Vatican II, the congregation was left to itself to handle the consequences of this self-conversion. It mainly shifted the focus of its work from mission to dialogue and improved mutual understanding between Christians and Jews. This shift of attitude toward Jews and the necessity of evangelizing them was part of a broader trend among French Catholic theologians. It played an instrumental role in leading to the promulgation of Vatican II's *Nostra aetate* declaration (October 1965).

Caught up in between its desire to give a new impulse to evangelization and the somewhat extraordinary development of its dialogue with the Jewish world, the Magisterium of the Catholic Church was much slower to single out the implications of *Nostra aetate*'s *aggiornamento* for its concept of *missio ad Iudaeos*. If Jews were no longer to be considered cast out of God's salvific design, to what extent was it still relevant to promote the good news in their midst?

Doubtlessly, the acknowledgment that organized forms of missionary activity would inevitably lead Jewish converts to renounce their Jewish identity once they entered the Catholic Church stands behind the statement that one reads in "The Gifts and the Calling of God Are Irrevocable", the 2015 document of the Vatican Commission for Religious Relations with the Jews: "The Catholic Church neither conducts nor supports any specific institutional mission work directed towards Jews."[7] This stance was reaffirmed and developed by Pope Emeritus Benedict XVI a couple of years later. Commenting on the verses that are at the core of the Great Commission doctrine (Mt 28:19), he writes: "Mission to all peoples and cultures is the task entrusted by Christ to his disciples. What is at stake is acquainting all men with the 'unknown [G]od' (See Acts 17:23). Human beings are entitled to make the acquaintance of God since only those who know God have the capacity to live as they ought to. This is why mission ministry is universal—with one exception: a mission to the Jews was never contemplated nor deemed to be necessary because, from all the peoples, they were the only ones to be acquainted with the 'unknown God'."[8]

Obviously, from a Catholic and, more broadly, Christian point of view, the knowledge of God that can be derived from the teachings of what is commonly designated as "Old Testament" are not enough to achieve salvation, at least through "ordinary means", as the Magisterium would say—otherwise, the sending of the Son of God as Savior would lose its purpose. If it behooves Jews to hear about salvation in Christ, how could the Church renounce its missionary calling toward Jews without betraying the reason that justifies her establishment? Most probably, what is implied here is a distinction between goals and means. Missions are institutional means that can be replaced with other means. Meanwhile, the goal—reaching out to Jews in the name of Christ—remains identical. The 2015 document and other recent declarations replace the term "mission" with that of "witness": "Christians are nonetheless called to bear witness to their faith in Jesus Christ also to Jews, although they should do so in a humble and sensitive manner, acknowledging that Jews are bearers of God's Word, and particularly in view of the great tragedy of the Shoah."[9]

Paradoxically, as we read in the same document, this new emphasis on witnessing as an alternative to developing missionary activities echoes the deep theological sense of "mission":

> The concept of mission must be presented correctly in dialogue between Jews and Christians. Christian mission has its origin in the sending of Jesus by the Father. He gives his disciples a share in this call in relation to God's people of Israel (cf. Mt 10:6) and then as the risen Lord with regard to all nations (cf. Mt 28:19). Thus the people of God attains a new dimension through Jesus, who calls his Church from both Jews and Gentiles (cf. Eph 2:11–22) on the basis of faith in Christ and by means of baptism, through which there is incorporation into his Body which is the Church (*Lumen gentium*, 14).[10]

It is difficult not to notice the tension between the new role assigned to "dialogue" and the insistence on the Church's faithfulness to "mission" understood in its original sense.

Significant segments of the rabbinic world—precisely those that are involved in the dialogue with the Catholic Church—are prepared to view the Church as an entity that somehow leads a considerable part of non-Jewish mankind to God. For them, dialogue is about a respectful sharing of knowledge and reflection on the core values of the two religious traditions that take part in it. The problem is that the Catholic partner does not seem equally accepting of the idea that Judaism, in its current condition, is the most adequate way for Jews to hear about God's saving truth. Indeed, what if, on the Catholic side, dialogue with the Jewish world can never be separated from a goal that, ultimately, consists of "incorporating" Jews into the Body of the Church through a strategy that the Magisterium calls "witnessing"? To what extent is such a "witnessing dialogue" fundamentally different from "mission", understood as a tactical means to obtain the conversion of Jews to the Catholic truth?

True, the reflection on the Shoah led the Catholic Church to credit ongoing Jewish existence with theological significance in God's design of salvation over mankind. And yet, despite all its efforts, the Catholic Magisterium seems at pains to conceive a way of engaging with the Jewish world that would be free of the suspicion of ultimately aiming at canceling Jewish existence through the incorporation of Jews into the Church. Where is the presentation of the Christian message that would not entail the destruction of the very idea on which a sovereign Jewish state is established, namely, the preservation of Jewish existence against all efforts to annihilate it? Where is the presentation of this message that would reckon not only with the freedom of a Jew but also with that of an Israeli Jew to accept or reject it for what it is and says, and not because of the practical consequences this acceptance or rejection would occasion?

The Protestant World: A Jewish Mission to the Jews

In the traditional Protestant—mostly Lutheran—world, the notion of dialogue became more and more sharply set against that of mission from the beginning of the 1970s onward (meetings of the Lutheran World Federation in Asmara 1969, Bossey 1982, Stockholm 1983, and so forth). Most certainly, the reason for this tension lies in the fact that this part of the Protestant world, unlike the Catholic Church, never gave up the idea of promoting "organized missions".[11] Accordingly, the Protestant leadership faced a choice of theological, "diplomatic", and financial priority. Should the thrust of its efforts and means be devoted to mission work at the expense of dialogue with the Jewish world? Was the opposite decision not more appropriate? Indeed, there was no practical way in which the unilateralism of an organized *missio ad Iudaeos* could be reconciled with the respectful bilateralism that is the defining element of authentic dialogue.[12]

Be that as it may, a tectonic change took place in another sector of the Protestant world during the same period—the beginning of the 1970s. In the aftermath of the Six-Day War, when the protest movement was in full swing in the United States, movements like "Jews for Jesus" and "Messianic Jews" emerged out of the Evangelical constellation. This phenomenon featured a major reshuffling of the cards. Far from promoting an escape from the Jewish condition, these movements received their impetus from the new sense of pride that overwhelmed Jews all over the world after Israel's 1967 victory. Being an intrinsically Jewish and fairly autonomous organization, Moshe Rosen's "Jews for Jesus" were less liable to the accusation of working to gentilize Jews. As for Messianic Jews, was there more tangible proof of a new commitment to the life of the Jewish nation than their claim to set up communities that would refuse to be called "Christian" and promote a number of elements borrowed from the Jewish rabbinic tradition? Messianic Judaism had all the appearance of some heaven-sent revenge for the frustrated aspirations of Hebrew Christians throughout the nineteenth century.

In addition, even if charitable works were not foreign to "Jews for Jesus" or Messianic congregations, they could no longer be assimilated into the "deceitful tools" that nineteenth- and early-twentieth-century Protestant missionary activities allegedly forged to "attract Jews". The world had changed. Jews, especially in Western countries and *a fortiori* in Israel, were no longer a group of socially marginalized, economically oppressed individuals who would be tempted to collect the material benefits provided by missionary organizations in order to ameliorate their condition.

Speaking of organized missions, it is but natural that these two sectors of the Protestant word—the "old" institutions of traditional Protestantism and the emerging Jewish movements of Jesus' discipleship—would join forces at some point. The problem of the former was gentilization, an endemic flaw to which "indigenous" Jewish congregations were the antidote. Meanwhile, the latter were vulnerable and isolated, lacking expertise and financial means, all deficiencies that the support of established missionary societies could help to remedy. A new paradigm based on the cooperation between the two became standard in the Protestant world.[13] It found a concrete embodiment in the Lausanne Consultation on Jewish Evangelism, an umbrella organization launched in 1980 that gathers groups, movements, and congregations across the spectrum of Protestantism involved in the *missio ad Iudaeos*.

The new framework provided a degree of response to the bimillennial Jewish anxiety about gentilization. Fundamentally, however, it only strengthened the conundrum rooted in Protestant chiliasm. On the one hand, the contemporary *missio ad Iudaeos* acknowledges the providential nature of the ongoing existence of the Jewish nation, a doctrine at the core of Christian Zionism.[14] On the other hand, following the whole tradition of the Reform, it fails to conceive how a religious-ethnic body that sees in the explicit dismissal of Christ as Savior as a condition for its ongoing existence could convey God's grace and keep its members on the right path.[15] More prepared than the Catholic Church to ascribe the establishment of the state of Israel to a benevolent decree of God's providence, the Protestant world is also more radical than the Catholic Church in its rejection of a path toward salvation that does not rely on the explicit recognition of Christ as Savior. While most educated Catholics would describe the Christian faith as the accomplished fulfillment of the Jewish one, Christians with a Protestant background would be more inclined to contrast faith in Jesus with rabbinic tradition as truth contrasts with error. The question is, How can the *missio ad Iudaeos* ask Jewish Israelis to turn away from rabbinic tradition as incompatible with the true Word of God when it sees the hand of God in a state that owes its existence to the rabbinic tradition? Is this tradition not the force that has prevented—and continues to prevent—the Jewish nation from dissolving in the Christian world? How come the structurally erroneous denial of Christ associated with Judaism did function and is still called to function as the main instrument of God's design of salvation over mankind? If it is true that Rabbinic Judaism plays such a providential role, why should Jewish Israelis turn away from it? And if the *missio ad Iudaeos* actively promotes this renunciation, is this *missio* not working against God's design of salvation instead of advancing its realization?

Whichever answers to these questions can be brought up, it remains a fact that Jewish Israelis associate evangelizing efforts coming from the Protestant world and the Messianic one with the invitation to discard the implicit, albeit powerful, bond between the state of Israel and the religious tradition that preserved the Jewish nation in the course of history. This perception applies to Jewish Israelis of all persuasions—and even to those of no persuasion at all. While being what people call a *chiloni*, a nonobservant and maybe atheistic Jew, a citizen of Israel cannot ignore the objective debt that his state owes to the religious tradition he personally dismisses. And this awareness remains true, whatever the patriotic commitments, the openness to elements from the rabbinic tradition, and the proportion of halachically Jewish faithful that one currently finds in a number of Jewish Messianic communities in Israel. One is not free to heed the message of the gospel as it is actively spread by Protestant and Messianic communities when one knows that accepting it will ipso facto translate into a rupture with the principles of a state one wants to be fully part of—into the adoption of a vision where the reasons for the distance of Jews from Christianity are conceived as lethally erroneous, and their incorporation into the cosmic Body of Christ remains the ultimate ideal. It is essential to understand that the issue is not whether this rupture with the state and this vision of a cosmic Church are literally professed by the disciples of Christ living in Israel. The problem is that any attempt at active evangelization will be *automatically perceived* as part of the bimillennial effort of the Christian Church to dismantle the Jewish nation and absorb it into the far broader body of the *Goyim*.

In conclusion, neither the Catholic current stance on the *missio ad Iudaeos* nor the one originating in the Protestant world offers a satisfactory solution to the challenge of conveying an unalloyed—impervious to the noise rising from almost two millennia of Christian anti-Semitism—gospel to the public of an "open society" (blessed be the memory of Karl Popper!) as that of the state of Israel. Still, I find in both stances, as different and even mutually opposed as they are, elements that point toward a more satisfactory answer.

The Messianic Secret and Proclamation of the Gospel

Neither the Catholic Church nor any other Christian denomination, for that matter, will ever renege on the principle of the Great Commission, a principle that, according to the Gospel, applies to the Jews as well as to all the nations of the earth, even if it applies differently to the one and the others, as I showed earlier. The question has to do with its adequate implementation in a context where, for the first time in history, Jews *as a nation* have set themselves free from external pressure to accept the message conveyed by Christian missionaries.

The attempt of Catholic theology to promote a type of witness, even in the framework of interreligious dialogue, that would still be faithful to its lofty understanding of Christ's messianic mission to the Jews without translating into organized ministry might sound sophistic. Is not such systematic witness a type of "organized ministry" that simply avoids saying its name? Still, one should pay attention to the *intention* lying behind the effort to suppress any unilateral mission ministry directed at Jews. There is a clear awareness that words and discourses, the one and only purpose of which is to convince Jews of the truth of the Gospel, are counterproductive. This is not only due to the fact that these discourses immediately elicit an adverse reaction among those whose minds and hearts they want to reach.

The suppression of organized forms of the *missio ad Iudaeos* goes with an increasing awareness of the providential character of the Jewish nation's ongoing existence.

Indeed, the Magisterium of the Catholic Church recently made a decisive step forward by declaring that God's covenant with Israel was never rescinded.[16] Contrary to what is frequently assumed in the Protestant world, this teaching does not affirm the coexistence of two parallel ways of salvation. The promises contained in the covenant with Israel are accomplished in the covenant in Christ, and there can be no salvation through the former independently of the latter.[17] Still, mysteriously, the only name through whom there is salvation can be a source of salvation for those who do not confess it.[18] Accordingly, there is one way of salvation and two coexisting covenants. That the covenant in Christ accomplishes the covenant with Israel does not mean that the former cancels the latter.[19] The covenant with Israel is, according to its content and addressees, distinct from the New Covenant.[20] It never ceases to bolster the unique journey of Israel throughout human history.[21]

Naturally, one must still ask about the nature of a "witness" to the Jews that, out of respect for the providential *Sonderweg* (the unique historical path) of their nation, would not take the form of an organized ministry. Here, I would like to bring forward an understanding of this witness that, in my opinion, addresses the inherent problem affecting the dialogue between the Church and Rabbinic Judaism. The Church cannot forgo the desire to tell Judaism that its ultimate truth lies in recognition of Jesus as the Messiah of Israel. However, she knows that human words and demonstrations will only do so much since no conviction in this regard can be achieved without a supernatural illumination that pertains to the direct and sovereign action of God exclusively. Words and demonstrations can only "show" in the sense in which the finger of John the Baptist points in the direction of Jesus. Behind the words, there is the eloquence of a silence that makes Yeshua seen and lets him occupy center stage. Silence can be a unilateral cancellation of witnessing. But silence can also be a specific and powerful type of witness, provided it manages to show what words and demonstrations are unable to show. Still, what would this "eloquent silence" of Christianity look like in the Israeli context?

Let us further reflect on the state of the *missio ad Iudaeos* in the world closely or loosely associated with the Reformation. Doubtlessly, the implantation of Jewish Messianic communities in Israel has been a considerable achievement from an ecclesiological point of view. It would be difficult to find the equivalent of these congregations in the Catholic Church as she is currently established in Israel, let alone in other parts of the world. Whether elements borrowed from the rabbinic tradition are part of their liturgy and teaching or not, all Jewish Messianic congregations in Israel emphasize their connection with Jewish identity and strive to be actively part of the surrounding society. The closest Catholic equivalent to Jewish Messianic congregations, the *kehillot katolim dovrei ivrit*—Catholic communities of Hebrew speakers (the so-called of Saint James Vicariate)—position themselves differently. Even if they count Israeli citizens among their members, the formal integration of these *kehillot* into a patriarchate rooted in a population of Arab Christians and their awareness of "representing" the universal Catholic Church in the Jewish sector of the state of Israel, together with the percentage of migrant workers without citizenship in their midst, shape a relationship to the state of Israel that is more one of discussion partners than one of citizens to their shared homeland. More importantly, while these *kehillot* are generally eager to display signs of attachment to the rabbinic tradition and foster ties with local synagogues, Jewish identity is not given any role in their implicit but very concrete ecclesiology *ad intra*. Jewish members are treated precisely the same way as non-Jewish members, and the primary concern of a mostly non-Jewish clergy is to develop a worthy antenna of the Catholic Church in Israel as a foreign land.

To summarize, little distinguishes the *kehillot katolim dovrei ivrit* from classical Catholic "expat" communities. The "ecclesiological horizon", so to speak, of Jewish Messianic congregations in Israel is very different. We speak here of local communities overwhelmingly formed of Jewish citizens of Israel that discard the qualification of "Christian" due to their desire to belong to the Jewish world. They want to embody this segment of the Jewish world that acknowledges Jesus as the true Messiah of Israel, and as such, they claim to be citizens of Israel, the only sovereign Jewish state, on the same footing as all other citizens. Just as elsewhere, these Messianic congregations do not exclude non-Jewish members *ex principio*—in this sense, they are "apostolic" without being "Christian", at least name-wise.

As mentioned earlier, what triggers the hostility of large swathes of the Israeli population against these congregations, preventing further integration into the wider Israeli society, is their way of implementing the Great Commission. The more Messianic Jews openly promote the possibility of being Jewish while believing in Jesus, the more they are perceived as striving to destroy the cement of Israeli society by deceitfully enticing Jews to dissolve into the broader body of Christianity. They are generally viewed as *de facto* reducing Jewish identity to a pretense of political patriotism and an arbitrary collection of folkloric elements taken from the rabbinic tradition. What the wider Israeli public does not understand is what constitutes Messianic Judaism's most interesting ecclesiological insight. While the ultimate goal of the Great Commission is to gather Jews and gentiles in the living Body of Christ, this goal does not imply or advocate the dissolution of the Jewish nation in the mass formed of gentile faithful. There is room for a Jewish church—a church that, in the living Body born out of the New Covenant, would preserve the ongoing life of a nation rooted in faithfulness to the first covenant.[22]

At this point, the question that needs to be asked to Jewish Messianic congregations is, Is the active proclamation of the gospel—what is perceived in Israel as Christian proselytism—the only way to implement the Great Commission? It is often difficult to avoid the sense that the Messianic *missio ad Iudaeos* derives less from a concern about the salvation of the souls who still ignore the good news than from a concern about the salvation of those who know it and preach it. The bad conscience of being an unworthy disciple of Christ as long as one does not spread the good news is not necessarily a manifestation of disinterested apostolic zeal or a sign that active ministry is the answer to a divine calling. Surely, the notion that those who have not heard the gospel are necessarily going to some eternal doom should incite the hesitant faithful to take action. But is it that certain that the Word of God is not somehow intimately connected with the Torah, so that there is a path to salvation within Rabbinic Judaism, as argued by the 2015 Vatican document? How are Christian Zionism and Jewish Messianic theology able to ascribe a divine mission to a nation that owes its survival to the collective denial of Christ's Messiahship otherwise?

What I would suggest is that the work of building authentic and fraternal Jewish Messianic communities *ad intra* is not a less faithful implementation of the Great Commission than trying to evangelize Jews *ad extra*. Quite to the contrary. While the *missio ad Iudaeos* cannot avoid being misinterpreted and therefore being widely counterproductive in the Israeli context, dismissing all proselytizing activities can deliver the most potent form of witness in the same context: "They do not talk. They do not pursue an agenda aimed at turning Jews away from Judaism and the state of Israel. They simply *are*. And they are ready to go through many trials in order to live according to their faith and be whoever they want to be." This type of attitude is an undeniable sign that there is something worth paying attention to here, and also an indication that the Jewish identity of these communities might not be the Trojan horse it is widely suspected of being.

The point I want to make is the following: *The form that would render eloquent the Catholic silence around the* missio ad Iudaeos *could be the establishment of congregations inspired by the example of Jewish Messianic communities.* Conversely, *the type of* missio ad Iudaeos *that would best correspond to Jewish Messianic congregations can be derived from the Catholic dismissal of "organized missions" and the emphasis on pure witnessing.*

After all, it might be the case that we are here rediscovering one of the reasons for Jesus' most constant attitude vis-à-vis his disciples and all the people he comes in contact with during the days of his earthly existence. Jesus never explicitly declares his identity as Messiah of Israel and Savior of the world. He instead lets his disciples come to this acknowledgment (see Mt 16:16; Mk 8:29–30; Jn 1:41). When Pilate asks Jesus whether he is the King of the Jews, Jesus replies, in essence: "You said it" (see Mk 15:2; Lk 23:3; Jn 18:37). Sending out his disciples, Jesus does not ask them to proclaim a new religious creed but to announce the proximity of the kingdom of heaven (see Mt 10:7; Lk 9:2; 10:9). At one point, Jesus sternly asks a leper whom he had cured not to tell anyone anything so that if the latter spreads the news about, it is not because of a will to advertise the miraculous deeds of Jesus, but *in spite* of Jesus' order to keep silent about it (see Mk 1:43–45).

It is safe to assume that things radically changed after the Resurrection. The swift and loud proclamation of the kerygma to all the nations "starting from Jerusalem" bears witness to the fact. However, as the kerygma goes back to Jerusalem after almost two thousand years marked by the tragedy of Christian anti-Semitism, the time to rediscover the power hidden in the silence of the messianic secret might have come.

This is a time when nothing should interfere between the newly recovered freedom of the children of Israel and their Messiah. This is a time when those who are convinced of the importance of this encounter should strive to be like a book forgotten on the seat of a stagecoach that a bored passenger would be free to leaf through or not. This is a time to understand that all the rest is in no one else's hands but God's.

10

Jesus and Jewish Identity: From Mosaic Judaism to the Church

Elias Friedman*

The passage from Judaism to Christianity rouses the passions of Jew and gentile alike. The Jew accuses the Christian missionary of attempting to destroy the physical integrity of the people, though not, of course, by physical means. Father Hruby seems to accept the assessment, for he says: "If Israel refuses to identify itself with the new Israel, which the Church pretends to be, it is because such an identification would lead, ipso facto, to the end of the Jewish people."[1] We find the forecast alarmist—at any rate avoidable—but the ground has to be cleared of the multiple ambiguities in the terms employed before light appears.

Christians are surprised to learn that belief in a Jewish Messiah should appear to imperil the existence of the Jewish people. They are bewildered and hurt at the resentment their well-intentioned missionary overtures encounter among Jews. When the so-called Anti-Mission Law was passed in the Knesset, the parliament of Israel, the reaction of Christians was one of heated indignation. We concede that they had a case to air; what we do not justify was the absence of any effort of comprehension among Christians of the Jewish point of view. Standing on their side of the fence, Jews have always observed with feelings of outrage the alienation of the convert from his people and the assimilation of his descendants into the gentile community. What is more, the very thought of adding the religious pluralism of the Christian world to that obtaining already in the Jewish world is enough to fill the Jew with horror. Is it to be wondered at that religious and secularist Jews combine forces to resist the Christian missionary, who proclaims salvation for the individual and prepares the earthly extermination of the people?

Jesus of Nazareth had no such intention. Had he not come to save the Jews (see Mt 1:21)? He himself was a Jew, born in Bethlehem of a Jewish mother, Mary, and circumcised on the eighth day of his life. He was of the tribe of Judah (see Heb 7:14), a scion of the royal house of David (see 2 Tim 2:8; Rom 2:26). Jesus directed his public ministry to the lost sheep of Israel, whom he loved and for whom he was to die before dying for others (see Jn 11:51–52).

When the Samaritan woman rounds on him pertly, saying: "You are a Jew. How can you ask me, a Samaritan and a woman, for a drink?" (Jn 4:9),[2] he does not reject the attribution. By announcing to the confused woman that "salvation is from the Jews" (4:22), he implicitly acknowledges that he is a Jew. The author of the Apocalypse bestows on the Risen Christ the epithet "Lion of the tribe of Judah" (Rev 5:5).

Saint Peter teaches that Jesus had come to grant "repentance to Israel and forgiveness of sins" (Acts 5:31), not a destructive aim, surely.

Some are of the opinion that "there is no shred of evidence that Jesus, at any point, repudiated his obligation to the Law, to which both his birth and circumcision committed him."[3] The statement is true, as far as it goes. Jesus had no plan to change Mosaic Judaism *during his lifetime*. The passage "not an iota will pass from the Law, till all has been accomplished" (Mt 5:18, adapted) may be an interpolation from Judaizing elements in the primitive Church, as some exegetes are inclined to think; they certainly express the attitude of Jesus to the Law, prior to Calvary. Modern revolutionaries are different. They are men in a hurry; they strive to introduce radical changes in the established order before their death. Not so Jesus! Two swords were enough for his purposes. The Church that he aimed to set up was to be the work not of Jesus himself but of his Spirit; to procure this gift for mankind, Jesus knew he had first to die and rise again from the dead.

It was a principle of Mosaic Judaism that a Judaite was bound to the observance of the Law as long as he lived; death liberated him from his obligation (see Rom 7:1–2; 1 Cor 7:39). Jesus remained faithful to the Law until his death. On the third day, he rose from the dead, free to institute his Church. He was no more a Judaite; he was an Israelite of a Judaean ancestry, of David's line (see Rev 22:16) and of Judaite origin.

The same principle holds good for the convert. In baptism, he dies with Christ and is absolved from the obligation to observe the Law of Moses. After baptism, he rises to a new life, an Israelite but no more a Jew, subject to the Law of Christ only. "It was through the law that I died to the law, to live for God" (Gal 2:19–20). One commentator finds the passage obscure. A reference to rabbinic teaching will make its meaning clear. In setting up his Church, Jesus did no violence to Mosaic Judaism, contrary to what many Christians imagine. Jesus and Mosaic Judaism died together on the Cross; they rose together on the third day, transfigured.

We are now in a better position to judge how erroneous are certain positions summarized by Eugene Fisher. Some scholars, for instance, hold that post-Christic Judaism and Christianity are both "in full and valid covenant with God", that "Christianity is an alternate form of the Sinai covenant, which remains in force"; or again, "that the Christian covenant thus perfects and fulfills, not Sinai, but the covenant with Noah." One asks oneself in astonishment, if what these positions pretend are true, why any Jew should ever have become a Christian, beginning with Saint Peter and Saint Paul.

Whereas some appear to hold that Jesus left Mosaic Judaism intact, Larcher goes to the opposite extreme: "He [Jesus] foresaw and posed successively the acts which were to lead to a rupture with Judaism."[4] To give Larcher his due, his thesis vacillates between continuity and a break in the passage from Mosaic Judaism to the Church. Elsewhere he modifies his previous stances: "Jesus, in virtue of the same divine authority, could have declared the Torah abrogated, incomplete and imperfect word of God, eclipsed by the perfect and definitive Word. He did not do so." Again, he concedes that the Torah "continues to indicate the will and intention of God".

Larcher, expressing a broad current of opinion among Christian theologians, maintains that Jesus put aside all that was material, temporal, and nationalist in Mosaic Judaism. What, then, is the residual value of the Old Testament for the Christian? The Old Testament, Larcher replies, retains no more than a "pedagogic value" for the new Israel. In consequence, Larcher regards as illegitimate any attempt to apply the prophecies of the Old Testament for the purpose of explaining the return of Jews to the Holy Land. How should a Christian explain it? "The answer to those questions", he writes "escapes us entirely, for the designs of God are impenetrable in advance. We incline our head piously at the thought, but, in fact, have not the designs of God advanced? Is not the reestablishment of the Jews in the Holy Land a reality?" Larcher finds facts embarrassing. His rejection of Zionism is short and harsh. The most he is prepared to admit, and that grudgingly, is that maybe the Jewish people constitute a special case. We see no sign that Zionists are going to fold up their tents and steal away, in order to facilitate matters for Larcher.

Rijk was more candid. He confessed that theologians are, ultimately, uncertain about the residual value of the Old Testament for Christians.

Adolf Darlap was positively humble. On the status of the Old Testament in Christianity, he admitted "that it is not so easy to define what remains and what has been suppressed".[5]

Perhaps Darlap's question should not be raised at all. The passage from Mosaic Judaism to the Church was the work of the Holy Spirit, and its results are transmitted to us by Tradition. The theologian registers them retrospectively. Seventh-day Adventists appear to enter where angels fear to tread when they conclude that the sanctification of Saturday is preceptive for Christians.

In the meantime, the Church tenaciously held to the belief that books of the Old Testament had been composed under the inspiration of the Holy Spirit, no less than those of the New Testament. Catholic theology taught that the Old Testament was a legitimate source for demonstration of theological propositions, on a par with Tradition and the teaching authority of the Church. Ecumenical councils quoted the Old Testament as if its quotations were demonstrative, not merely illustrative.

The truth is that the redemptive death of Jesus introduced a dual ferment of continuities and discontinuities into every order of Mosaic Judaism. Jesus compared the action of the kingdom of God to yeast fermenting a paste. Newman used the image of a caterpillar that undergoes metamorphosis in its silky cocoon, to issue therefrom a butterfly.

Newman, in fact, succeeded where others failed. He laid down the principle that explained the transition from Mosaic Judaism to the Church. "Let us recollect", he began, "*why* [the prescriptions of the Law] are abrogated, and we shall understand *in what sense*. They are abolished, because they were types, and because Christ, their Antitype, is come. True, *so far then* as they are types they are abolished; but not as they are religious services, and principles and elements of religious worship. That is, we must distinguish between the precept itself, and the particular fulfilment of it under the Jewish Law, that is, the Jewish rite."[6]

Continuing in the same line, Newman went on:

> Not only do forms and ordinances remain under the Gospel equally as before; but, as is plain from the very chapter on which I am commenting, what was in use before is not so much superseded by the Gospel ordinances, as changed into them. What took place under the Law is a pattern, what was commanded is a rule, under the Gospel. The substance remains, the use, the meaning, the circumstances, the benefit is changed; grace is added, life is infused; 'the body is of Christ;' but it is in great measure that same body which was in being before He came. The Gospel has not put aside, it has incorporated into itself, the revelations which went before it.[7]

Newman summed up his thought on the passage from Mosaic Judaism to the Church in a lapidary sentence: "The Jewish Church and the Christian Church are one."[8] David Flusser, surprisingly enough, comes to a similar conclusion, to be interpreted, naturally, in terms of his own premises.[9]

Let us apply Newman's illuminating distinctions in some detail.

Doctrine

The rigorous monotheism of the Old Testament prophets was unhesitatingly accepted by the Gospel. On one occasion Jesus recited the opening sentence of the *shema*: "Hear, O Israel, the Lord our God, the Lord is one God." To this monotheism was added the doctrine of the Trinity. The Christian accepts that monotheism is a dogma or revealed truth of the Old Testament and, if revealed, then preceptive.

The eschatology of Mosaic Judaism was taken over almost in its entirety by the Church. The Apocrypha and the pseudepigrapha of the Old Testament dealt in a vivid and imaginative way with last things, the end of history, the ultimate destiny of souls. To these beliefs and others the Church added that on the last day it would be Jesus the Lord, come in glory, who would judge the living and the dead.

Morals

Christianity retained the Ten Commandments, only illustrated, tempered, and spiritualized, as Newman would have said. Cicognani and others have argued that the Ten Commandments reappear in Christianity because they represent the natural law. The remark does not cover the precept of Sabbath observance. The Jewish Sabbath became the Lord's Day in Christianity on the authority of Tradition. The Lord laid down no precept concerning it. It was sufficient for Christians to consecrate one day a week to God, which day being of secondary importance. Not even the Jewish component of Sabbatical repose was retained, for in the first centuries of the Christian era, the Church lacked the political power to impose one day of rest a week on Christians. If courts, banks, businesses close down on Sundays, we are beholden for it to Constantine the Great. It may come as a surprise to Christians to be reminded that the Sabbatical repose they practice on Sundays is not of divine but of ecclesiastical law.[10]

Newman wrote in confirmation: "And so again the Ten Commandments belong to the Law, yet we read them still in the Communion Service as binding upon ourselves, yet not in the mere letter; the Gospel has turned the letter into spirit."[11]

Marriage

Monogamy and the indissolubility of Christian marriage are preceptive for Christians. Jesus defended these principles by invoking Genesis 2:24. Cicognani inferred from this that Christian marriage is indissoluble only because Jesus confirmed the teaching of Genesis. Did he not force an interpretation on the text from *a priori* motives? To us, the more natural reading is that Jesus invoked Genesis because it contained a teaching preceptive for the People of God in both phases of its existence.

Scripture

The Church retained the Sacred Scripture of Mosaic Judaism in the most spontaneous manner imaginable. Where Christianity differed from Judaism was in its interpretation of the messianic prophecies and the provisional status it accorded to the institutions of the Mosaic Law (see Mt 23:1–3).

Ritual

The sacrifice of the Cross rendered obsolete the bloody offerings of the old order (see Heb 9:11–14). It was not the principle of the sacrifice that was abolished, but the kind of sacrifice offered. Simultaneously the ministerial priesthood of Aaron was replaced by the priesthood of Jesus. Protestants err who assert that Jesus ever intended abolishing a sacrificing priesthood.

Newman expounds the matter with his customary energy and clarity: "Persons sometimes urge that there is no code of duty in the New Testament, no ceremonial, no rules for Church policy. Certainly not! They are unnecessary; they are already given in the Old. Why should the Old Testament be retained in the Christian Church but to be used? There we are to look for our forms, our rites, our policy, only illustrated, spiritualized by the Gospel. The precepts remain, the observance of them is changed."[12] How far are we not from Larcher!

In the light of Newman's teaching, we stand dismayed when Hruby affirms: "Israel is entitled, legitimately, in the order which is theirs, to expect that in time the Temple will be restored."[13] Christians, in the order that is theirs, may think otherwise. At all events, one Israeli religious leader has expressed his disappointment at the marginal degree of enthusiasm the project of restoring the Temple arouses in the Israeli public. In the first place, the Temple would have to be built on the site now occupied by world-renowned Muslim sanctuaries, an unthinkable violation of the status quo governing holy places in Jerusalem. What is more, bloody sacrifices being offered in public would hardly be an agreeable sight.

Christianity inherited from the old dispensation its ministerial priesthood and the distinction between the priesthood and the laity, one which lives on in the consciousness of Jews to the present day, though the Jewish priest or *cohen* has not exercised his functions for nigh on two thousand years. Lastly, the Christian Church abided by the rule of Mosaic Judaism, which reserved the priesthood to males, in opposition to the pagan world, where the priestess was an accepted institution.

Ecclesiastical Authority

After recounting the parable of the homicidal vine-dressers, Jesus added the ominous words: "For this reason, I tell you, the Kingdom of God will be taken away from you and given to a nation that will yield a rich harvest. When the chief priests and the Pharisees heard these parables, they realized he was speaking about them" (see Mt 21:43–45).

If we delete the phrase "and the Pharisees" as a gloss, which some exegetes recommend, the passage suits our purpose even better. Jesus is using the passive voice to avoid pronouncing the name of God, in accordance with the custom of his time. What he meant to say was, therefore, that God was about to withdraw whatever kind of divine authority had been bestowed on the priesthood of Mosaic Judaism in order to transfer it to others. Protestants argue from this passage that Jesus intended to transfer authority to Peter, in the latter's merely individual capacity. They err. The authority in question was not the authority of the chief priest of that time but of his office, which had existed for centuries before.

The priesthood of the Old Law had been established as preceptive for the People of God in whatever phase of its existence. The discontinuity introduced by the Gospel ferment lay in the transfer of the same authority from the house of Aaron to Peter, the apostles and their legitimate successors. Since none of these came from the Jewish priesthood, Jesus effectively opened the priesthood to any man qualified for the office.

The transfer of priestly authority, announced prophetically by Jesus, is one of the principal axes in the transition from Mosaic Judaism to the Church. The corollary is that the Church is in formal continuity with Mosaic Judaism, which is the burden of Newman's magnificent essay on the subject. The transfer of authority establishes on an unassailable foundation the essential identity between the two great phases of the public revelation of God to mankind. Mosaic Judaism was the People of God under the Law of Moses; the Church was the same people under the Law of Christ.

The second corollary is that when the transfer of divine authority had come into effect, it left Jewish religious leaders destitute of divine authority. Indeed, the obsolescence of the Temple system in the generation that followed the Resurrection of Jesus was rapid, ending in its physical destruction in A.D. 70, when providence confirmed the dispositions taken by God. The Temple burned, and with it the genealogical records required to demonstrate the validity of the Jewish priesthood. Today a Jew bearing the name Cohen can only adduce family tradition in support of his claim to be of priestly descent. What court of law would deem that sufficient evidence after an interval of two thousand years?

Even more so than the Jewish priesthood was Rabbinism, which succeeded Mosaic Judaism as the religion of the people, deprived of divine authority. True, the people who now came under the control of the rabbis were still authentic Israelites; their history would unfold under the *régime* of the election; despite the exile, they would retain a link with the land of Israel. But these were attributes of the people, not of their new religious *régime*. They held for secularized Israelites no less than for religious ones, for the material object of the election is the people, not its religious beliefs or opinions.

We gladly concede that Rabbinism possesses values, many of which have been gravely neglected by the Christian clergy, and which the latter can recuperate in friendly discussion with Jews. However, all religions have their respective values, though one and one only is valid, the religion of Jesus Christ.

The Legal Prescriptions

The sacrifices of the Old Law were replaced by a new one, more efficacious than the blood of goats and bull calves (see Heb 9:12), the old priesthood by a new one, the old legal and ritual prescriptions by a new legislation and a new ritual. The Law, it is said, was abrogated. Notwithstanding, the idea of abrogation can only be analogical when applied to the supernatural order. Christianity abrogated the prescriptions of the Old Law, to replace them with others. The kingdom of God was to be taken away from the chief priests; it had therefore existed in Mosaic Judaism. In the Church, the kingdom entered a new phase, without loss of its essential identity and structures.

Cicognani recognized the similarity between the institutions of Mosaic Judaism and the Church, without being able to account for it. Was it therefore accidental? Larcher found Mosaic Judaism unrecognizable in the Church. For Newman, the similarity is essential. Are there not in both a chief priest, assisted by secondary priests and counseled by legal experts? Are there not found in both priests ordained to offer sacrifices on consecrated altars? Both have a priesthood distinguished from a laity also called to holiness of life. Both have a Holy Scripture, a large part of which is shared. The histories of both are illustrated by prophets, monks, saints, martyrs, and confessors.

Post-Christic Rabbinism, in contrast, has no chief priest, no Sanhedrin, no sacrificing priesthood, no altars, no monastic institutions. Yes, Rabbinites can be saved in the synagogue, like Muslims in Islam and Buddhists in Buddhism. Their salvation depends on the good disposition of individuals, encouraged by the occasions that their religion may offer them to pose saving acts of faith. Their salvation does not demonstrate the validity of Rabbinism.

For Eugene Fisher to pretend that the Jewish covenant-unbiblical expression remains valid after Christ, that Rabbinism is sufficient for salvation on its own terms, that it does not need to be perfected by Christianity, and other sophisms of the like is to deny that Jesus Christ died to save all men, the Jews first. We welcome Father Fisher's appeal for a revision of the theology of post-Christic Judaism and the Jewish people; we agree that the revision involves a change of heart for Christians, not only a change in theological perspectives. But must Fisher revise Christian truth in the process? His book is titled *Faith Without Prejudice*; it is certainly not a book about faith without bias.

Cardinal Newman speaks the mind of the Church when he denies forcibly that any essential change of identity took place in the transition from Mosaic Judaism to the Church. He asks rhetorically: "What likeness is there between a church spread over the whole earth and a church pent up in one comer of it, between a national church and a Catholic? I answer, surely the mere extent of a church and its fortunes generally are but an accident of its being; externals cannot destroy identity if it exists, which is something inward."[14]

"But further," he continues, "it may be objected that the change was internal, not external; not only did the Church change from local to Catholic, but it became a Church of the Gentiles instead of a Church of the Jews."[15]

"I consider", he answers in reply, "that the word remnant, so constantly used in scripture, is a token of the identity of the Church in the mind of her Divine Creator, before and after the coming of Christ. Express and precise as are the sacred writers in declaring that the Gentiles shall be rejected, still, instead of stating the solemn appointment of God in a simple contrast between the two dispensations, they are accustomed to speak of the Remnant of Israel inheriting the Gentiles."[16]

Father Benoit is of the same opinion, that this universal expansion of the new elected people is not, in any way, brought about by the expulsion of the Jews, but by the addition of the pagans. The latter were not substituted for the former, as one says sometimes; they were associated to them.

The gentiles were branches of the wild olive tree, grafted against their natural inclination into the cultivated olive tree (see Rom 11:19), not by any metaphysical necessity, but by the decree of a merciful God and, conditionally, on their remaining faithful to their calling (see Rom 11:20–21).

The Church of Christ was, therefore, not in contradiction to Mosaic Judaism. It did not oppose Mosaic Judaism; it was opposed to the survival of Mosaic Judaism. Mosaic Judaism did not disappear like a child who is reported missing to the police. It grew up. The adult does not abrogate the child. The child is assumed into the adult. They are the same person in different stages of its existence.

Christianity and the Social Régime of Mosaic Judaism

Jesus did not neglect to provide his people with new institutions to take the place of the old. He chose the Twelve and instructed them in the mysteries of the kingdom. He guided their first steps in the field of the apostolate. At Emmaus, the Risen Christ continued his teaching office (see Lk 24:13–35). After Pentecost, the Twelve appeared as a well-organized group, Peter at the head, John and James his intimate confidants. The group was able to make serious decisions, to replace Judas the traitor with Matthias, and to admit the gentiles.

Jesus left behind him an organized Church, the members of which were all Israelites, a Church of the Hebrews. Christ, its mystical head, was himself an Israelite; Mary and the apostles were Israelites. Since the Church existed before the admission of the gentiles, it is in essence Israelite. Gentiles only belong to the integrality of the Church, given that Christianity cannot be rightly conceived without the mission to the gentiles.

The Church of the Hebrews was not a new sect of Judaism, not a kind of Reformed Synagogue. It represented the definitive form of the kingdom of God on earth, eschatologically oriented.[17]

Mosaic Judaism had been a *dat*. The word is of Persian origin, signifying "decree" or "royal decree". It was extended to describe the religion of Moses, which appeared to Jew and gentile alike as representing a system of divine decrees. The sense of *dat* is excellently brought out in the book of Esther. Haman complains to his king about the Jews: "Their laws [*dateihem*] are different from those of all the nations and they ignore the royal edicts [*datei Hamelech*]" (Esther 3:8, adapted). The Latin word *religio* has a wider and a narrower sense. The wider sense corresponds to the ordinary sense of the word "religion". The narrower sense is confined to ecclesiastical circles: It signifies a religious order under its rule and constitutions. It is this second and narrower sense of the word *religio* that the Hebrew *dat* approximates.

The Risen Christ had abolished the Jewish *dat*, though all his immediate disciples did not appreciate the extent of the change that he had effectuated in Mosaic Judaism. Many continued to circumcise their children, pray in the Temple, frequent the synagogue, and call themselves Jews. Nor was there, at first, a proper name for the new religion. Jews such as Saint James and the members of the community of Jerusalem held that the Law of Moses was still necessary for salvation. They were Judaeo-Christians.

On certain occasions Saint Paul, too, calls himself a Jew (see Acts 22:3). In a famous confrontation between them, Saint Paul upbraids Saint Peter, saying: "You who are a Jew are living according to Gentile ways" (Gal 2:14). Was Saint Paul justified in calling Saint Peter a Jew?

On the face of it, he was not! Saint Paul had a very clear notion of whom he thought was a Jew, and whom he thought was not a Jew. A Jew, for Saint Paul, was one who trusted in the Law (see Rom 2:17), who knew God's will through the Law, who was a subject of the Law (see 3:19). The gentiles, on the other hand, were those "who do not have the law" (2:12).

What Saint Paul had in mind and what he should have said, perhaps, was that he and Saint Peter were of Jewish origin, for they had now "died to the law" (7:4).

At such an inchoative stage in the history of Christianity, it would be unfair to expect from Saint Paul a more rigorous and consistent terminology. Ultimately, Saint Paul directed his mission to the gentiles. The Jewish adherents to the new way were few in number. Saint Paul did not positively enjoin them to abandon the customs of their ancestors, but he had undermined their *raison d'être*. If the Law was not necessary for the salvation of the gentiles, neither was it necessary for the salvation of the Jews. Saint Paul himself was prepared at times to practice the Law. He circumcised Timothy; he fulfilled his vows in the temple; but these were done in pursuit of his missionary policy of being all things to all men. The fact remains that Saint Paul was still entitled to pose such acts, for the converts had not yet been expelled from the synagogue. They were obliged to leave the synagogue only after the destruction of the Temple.

The right to pose acts of the Jewish religion entitles a person to be called a Jew. The principle holds to this very day in rabbinic law. For instance, a convert man may give his Jewish wife a bill of divorce, valid in the eyes of a rabbinic court. In the same measure, the convert is a Jew in the act for Rabbinic Judaism and not only in potency, as Kurman would have it.

But Saint Paul no more considered that the Law of Moses bound his conscience. He was not a Judaeo-Christian in the strict sense of the term. What is more, his teaching on the caducity of the Law of Moses plunged the Judaeo-Christians into a profound dilemma. Saint Paul declared the wall of separation between Jew and gentile to have been overthrown by Jesus Christ. The special consequence was that the régime of social separation between Jew and gentile was suppressed. A Christian of Jewish origin was now free to marry a Christian of gentile origin. As the Judaeo-Christians saw it, and the rabbis with them, the way now lay wide open for the dissolution of the Jewish people in a flood of gentile proselytes to the new religion.

The Judaeo-Christians recoiled from the prospect. Unable to find a solution to their dilemma consonant with the spirit of Christian fraternity, they entrenched themselves behind the régime of social separation between Jew and gentile, so characteristic of Mosaic Judaism. Their bishops turned down the invitation to attend the Council of Nicaea, thus branding Judaeo-Christianity as heretical in the eyes of the Catholic world. The hostility of gentile Christians from without and sectarianism from within brought about the disappearance of the various currents that together made up the church of the circumcised.

Testa and Bagatti have pioneered studies in the remarkable world of the Judaeo-Christians. They have traced the manifold influence of their culture on the development of Christianity. Our purpose requires from us to insist on the fact of their disappearance from the stage of history.

Daniélou maintained that even if all Israel had embraced Christianity, the continuity of Israel would not have been threatened. How could he know? The history of Judaeo-Christianity belies his facile optimism. It was an experiment that failed, in which Christianity did not succeed in conserving a community of Israelite Christians. The lesson for us is that not every community of Israelite Christians bears with it a guarantee of survival. How much more successful have not the rabbis been!

In the personal experience of the author of these pages, to guarantee the continuity of Jewry's history, in the hypothesis of an entry en masse of Jews into the faith, steps would have to be taken and obstacles overcome that Daniélou either ignored or preferred not to mention.

The problem of terminology vexes converts to this day, as we see in the case of Father Daniel. Many designate themselves Jews, relying on the example of Saint Paul. But circumstances have changed since the first days of the Church, making it inexact for converts to apply to themselves the term "Jew". If they insist on so doing, they invite the question as to what they mean by the word.

Protestant circles favor "Hebrew-Christian". So did David Goldstein. The trouble is that the word "Hebrew" has come to have a double nuance. It could signify an Israelite, abstraction being made as to whether Israelites are the Elect People or not; or it could signify an Israelite in the mouth of the one who actively denies that post-Christic Jewry, in particular, is still the object of the Election. The latter is the use adopted by the Canaanites. The courts of the state of Israel have declared that "Hebrew" and "Jew" are synonymous in the eyes of the law.

During World War II, Christians of Jewish origin were classified as "Christians of Jewish descent". The Nazis, who employed a racial criterion in the determination of Jewish identity, were known to round up Jewish converts and send them to the camps of extermination, where they met with the same fate as their fellow Jews.

The expression "Jewish Christian" is often carelessly bandied about. It appears to us incorrect and thoroughly ambiguous.

Gentile courts of law are willing to accept the declaration of any person that he is a Jew, but facts of that kind have no theological value.

An Israelite who today accedes to the Christian faith is not a Judaeo-Christian. Not only did Judaeo-Christians frequent the synagogue until their expulsion from it around the year 80 of the Christian era, they believed that the Law of Moses was still valid. Today Jewish converts may not attend synagogue services habitually. Such behavior would be considered inconsistent with their Christian confession of faith by both Jews and gentiles alike.

Messianic Jews number about three thousand in the state of Israel. They have been the object of study by Pastor Kvarme of the Norwegian Church, Haifa. Some accept the divinity of Christ and have been baptized. Others, like the Ebionites of old, reject the doctrine. The different currents agree in believing Jesus to be the Messiah. They resemble the early Judaeo-Christians in their resolve to retain their historical identity. This attitude expresses itself in their rejection of the title "Christian", which they confine to gentile Christians, classical persecutors of the Jewish people. Another tendency is to adopt a régime of social separation from recognized Christian denominations.

According to Pastor Kvarme, the Messianic Jews in Israel are already divided among themselves on doctrinal issues. If a house divided against itself must fall, then their future is not assured. Nor can their fragile organization offer the Jewish people what it is obscurely seeking, a firm guarantee against the dissolution of their historical identity, in the event of its embracing the Christian faith.[18]

11

The Catholic-Messianic Jewish Conversations

David Neuhaus

The significant changes in Catholic teaching about Jews and Judaism since the Second Vatican Council (1962–1965) and the dialogue it has nourished between Catholics and Jews have been the subject of many studies. In the aftermath of the Council, Catholic hierarchs and theologians have been working to transform the "*teaching of contempt*" into a teaching of respect. This is an ongoing project. However, there is another dimension of the encounter with Jews after the Council. The Catholic Church reaffirms that the Church is the unity of Jewish and gentile believers in Christ as explained in the New Testament (see Rom 11; Eph 2:15–16). The *Catechism of the Catholic Church* teaches:

> The glorious Messiah's coming is suspended at every moment of history until his recognition by "all Israel," for "a hardening has come upon part of Israel" in their "unbelief" toward Jesus (Rom 11:20–26; cf. Mt 23:39).... St. Paul [writes]: "For if their rejection means the reconciliation of the world, what will their acceptance mean but life from the dead?" (Rom 11:15). The "full inclusion" of the Jews in the Messiah's salvation, in the wake of "the full number of the Gentiles" (Rom 11:12, 25; cf. Lk 21:24), will enable the People of God to achieve "the measure of the stature of the fullness of Christ," in which "God may be all in all" (Eph 4:13; 1 Cor 15:28).[1]

In this essay, I seek to examine a dialogue in the margins of the Catholic-Jewish dialogue, one that has evolved between the Church and Jewish believers in Christ who continue to identify as Jewish. The issue is particularly sensitive as the Church seeks to build relationships with mainstream Jewish communities, insisting that it no longer preys on Jews, proselytizing them and ushering them into the ranks of a Church that has no place for Jewish particularity. However, the Church is challenged by a new phenomenon: Jews who have come to faith in Jesus as the Messiah and Son of God and who insist that they remain Jews and part of the Jewish community. Although there is a diversity of Jewish believers in Jesus, some integrated into the ranks of the established churches (including the Catholic one) and other ecclesial communities, there are those who insist they remain part of the Jewish community and remain outside any Christian community. They will be referred to here as Messianic Jews.[2]

A Jew according to traditional Jewish law is the child of a Jewish mother or someone who converts to Judaism.[3] Despite the fact that the definition says nothing about faith or religious practice, Jews were defined as such by their Jewish religious practice up to the beginning of modernity. *Halakhah* (the Hebrew term for walking with God) gave the contours of Jewish identity (circumcision, Sabbath observance, dietary laws, and so forth). However, modernity not only shattered the religious unity of practice at the heart of traditional Jewish identity through the development of different streams of Judaism (ultra-Orthodoxy, modern Orthodoxy, Conservative Judaism, Reform Judaism, and so forth) but also saw the emergence of a Jewish secular identity that rejected religious practice altogether. Many Jews in the contemporary world, whether religious or not, see themselves as belonging to a people, sharing a history, a culture, and a worldview. Debate rages among Jews today about what constitutes being a Jew. Is being Jewish primarily a religious reality, or is it a national/cultural/ethnic one? Whereas few today dispute that a Jew can be thoroughly secular, can one claim to be Jewish when one practices another religion rather than no religion at all?[4] And Messianic Jews? They claim that their form of Judaism includes a belief in Jesus as Messiah and Savior, a claim that often arouses the ire of many Jews, religious and secular.

Who Are the Messianic Jews?

The roots of the phenomenon of Jews who have come to faith in Christ but do not belong to Christian churches and insist that they remain Jewish are to be found in modern times.[5] Renewed Christian interest in the Old Testament and the Holy Land as well as the development of modern nationalism influenced the emergence of individuals and groups of Jewish believers in Christ. Currents of Christian Zionism had already begun to emerge in the Anglo-Saxon world from as early as the seventeenth century.[6] Strongly eschatological, they promoted the idea that the end of times and Christ's return were imminent and that the fulfillment of promises to the Church must be preceded by the fulfillment of the biblical promises to the Jews. Later, the development of nineteenth-century nationalism facilitated acceptance of the idea that the Jews not only were a religious community but also defined themselves as a people, an increasingly common Jewish self-understanding in the modern era. Jewish Zionism, which appeared in the course of the nineteenth century, promoted the idea that Jews must take their place alongside other peoples, affirming their national identity at the time that Italians, French, Greeks, and Poles were doing the same. Jewish Zionism evolved within the context of these European national movements, which were too often prone to modern anti-Semitism. Jewish Zionists proposed not only that Jews were a people like any other but also that they had a right to a homeland in Palestine, pointing to the Bible as their source. They insisted that Jews preserve their identity, and a sure way of doing that was by immigrating to a homeland in which they would constitute a majority.

In the Protestant world, interest in the vocation and destiny of the Jewish people inspired the foundation of structures that encouraged belief in Jesus among Jews but did not constrain them to renounce their Jewish identity.[7] A joint Anglican-Lutheran mission to the Holy Land was founded in 1840, headed by the first Protestant bishop of Jerusalem, a converted Jew by the name of Michael Solomon Alexander. Although some see this as a beginning of modern Jewish Christianity, the pioneering attempt failed to establish a community of Jews who accepted faith in Christ. The Hebrew Christian Alliance, founded in 1867 in Britain, and the International Hebrew Christian Alliance, founded in 1925 in the United States, celebrated the Jewish identity of those who had come to faith in Jesus, predominantly through Protestant missions. The Israelites of the New Covenant, active in Kishinev in Russia (today Moldavia) from the end of the nineteenth century, is another precursor of the contemporary

Messianic Jewish movement because it promoted a Jewish expression of corporate life in Jesus, including forms of Jewish observance and liturgical worship based on traditional Jewish prayer.[8]

Focusing on the Shoah and the establishment of the state of Israel, many contemporary Jews maintain that their identity is independent of a religious component. The Nazi program to annihilate all Jews ignored religious practice and united all Jews in a supposed ethno-genetic community. Jews who believed in Christ went to their death with all other Jews, as the Nazis made no distinction between Jews who practiced their religion and those who did not, Jews who believed in Christ and Jews who did not. After the Shoah, Zionist thinking became dominant in the Jewish world, and many Christians also endorsed Zionism as a way of making amends for Jewish suffering at Christian hands. The establishment of a so-called Jewish state in 1948 deepened an increasingly commonly held conviction that the Jews were a people in the modern, nationalist sense. They were united regardless of faith, religious practice, or ideological conviction. Although Jews who had converted to Christianity or those who professed faith in Jesus Christ were still viewed by many Jews, both secular and religious, as having put themselves outside the community, it was easier for them to integrate discreetly within the Jewish community, particularly in the state of Israel.[9] This was often accomplished through an identification with Zionism. For many Jewish believers in Christ and their Christian supporters, Christian Zionism and Jewish Zionism were seen to converge in the insistence on Jewish aspirations to be recognized as a people as well as in the conviction of a continuing role for Jews in the history of salvation.

The contemporary wave of Messianic Judaism has its roots in the period after 1967. The Jesus Movement in California and the 1967 war in the Middle East, which was seen by some as a divinely inspired victory for Israel, both contributed to bringing some Jews to belief in Jesus. Charismatic faith and renewed Jewish national pride were intertwined. In 1975, the Hebrew Christian Alliance in the United States was renamed the Messianic Jewish Alliance of America, a change signaling the new orientation: more Jewish identity and less Christian tradition. This had implications for self-understanding and ecclesiology, for worship and lifestyle, for biblical exegesis and theology in the Messianic movement.[10] Many Messianic Jews were seeking out ways to live corporately as Jewish disciples of Jesus, outside traditional Jewish and Christian institutions and structures.

Messianic Jews can be found today in a vast array of congregations, particularly throughout the Anglo-Saxon Jewish diaspora (the United States, Britain, Australia, South Africa, and so forth), in the countries of the ex–Soviet Union, in Europe, and in Israel. Worldwide, Messianic Jews number between 50,000 and 150,000.[11] One issue that is strongly debated among Messianic Jews is the possibility of non-Jews joining Messianic Jewish communities. Many communities accept non-Jews, and some even have a majority of non-Jewish members. The ways that Messianic Jewish communities express their Jewish identity, formulate their faith in Jesus Christ (often referred to in Hebrew as Yeshua *HaMashiah*), live, and worship are very diverse. Some closely resemble various currents of Protestant and Evangelical Christianity, whereas others have adopted traditional Jewish practice and worship, some even choosing an Orthodox or Conservative Jewish way of life. Within this diversity, no central leadership exists to ensure commonality of discourse, definitions of dogma, and uniformity of practice. One leading Messianic rabbi, observing a traditional Jewish lifestyle, explained: "When we call our movement a type of Judaism, we are affirming our relationship to the Jewish people as a whole, as well as our connection to the religious faith and way of life which that people have lived throughout its historical journey."[12]

Messianic Jews are often distinguished by their observance of the Jewish calendar, Sabbath, and Jewish feast days instead of marking Sunday and the Christian calendar. Some Messianic congregations use Jewish forms of worship and liturgy, whereas others conform to Christian forms. Messianic Jews generally baptize their members, some practicing adult baptism only, and they celebrate forms of the Lord's Supper. In their adhesion to faith in Christ, they recognize the authority of the New Testament but often reject later Christian tradition. Some understand the Messianic movement in "restorationist" terms: the rebirth of the original Jewish component of the primitive Church, coexisting alongside the gentile component. As one Messianic leader claims: "Messianic Judaism is not a completely new movement, but rather the resurrection of a very old movement."[13] Another prominent Messianic leader insists:

> Just as the destruction of a Jewish national presence in the holy city and land in the first century opened the door for supersessionist ecclesiology, so the restoration of such a presence in the twentieth century challenges that ecclesiology.... The restoration of a Jewish national existence in the land promised to the patriarchs and matriarchs has also led to the restoration of the church from the circumcision in the holy land and the holy city. Jerusalem was the original centre of the church; could it be that Zion again has a central role to play in the life of the church?[14]

Protestant Christians, who historically supported missions to the Jews, have had a strong influence on the development of the discourse, theology, and attitudes of the Messianic Jewish movement. The vast majority of Messianic Jews believe that the one God is Father, Son, and Holy Spirit, but they rarely use the term "Trinity". Without using the language of the ecumenical councils, almost all Messianic Jews would affirm that Yeshua is fully divine and fully human. For them, the councils that defined the Christological doctrines pointedly excluded Jewish modes of discourse. Jewish Messianic theologians attempt to formulate their conceptual discourse within the context of the Bible, both Old and New Testaments, underlining the enduring witness of the Old. Many Messianic Jews have inherited a certain hostility to the Catholic Church that is rooted in Jewish historical memory and strengthened by Evangelical suspicion of Catholics.

Messianic Jews often see their vocation as remaining fully Jews, not assimilating into the gentile majority, in order to preserve the Jewish component in the universal Body of Messiah, the Church, a unity of Jews and gentiles, thus described in the New Testament. They point out that although they believe in Jesus, the only way to preserve Jewish identity is to nurture Jewish communities where Jewish believers transmit Jewish identity. The conversion of Jews to Christianity and their integration into the universal Church has in almost all cases led to the extinction of the Jews as a distinct people. A central concern is the preservation of Jewish continuity in the Body of Christ.

In the post–Vatican II era, some Messianic Jews have discovered that the Catholic Church has undergone a process of rethinking its own Jewish roots, beginning with the affirmation that Jesus is the Jewish Messiah. Furthermore, the Catholic Church is engaged in an ongoing dialogue with Jews in order to root out anti-Judaism in Catholic thinking and a concerted struggle in partnership with Jews against anti-Semitism. Among those working to reformulate Catholic attitudes toward Jews and Judaism have been Jewish Catholics who themselves affirm their Jewish identity.[15]

Jewish Particularity Within the Church

In former times, a Jew who confessed faith in Jesus as the Messiah and Savior was no longer considered a Jew. From the early centuries, the Church discouraged the preservation of a distinctively Jewish identity within the Church. Jews who came to faith in Christ and who frequented the synagogue or observed any Jewish practice were even threatened with excommunication or worse.[16] It was assumed that the Jew would give up his Jewish identity at the baptismal font: Jews were now Catholics, and Jewish identity was to melt away.

Whereas in days gone by, for baptized Jews, attending synagogue, observing the Sabbath, practicing Jewish dietary laws, or circumcising their sons might be condemned as heresy or worse, today Jews are free to continue valuing their Jewish identity, practice, and solidarity with the Jewish people. Parallel to the development of the Messianic Jewish movement, the Catholic Church has seen the evolution of individuals and groups of Jewish Catholics who affirm their own Jewish identity within the Catholic Church and celebrate it. For example, one prominent Jewish Catholic, Cardinal Jean-Marie Lustiger, archbishop of Paris (1926–2007), once wrote: “In becoming a Christian, I did not intend to cease being the Jew I was then. I was not running away from the Jewish condition. I have that from my parents, and I can never lose it. I have it from God, and he will never let me lose it.”[17]

This not only is a personal choice but also is sanctioned by the Church, recognizing the blessing bestowed by the Jewish people on humanity. Thus, Pope John Paul II described emblematic Jewish-Catholic Edith Stein in 1987 in his address to the Jewish community in Cologne as “a daughter of Israel who remained faithful, as a Jew, to the Jewish people, and, as a Catholic, to our crucified Lord Jesus Christ”.[18] In his homily pronounced at Stein’s canonization in 1998, John Paul II declared: “She understood that it was very important for her ‘to be a daughter of the chosen people and to belong to Christ not only spiritually, but also through blood’.”[19]

Jewish Catholics, although few in number, are very diverse.[20] From an institutional point of view, the two best-known structures that regroup Jews who are Catholics are the Saint James Vicariate for Hebrew Speaking Catholics in Israel (henceforth SJV) and the Association of Hebrew Catholics (henceforth AHC). Among the founding figures of both structures are two Jewish Catholics who became Carmelites and lived in the Monastery of Stella Maris in Haifa. SJV founder Daniel (Osvald) Rufeisen and AHC spiritual father Elias (John) Friedman had different perspectives on Jewish identity in the Catholic Church. Both Rufeisen and Friedman were Zionists, seeing the state of Israel as representing a new period in Jewish history that could inaugurate a new era in Jewish attitudes toward Christians and Christianity. However, the SJV developed in Israel, whereas the AHC developed mostly in the Anglophone diaspora. Language and cultural milieu also explain much of the difference between the two: The SJV was a European and predominantly Francophone phenomenon in Israel, whereas the AHC remains largely centered in the United States of America.[21]

Rufeisen and some of the other founders of the SJV believed that they were reestablishing the ancient "church of the circumcision",[22] the Church of Saint James in Jerusalem, a community of Jews who believe in Jesus without ceasing to be Jews. Rufeisen, referring to his own becoming a follower of Jesus, explained: "For me the acceptance of Christianity was a Jewish step."[23] He would insist that his move toward Jesus as Messiah was steeped in his Jewish identity, a move similar to the earliest Jewish disciples of Jesus. From a theological point of view, he and his SJV companions wanted the expression of their faith in Jesus as Messiah to be Jewish—not only deeply rooted in the Scriptures of Israel but also formulated in the expressions of the Jewish people throughout the centuries and thus at home in the Hebrew language, in a society in which the majority were Jews and in a state that defined itself as Jewish.

Friedman, on the other hand, was more reticent about Jewish identity in the post-Jesus period and insisted on using the term "Hebrew Catholic". A Hebrew Catholic was an Israelite, a member of the people of Israel; however, Jewish tradition, practice, and belief, based on Jewish religion formulated by the rabbis and unenlightened by the revelation of Christ, were no longer appropriate for the Hebrew Catholic. He wrote in his 1987 opus *Jewish Identity*: "An Israelite who today accedes to the Christian faith is not a Judeo-Christian.

Not only did Judeo-Christians frequent the synagogue until their expulsion from it around the year 80 of the Christian era, they believed that the Law of Moses was still valid."[24] According to AHC, vestiges of Jewish culture and ethnicity can be retained to encourage Jews to believe in Jesus without fear of losing their Jewish identity.[25] Sabbath observance or the Passover meal might be practiced within the Catholic context by Catholics of Jewish origin in order to express their Israelite identity. In an interview with David Moss, Archbishop Raymond Burke, the patron of the AHC, clarified that traditional Jewish practices are permitted because they are carried out in the light of Christ. The interview strongly underlined that baptized Hebrew Catholics remain part of God's elect, holding a special place as heirs of historical Israel.[26] The AHC states on its website: "The tragic exile of post-Christic Jewry was due to their incredulity, their refusal to acknowledge the divinity of Jesus. This thought should prompt Hebrew Catholics to redress the situation by their exemplary orthodoxy"[27]—orthodoxy in Catholic faith and practice.

SJV encourages a relationship of dialogue with mainstream Jews, including religious Jews, and does not engage in any form of missionary activity. In the spirit of the Second Vatican Council, SJV underlines the traumatic relations between Jews and Christians through the centuries, recognizing that mission in any form contributes to the negative heritage of Jewish-Christian relations in history. It seeks to incarnate a loving presence of Church in the midst of the people of Israel. On its website, it describes itself as working "to strengthen the relationship between Jews and Christians, sharpening the Church's awareness of its Jewish roots and of the Jewish identity of Jesus and his apostles" and seeking "to sharpen the awareness of Jews in Israel with regard to the history, teaching and contribution of the Church to society. Our faithful are engaged fully in the life of Israeli Jewish society and in the life of the Catholic Church."[28] The AHC avoids using the word "mission" and uses the word "witness" instead. However, the opening statement on its website says: "If you are Catholic, we hope that you will join us in the work of preserving the identity, heritage, and community of Jewish people within the Church."[29] The focus is on the Jews in the Church. Again, the diversity in approach is apparent, with SJV embracing a more dialogic approach to Jews, eschewing mission, and AHC promoting a more traditional approach that seeks to promote Christian faith among Jews.

Catholic-Messianic Jewish Dialogue

Without compromising the ongoing and important dialogue with mainstream Jews and the paradigmatic changes in the attitude to Judaism and the Jewish people inaugurated by the Second Vatican Council, the Catholic Church initiated a discreet but vibrant dialogue with Messianic Jews. The Roman Catholic and Messianic Jewish Dialogue Group was formed in the year 2000 at the initiative of Rev. Georges Cottier, O.P. (later Cardinal), then theologian of the household of Pope John Paul II, who gave his blessing and encouragement to the initiative. John Paul II, Cottier, and Cardinal Joseph Ratzinger (later Pope Benedict XVI) had all met with Messianic Jews in the years of preparation for the pope's act of repentance in 2000 for the sins of Christians, including sins committed against the Jews. That year also saw Pope John Paul II's momentous visit to the Holy Land.

The goals of the dialogue were to explore the meaning of the Messianic Jewish movement for the Catholic Church and the significance of the Catholic Church for Messianic Jews. While the dialogue was unofficial, it was a dialogue established under Church authority and not a private initiative. The group met annually, alternatively in Israel and in Rome. Under the guidance first of Cottier and later Cardinal Christoph Schönborn, archbishop of Vienna, the Catholic side was made up of a group of theologians, pastors, and experts in biblical studies and Jewish-Christian relations. It has included a number of Jewish Catholics over the years, including two of the clerics appointed to head the SJV, themselves Jewish Catholics.[30] The Messianic side was made up of Messianic leaders open to dialogue with the Catholic Church, representing a wide range of practice and thought inside the movement. A constant concern has been to what extent the Messianic participants can claim to represent a movement that is extremely diverse, with no central hierarchical leadership.

During a first phase in the dialogue, from 2000 to 2006, the focus was on establishing relations of trust. A central concern of the Messianic side was that the Catholic Church recognize the Messianic movement as a work of the Holy Spirit and "an eschatological sign". The Messianic participants pointed out that they were rejected by Jews who consider them Christians and by Christians who cannot understand why, if they indeed believe in Jesus, they do not integrate into existing churches. Among points treated in the first phase of the dialogue were the ongoing place of the Jewish people in the history of salvation (2002), the continuing significance of the biblical distinction between Israel and the nations (2003), and the election of Israel and the mystery of the particular and the universal (2004).

From 2008 to 2014, the group was able to discuss some of the more divisive issues in the conversation between Catholics and Messianics. In 2008, an important breakthrough was reached when one of the leading Messianic Jewish theologians in the group, Rabbi Mark Kinzer, presented a paper on the Vatican II document *Lumen gentium*, read from a Messianic perspective.[31] Kinzer expressed appreciation for the richness and comprehensiveness of the Council's teaching, especially the progress made in the Catholic understanding of the election of the Jewish people, although he also pointed out that there was more work to be done. The two sides engaged in deeper dialogue as soon as they agreed that the original constitution of the Church was the unity of the *ecclesia ex Judaeis* (the church from the Jews) and the *ecclesia ex gentibus* (the church from the gentiles). While major differences remained, this shared conviction provided a framework for subsequent meetings. From the discussion of ecclesiology (2008), the group proceeded to issues concerning baptism (2009), the Eucharist (2011), sacramentality (2012), and priesthood and apostolic succession (2013). The participants discovered the extent of agreement that does exist when both Church and Messianic believers together take seriously their shared faith in Jesus as Messiah and the rootedness of the earliest Christian tradition in the Jewish heritage.

The dialogue was transformed during the pontificate of Pope Francis, who himself had met with Messianic Jews when he was still a bishop in Argentina. He made the decision to make the dialogue public, although this too through a discreet but significant act. In 2015, an article that described the dialogue was published in the Holy See's review *Civiltà cattolica*.[32] During this period, it was decided that the dialogue group be transformed into a study group that would fall under the jurisdiction of the Congregation for the Doctrine of Faith. Meetings would now be held in Rome in the presence of a delegate from the Congregation, and discussions between Catholics and Messianic Jews would focus on the different understandings of the Jewish dimension of the Body of Christ. Since 2018, discussions have begun looking at the major issues raised in the conversation between Messianic Jews and Catholics. Can the Catholic Church discern Messianic

Judaism to have its origins in the work of the Holy Spirit? Should the Catholic Church revise its own vision of the integration of Jews into its ranks? Jews had been obligated to renounce what was deemed "Jewish superstition" in the past, but today, is not the Church invited to new ways of thinking about the Jewish identity of Jewish Catholics? Furthermore, should the Catholic Church, consonant with its renewed understanding of the Jewish tradition, actively encourage Jewish Catholics to preserve their Jewish identity and their expression of Jewish tradition?

Issues in the Dialogue

As the conversation between Catholics and Messianic Jews proceeds, it is clear that the two sides deepen their understanding of the nature of the Body of Christ and the People of God. They affirm together that this dialogue touches the heart of the relationship between Israel and the Church in the saving purposes of the one God: Father, Son, and Holy Spirit. However, there are differences that call for further study. Among these issues are the following:

1. How to guarantee Jewish continuity in the Body of Christ? To what extent can believers in Christ safeguard community boundaries that ensure the survival of a particular group, following a specific way of life? Does intermarriage between Jewish and gentile believers threaten this continuity due to assimilation into the majority?
2. Jewish particularism is in tension with Catholic universalism. Making a space for Jewish believers is a challenge for the Catholic approach that tends to be suspicious of borders that divide people. However, this same Jewish particularism needs to be an essential feature of a Church that seeks to be "catholic", bringing together Jews and gentiles. At the same time, Catholic universalism challenges Jewish particularism, particularly where worldly tribalism or nationalism might create borders that infringe on the rights of others and create situations of exclusion, inequality, and oppression.
3. The Catholic Church is committed to building a relationship of reconciliation and partnership with all Jews, religious and

secular, most of whom see belief in Christ as a Christian rather than a Jewish characteristic. The relationship of the Church with Messianic Jews is a challenge to this commitment because Messianic Jews straddle the border between the Church and the Jews. Particularly sensitive is the subject of proselytism and missionary work, often promoted by Messianic Jews within the Jewish community. The Church seeks to grow in understanding the diversity in the Jewish world and how best to engage with all sections of it respectfully and sensitively.

Jewish Continuity in the Body of Christ

Among the most prolific authors on the subject of Jewish continuity in the Body of Christ are two members of the study group, Messianic Jewish Rabbi Mark Kinzer[33] and Catholic Rev. Antoine Levy, O.P.[34] In dialogue with both Catholic Tradition and Messianic Judaism, they have presented their versions of a bilateral ecclesiology, a Jewish church and a gentile church existing alongside one another and together in unity making up the one Body of Christ. They find hints of this bilateral ecclesiology explicitly in post–Vatican II Catholic teaching. In *Lumen gentium*, the Dogmatic Constitution of the Church, the Church, underlining its continuity with the Old Testament people of Israel, is described as "the ancient olive tree ... whose holy roots were the Prophets and in which the reconciliation of Jews and Gentiles has been brought about and will be brought about".[35] Both Kinzer and Levy insist that in this reconciliation, Jews and gentiles maintain their specificity and focus on the characteristics of the Jewish component.

In his work, Kinzer has closely read Catholic teaching and discerns a development from *Lumen gentium* (*LG*) through *Nostra aetate* (*NA*) to the publication of the *Catechism of the Catholic Church* (*CCC*) in 1992.[36] He finds only ambiguous hints of the bilateral ecclesiology he promotes in *LG* and traces what he defines as an evolution in the later teaching. *LG* presents the Church as modeled on Israel in the Old Testament: "It was prepared in a remarkable way throughout the history of the people of Israel and by means of the Old Covenant."[37] However, according to Kinzer, *LG* gives the impression that with the inauguration of the Church, Jews no longer have ongoing significance and Jews who enter the Church are fully assimilated into the group of other believers. Yet Kinzer identifies another hint of the ongoing vocation of Jews in the Church when *LG* considers the Church's relations with members of other religions. *LG* points out that Jews are closest to the Christian faith and declares: "On account of their fathers this people remains most dear to God, for God does not repent of the gifts He makes nor of the calls He issues."[38] In this reference to Romans 11:29, Kinzer sees the ongoing vocation of the Jews who are believers in Christ.

In turning to the *CCC*, Kinzer identifies a subtle evolution in Church teaching, and he points out that it "affirms explicitly the irrevocable character of God's gifts to genealogical-Israel".[39] Drawing on *NA*, the *CCC* speaks of the Church's relationship with Jews: "When she delves into her own mystery, the Church, the People of God in the New Covenant, discovers her link with the Jewish People, 'to whom the Lord our God spoke first.'"[40] Kinzer claims that this should also be applied to Jews in the Church. The paragraph continues: "The Jewish faith, unlike other non-Christian religions, is already a response to God's revelation in the Old Covenant. To the Jews 'belong the sonship, the glory, the covenants, the giving of the law, the worship, and the promises; to them belong the patriarchs, and of their race, according to the flesh, is the Christ,' for the gifts and the call of God are irrevocable."[41] The next paragraph also insists on the commonality of Jews and Christians: "And when one considers the future, God's People of the Old Covenant and the new People of God tend towards similar goals: expectation of the coming (or the return) of the Messiah."[42] The document that commemorated the fiftieth anniversary of the publication of *NA* in 2015 made the bilateral ecclesiology Kinzer is seeking to enunciate even clearer: "It is and remains a qualitative definition of the Church of the New Covenant that it consists of Jews and Gentiles, even if the quantitative proportions of Jewish and Gentile Christians may initially give a different impression."[43]

In 2021, Levy published *Jewish Church: A Catholic Approach to Messianic Judaism* in which he engages in a discussion with Mark Kinzer. Levy espouses a traditional Catholic position on the unity of the Body of Christ under Petrine primacy and applies this to the Messianic Jews. He argues for the integration of Messianic Judaism into the Catholic Church in order to gain not only catholicity for the Church (not only gentiles but Jews too) but also universality for the Jews (not only Jews but gentiles too). A Catholic Church without Jews does not live up to the ecclesiological model of the New Testament and later Catholic Tradition: the unity of Jews and gentiles. A Jewish community of believers without gentiles does not live up to that same model, a body in which the wall of enmity between Jew and gentile has been destroyed. As Levy writes: "A Messianic Jew in the denominational sense of the term is a member of a movement that will not find its fully Catholic realization as long as this movement subsists independently from the wider Church. A Catholic Jew—or a (Christian-)Orthodox Jew for that matter—is a member of a Church that is still far from her fully Messianic accomplishment because its Jewish component is still insufficiently manifested."[44]

Levy affirms that there is a need for the preservation of Jewish identity within the Church. He mourns the determination to wipe out such distinctive identity of Jews entering the Church through the centuries. He also claims that Jewish believers in Jesus are as obligated by Torah as Jews who do not believe in Jesus. However, the precise content of the Torah that is observed by Jewish believers in Jesus is transformed, according to Levy: "Rabbinic tradition should be interpreted in the light of Yeshua. I would call it 'Messianic-Torah model'."[45] He explains: "It is simply impossible to imagine that the acknowledgment of Yeshua as Messiah of Israel would not have had consequences on the manner in which Jewish believers were to practice traditional Torah-observances."[46] Whereas Kinzer has a profound concern with the continued religious solidarity of Messianic Jews with the broader Jewish community in faith and practice, Levy's more speculative categories insist on the difference that belief in Jesus makes. In a polemical rebuttal of Kinzer, Levy declares: "Claiming, as Kinzer does, that a Jewish disciple of Jesus is on principle obligated to the same religious lifestyle as a Jew who is not a disciple cannot but reduce the purpose of the Gospel to nought. For these Jewish disciples, the Incarnation might as well not have happened, and Christ might as well not have given up his life."[47]

Levy's description of the Jewish church he envisages resonates to some degree with the ideas of the AHC, reserved about affirming too readily rabbinic tradition and emphasizing nationalist identity of the Jewish people. He writes: "The qualitative leap that proceeds from the revelation of Christ cannot but draw Messianic Judaism outside of the traditional setting of the Synagogue. The truth is that if Jewish disciples cannot be disciples of Yeshua in the same manner as their Gentile brethren because they are Jewish, they cannot either be religiously Jewish in the same manner as their Jewish brethren because they are disciples of Yeshua."[48]

In the third part of his book, Levy engages in making explicit what a "Messianic Torah model" would look like, alternatively applying his Christological readings to various and sundry parts of rabbinic tradition and his Jewish perspective to parts of Catholic Tradition. However, in the end, it is his theological affirmation of Jewish nationalism that is at the core of the identity dilemma: "The State of Israel is the living proof that the religious legacy of the Jewish nation is the object of God's ongoing favor. If on the one hand this legacy is not obsolete, as Christian thinkers have claimed for so long, and if on the other this living legacy pertains to the heart of the Church's faith, the State of Israel is a living sign that the Church needs to acknowledge that Jewish believers, as representative of Israel qua Israel, constitute an essential part of herself."[49]

In a final section, Levy argues that the Catholic Church has the potential to be fully the Church of Christ, a potentiality that must first set about healing the first schism: between the Church and the synagogue. According to him, the rejection of Jesus by the Jews was partly because of the Jewish people's fear of losing its identity. Levy claims: "The Church that truly corresponds to the First Council of Jerusalem could not endure due to the absence of a structure that would have guaranteed the survival of the Jewish nation, of Israel qua Israel within her visible boundaries. In our days, almost two-thousand years after the Council of Jerusalem, the Church is offered the opportunity to manifest her faithfulness to her most authentic nature through the establishment of a Jewish *ekklesia*."[50]

Kinzer and Levy's continuing debate serves to clarify some of the issues at stake in the dialogue between Messianic Jews and Catholics. The central question in the debate between Kinzer and Levy is the preservation of Jewish continuity in the Body of Christ. Together they established an ecumenical forum of Jewish believers in Christ across a spectrum including Catholic, Orthodox, Protestant, and Evangelical communities, as well as Messianic Jews. This forum began as a gathering of theologians known as the Helsinki Consultation on Jewish Continuity in the Body of the Messiah in 2010.[51] In 2018, the consultation formed a wider association called *Yachad BeYeshua* (Together in Jesus), founded in Dallas.[52]

Kinzer, Levy, and other participants in the forum, such as Messianic Jewish theologians Richard Harvey[53] and David Rudolph,[54] share certain presuppositions that have been questioned by the present author, who is an Israeli Jewish-Catholic priest engaged in the Catholic-Messianic Jewish dialogue and was a member of the Helsinki Consultation. In my view, the understanding of the Jewish people promoted by these thinkers is too strongly influenced by a discourse that evolved in the nineteenth century, shaped by European Romanticism and political Zionism. I question whether the uncritical theologization of this kind of modern nationalist discourse is compatible with Catholic thought and necessary for Jewish continuity. I propose that there are other ways to understand the ongoing vocation of Jews in the Body of Christ.

In a June 2013 paper delivered at the Helsinki Initiative annual meeting in Oslo, I challenged the definitions of peoplehood and identity proposed by Kinzer and Levy. I concluded by saying:

> Jews in the Body have a special vocation to raise the question of Torah and its mitsvot in every generation. The ongoing attachment to Torah is translated into the constant raising of the ongoing validity of the Torah: what about circumcision (bodies marked for God), what about Shabbat (bodies oriented to God) and kashrut (bodies cultivated for God). Torah is language that is ongoing in its relevance for relationship with God.... To speak Torah language is the vocation of Jews in the Church in the face of the millennial tendency of a Gentile Church towards philosophical speculation that is in danger of detaching God from incarnation and encounter.[55]

Clearly delineating an ongoing Jewish vocation in the Church does not necessarily entail the type of bilateral ecclesiology promoted by Kinzer and Levy.

Ultimately, Jews and gentiles invited into communion with Christ carry different crosses in their journeys of discipleship. Gentiles are called to rethink their gentileness, being grafted into the domestic olive tree that is Israel, adopting Israel's discourse and narrative. Jews, being naturally part of this same olive tree, are called to rethink the boundaries that keep gentiles out, welcoming them rather into the commonwealth of Israel. This is not ethnic or genetic, not national or cultural. The union of Jew and gentile is rather the glorious transfiguration of humanity as it takes on the features of Christ. Paul writes: "As many of you as were baptized into Christ have put on Christ. There is neither Jew nor Greek, there is neither slave nor free, there is neither male nor female; for you are all one in Christ Jesus. And if you are Christ's, then you are Abraham's offspring, heirs according to promise" (Gal 3:27–29).

This does not mean that ethnicity, economic distinctions, or sexual differentiation disappear but rather that they no longer have definitive relevance with regard to citizenship in the kingdom. In a 2011 address in Paris to the Helsinki Consultation, I explained that Jews, whether they believe in Jesus or not, have a common vocation: "The continuing witness of Israel is to the One God—a God who loves, a God who speaks.... This theocentricity reminds us of the radical conformity of Yeshua to his Father as he takes on the form of a slave and empties himself (cf. Philippians 2:7)."[56]

Ultimately, within the Body of Christ, Jews are also called to be custodians of the memory of the long centuries of the history of salvation, a memory that is both personal and experiential, the history of Israel, transmitted through a vital witness to the gentile part of the Church. Equally significant, Jews are a witness to the disastrous effects of forgetting this history and ignoring the Church's rootedness in it. Jews suffered the consequences of this forgetting on their flesh when Christians turned against the Jewish people. The Jewish vocation is to guarantee that the discourse of Israel, developed in the Scriptures, is never dissolved in sterile speculation about a God concept. Jews (those who are in the Church and those who are not) are called to be a choir always remembering the goodness of the Lord to Israel and singing God's praises. "Bless the LORD, O my soul; and all that is within me, bless his holy name! Bless the LORD, O my soul, forget not all his benefits, who forgives all your iniquity, who heals all your diseases, who redeems your life from the Pit, who crowns you with mercy and compassion" (Ps 103:1–4).

12

The Ecclesial Mission of the Association of Hebrew Catholics

Lawrence Feingold

The aim of this essay is to reflect on the theological fittingness that an association of Hebrew Catholics exists in the Church. I am using the term "Hebrew Catholic" to refer to members of the Catholic Church who also pertain to the people of Israel by their Jewish ancestry and heritage. Father Elias Friedman, who founded the Association of Hebrew Catholics (AHC) in 1979, chose the term "Hebrew Catholics" rather than "Catholic Jews" in order to make a distinction between Jewish identity outside and inside the Church. Ronda Chervin explains:

> He [Elias Friedman] suggests that the term "Jew" be used, as it was historically, to refer to those who accept the Judaic religious law. The word "Hebrew", on the other hand, refers to the people of the election, whether they accept the Jewish rabbinic law or not.... If such a distinction is accepted, it follows that so-called "Jewish converts" to Christian religions should not call themselves Jewish Christians, or Jewish Catholics, but instead Hebrew Christians, or Hebrew Catholics, for they are no longer under rabbinic law, but they should conceive of themselves as still part of the people of the election.[1]

This terminological distinction is admittedly unsatisfactory and artificial since Jewish identity cannot be neatly defined. The point is to acknowledge that Jewish identity in the Church is something analogous, for a Hebrew Catholic is simultaneously a member of the people of the Old and of the New Covenant. Saint Paul, for example, speaks of himself as a "Hebrew born of Hebrews" (Phil 3:5) but also considers that he is not "under the law" of Moses but "under the law of Christ" (1 Cor 9:20–21).

Covenant and Election Not Revoked

The founding of an Association of Hebrew Catholics is a fruit of the teaching of the Second Vatican Council. The declaration *Nostra aetate*, no. 4, teaches that God, who is faithful to his callings and promises, has not annulled his covenant with Israel by the new and eternal covenant in Christ: "God holds the Jews most dear for the sake of their Fathers; He does not repent of the gifts He makes or of the calls He issues—such is the witness of the Apostle."[2] *Nostra aetate* is alluding here to Romans 11:29: "For the gifts and the call of God are irrevocable." God remains faithful, despite human infidelity. In Romans 3:3, speaking of the Jewish people, Saint Paul says: "What if some were unfaithful? Does their faithlessness nullify the faithfulness of God?"[3] Similarly, in 2 Timothy 2:13, he writes: "If we are faithless, he remains faithful—for he cannot deny himself."

Pope Saint John Paul II clarified this teaching of *Nostra aetate* in a discourse to representatives of the Jewish people in 1980. Speaking of Jewish-Christian dialogue, he said: "This dialogue, that is, the meeting between the people of God of the Old Covenant, never revoked by God [cf. Rom 11:29], and that of the New Covenant, is at the same time a dialogue within our Church, that is to say, between the first and the second part of her Bible."[4] This teaching was taken up by the *Catechism of the Catholic Church*, no. 121, which relates the permanent value of the books of the Old Testament with the fact that "the Old Covenant has never been revoked." It has also been reaffirmed by Pope Francis in *Evangelii gaudium*: "We hold the Jewish people in special regard because their covenant with God has never been revoked, for 'the gifts and the call of God are irrevocable' (Rom 11:29)."[5]

The Continuing Mission and Witness of the Jewish People

This principle that Israel's covenant has not been revoked has numerous implications that have yet to be fully contemplated by theologians.[6] First, God's continuing covenant with the people of Israel implies that they continue to have a mission in salvation history to give witness to that covenant. Covenant partners, like spouses, give witness to the covenant that joins them in a relationship that is both intimate and social.[7] Israel's very existence and vibrant faith through forty centuries point to God's election, revelation, and gracious providence that has instilled them with messianic hope, a culture formed by the Torah and their faith, and sustained them in the midst of so many trials and persecutions.

From the Christian perspective, does this still have relevance after the coming of the Messiah? Yes, in many ways. The Jewish people, by their faithful existence, point to and make visible, as it were, Christ's Jewish humanity and fully Jewish life, God's long preparation for the Incarnation by calling and electing Abraham and his descendants, and his fidelity to the covenant. The glories of Israel described by Saint Paul in Romans 9:4–5 pertain to all Jews, now as before. After expressing his profound sorrow that many of his fellow Israelites had not come to faith in Jesus, he speaks of their glories: "They are Israelites, and to them belong the sonship, the glory, the covenants, the giving of the law, the worship, and the promises; to them belong the patriarchs, and of their race, according to the flesh, is the Christ, who is God over all" (9:4–5).

A second implication of God's continuing covenant with the people of Israel is that it is not revoked for those members of the Jewish people who enter into the New Covenant through faith in Christ and baptism. The glories of Israel pertain no less to Jews who enter the Church, for they offer a unique ecclesial witness to God's faithfulness to his people whom he has not cast off but has redeemed as foretold.[8]

The Mosaic covenant and the New Covenant established by Christ should not be conceived as in competition with each other, as if they were two parallel covenants on basically the same level, one of which replaces the other (supersessionism). The New Covenant is the *messianic fulfillment of God's covenants with Israel.* It follows that there is no contradiction involved in the fact that some members of the New Covenant are also members of the covenantal people of Israel. This was the case of the entire Church at Pentecost. It continues to be the case for Jews who enter the Church. In his homily for the canonization of Saint Teresa Benedicta of the Cross (Edith Stein), John Paul II emphasized the fact that the new saint pertained to both covenants:

"She understood that it was very important for her to be a daughter of the chosen people and to belong to Christ not only spiritually, but also through blood."[9]

By pertaining simultaneously to both covenants, Hebrew Catholics have a special collective witness and mission. They are aided by their heritage in bearing witness to the deep Jewish roots of the Catholic faith, the continuity of God's plan in salvation history, and its apostolic origin.

The Dividing Wall Between Jew and Gentile Broken Down by Christ: Bilateral Ecclesiology

The principle that God's covenant with Israel has not been revoked clarifies various texts of the New Testament that speak of the Church as being formed from the reconciliation of Jew and gentile. *Nostra aetate* draws attention to this: "Nor can she forget that she draws sustenance from the root of that well-cultivated olive tree onto which have been grafted the wild shoots, the Gentiles. Indeed, the Church believes that by His cross Christ, Our Peace, reconciled Jews and Gentiles, making both one in Himself."[10]

Christ's reconciliation of Jew and gentile in his Body is developed in Ephesians 2:14–16: "For he is our peace, who has made us both one, and has broken down the dividing wall of hostility, by abolishing in his flesh the law of commandments and ordinances, that he might create in himself one new man in place of the two, so making peace, and might reconcile us both to God in one body through the cross, thereby bringing the hostility to an end."

The dividing wall of hostility is broken down by incorporating gentiles into messianic Israel, so that the gentiles become "no longer strangers and sojourners, but ... fellow citizens ... and members of the household of God" (Eph 2:19).[11] The gentiles are welcomed into a Jewish household made new and catholic by the Messiah.

The union of Jews and gentiles in the Church is also graphically expressed in Galatians 3:27–29: "For as many of you as were baptized into Christ have put on Christ. There is neither Jew nor Greek, there is neither slave nor free, there is neither male nor female; for you are all one in Christ Jesus. And if you are Christ's, then you are Abraham's offspring, heirs according to promise."

These texts can be interpreted in different ways with regard to the distinction of Jew and gentile in the Church. The breaking down of the "dividing wall of hostility between Jew and Gentile" has often been taken to mean the elimination of the distinction. Jews would cease to exist in the Church as distinct from gentiles. This has been the dominant practical interpretation of the Church through the centuries as expressed in the policy of assimilation of Jewish converts.

But this cannot be the meaning of these texts if the election of Israel has not been revoked and if God wills the continued existence of the Jewish people. Similarly, baptism does not abolish the distinction between male and female,[12] nor the cultural differences mentioned in Colossians 3:11. What is being vigorously affirmed is the equal ecclesial dignity of all the complementary members sacramentally inserted into the Body of the Messiah.[13]

Although male and female are one in Christian dignity, their complementary union in marriage sacramentally manifests the union of Christ with his Church (see Eph 5:32). The communion between Jew and gentile in the Church also manifests, although not in the same sacramental way, the reconciliation that Christ has won on the Cross and the origin and the foundation of her catholicity.

The Messiah has broken down the dividing wall of hostility not by eliminating the Jewish root but by ingrafting the gentiles into it, according to the metaphor of God cultivating an olive tree used by Saint Paul in Romans 11:16–24. The olive tree is Israel, which then undergoes enlargement through ingrafting, as well as the loss of some original branches:

> If the root is holy, so are the branches. But if some of the branches were broken off, and you, a wild olive shoot, were grafted in their place to share the richness of the olive tree, do not boast over the branches. If you do boast, remember it is not you that support the root, but the root that supports you.... And even the others, if they do not persist in their unbelief, will be grafted in, for God has the power to graft them in again. For if you have been cut from what is by nature a wild olive tree, and grafted, contrary to nature, into a cultivated olive tree, how much more will these natural branches be grafted back into their own olive tree. (11:16–18, 23–24)

This communion in the Messiah represented by the ingrafting of wild branches into God's cultivated olive tree does not eliminate the distinction between wild ingrafted branches and natural branches. The natural branches include both those that were never separated, such as the apostles, and those that have been separated from the visible Church of the Messiah by unbelief and then later regrafted "into their own olive tree". Jewish identity remains in the natural branches when they are regrafted into the Church.

The Jewish-Catholic cardinal and archbishop of Paris, Jean-Marie Lustiger, emphasizes this foundational dimension of the Church's catholicity: "The Church appears as 'catholic,' ... because she is composed of both Jews and pagans. She fulfills the mystery of the salvation of all nations because she brings together the two groups according to whom history is divided: those who participate in the Election, Israel, and those who had no right to it, the pagans. For both groups, salvation is given as a grace, and a grace unmerited.... In this mystery of reciprocal recognition of God's freely given grace, each party bears witness to the other."[14]

This conviction that the Church should always manifest this reconciliation of Jew and gentile in her bosom has been called "bilateral ecclesiology". The Messianic Jewish theologian Mark Kinzer has written extensively on bilateral ecclesiology, according to which the one catholic Church consists of "both an *ecclesia ex circumcisione* and an *ecclesia ex gentibus*".[15]

The question is sometimes posed as to whether the AHC is like an association of Irish, Polish, or Chinese Catholics. No gentile ethnic group or culture is asked to give up their ethnic and cultural identity in entering the Catholic Church.[16] The visibility of every gentile culture in the Church is a witness to the identity of the Catholic Church precisely as *catholic*. Jesus is the Bridegroom, and all the nations of the world are his Bride. The multiplicity and diversity of the cultural traditions of the world glorify the Son of Man, who "was given dominion and glory and kingdom, that all peoples, nations, and languages should serve him" (Dan 7:14). There is no competition between the Catholic Church and a particular cultural identity that predates her and is elevated by her through evangelization.[17] Only those elements in contradiction with the Gospel are to be radically transformed.

Is it the same with Jews in the Church? Yes, but with an additional title. The Jewish component is not just another ethnic component of the Catholic Church whose mission extends to all nations. Catholics of Jewish heritage have a unique mission in the Church to be a witness of the Church's constitution from Jew and gentile and to be a contemporary witness to the people chosen for the glories enumerated in Romans 9:4–5, which culminates with the fact that "of their race, according to the flesh, is the Christ, who is God over all" (9:5).

The ecclesial presence of the gentiles is secured by the existence of the local churches spread throughout the world with bishops drawn from all nations representing all peoples. But since Jews were scattered around the world in the diaspora and since they were assimilated when they entered the Church, there has been no visible ecclesial representation of Catholics from the circumcision from the disappearance of the Church of St. James in Jerusalem and of the Nazarenes until our time with the AHC. There have always been some prominent Hebrew Catholics, such as Edith Stein, but no collective presence.[18]

How Can Jewish Identity Be Preserved over Time Inside the Church?

Since the covenant with Israel has not been annulled, it follows that God wills the continued existence of the Jewish people until the end of time. Jews outside the Church have maintained their corporate existence in extremely adverse conditions through fidelity to the twofold Torah, written and oral, as interpreted by the rabbinic tradition. Inside the Church from the second century, by contrast, Jewish identity was quickly lost because of a pastoral policy prohibiting Jewish converts from practicing elements of Jewish prayer, worship, or other aspects of the ceremonial Law of Moses.[19] This resulted in a pastoral régime of complete assimilation of Jewish converts such that Jewish identity was lost in the space of a few generations. How can Jewish identity be maintained in the Church without being nourished by any form of common worship or any ecclesial association such as the AHC?

This leads to a theological problem that has been formulated by Bruce Marshall.[20] How could it be true that God continues to will the existence of his Chosen People if he also wills them to enter into the Church, where, under this pastoral policy of assimilation, they would lose their distinct covenantal identity within a few generations?

In a similar vein, the eminent Jewish theologian Michael Wyschogrod asks whether, despite the contrary affirmation of *Nostra aetate*, the Church in her practice of assimilation for Jewish converts implies that the election of Israel has been superseded. He responds: "The Church claims to be the new people of God.... Does this mean that the old Israel, the sons of Abraham according to the flesh, ought to disappear from the stage of history? This is not clear. It would seem that the answer is 'Yes' because the Church, with the exception perhaps of the very first decades, did not insist that Jews who embraced Christianity retain their identity as Abraham's offspring. Instead, Jews who entered the Church intermarried and their descendants quickly lost knowledge of their origins."[21]

In other words, if the Church truly holds that Israel's covenant has not been revoked by God, there should be some way for members of the covenantal people of Israel who enter the Catholic Church to preserve their covenantal identity as Jews in the Church.[22]

The Messianic Jewish theologian Mark Kinzer poses a similar question to the Church:

> Is it sufficient for these Jewish members of the Church to be hidden like leaven in her universally expanding dough? Should their identity as Jews not be treasured, celebrated, and visibly expressed? And is it sufficient for these Jewish members of the Church to live dispersed among their gentile brothers and sisters, isolated from one another and without any distinctive corporate identity among themselves? Is the *ecclesia ex circumcisione* an invisible community of unrelated individuals, or is it called to be a manifest social reality, like the universal *ecclesia* of which it is part? These are questions that must be addressed in any twenty-first-century interpretation of *Lumen Gentium* in light of *Nostra Aetate*.[23]

The main purpose of the AHC is to aid Catholics of Jewish heritage in maintaining that identity while living a Catholic sacramental and liturgical life in full communion with the Church. This requires rethinking the practice of complete assimilation for Jewish converts going back to the post-apostolic age and instead affirming the value of the free practice of aspects of Jewish prayer and tradition by Jews who enter the Church through baptism. If the AHC is to help preserve an awareness of Jewish identity in Hebrew Catholics, there should be ways available for them to make use of the richness of Jewish forms of prayer and tradition, individually and communally, in the light of faith in Christ.[24]

The fact that the Old Covenant has not been revoked requires rethinking a longstanding theological position that viewed such practices in a very negative light. We shall briefly examine five witnesses of this tradition: Melito of Sardis, Saint Augustine in his controversy with Saint Jerome, Saint Thomas Aquinas, the Council of Florence, and Benedict XIV.[25]

Melito of Sardis

In the second century, Melito of Sardis, in his sermon "On the Passover", argues against the continued practice of rites of the ceremonial Law of the Old Covenant. He sees the rites of the Old Covenant as types prefiguring the sacraments of the New Covenant. As types, he compares them to a wax or clay model or of a statue that would lose its value and be destroyed when the final statue is finished.[26]

Melito's analogy is interesting because it fails to demonstrate his conclusion. The reasoning would be valid only if the model had no other purpose than to serve as a mere blueprint for the final product. Artistic models, however, are valuable for many reasons other than the making of the final statue. They reveal more of the mind of the maker and help one to appreciate the artistry leading to the finished work, and very often they are works of magnificent beauty in themselves. If we preserve and exhibit the models and sketches of Michelangelo and Bernini, how much more reverence should be shown to the sacramental rites of the Old Covenant that manifested the divine pedagogy and formed the living bond of communion of the Chosen People with God and one another.

Saint Augustine

Saint Augustine justified the practice of the Church in his day of prohibiting Christians from practicing any aspects of the ceremonial Law by an interesting argument distinguishing three periods of time:

before Good Friday, after Good Friday but before the promulgation of the Gospel, and after the promulgation of the Gospel. Against Saint Jerome, he argued that sacred rites of Israel were legitimately practiced by Jewish believers in Christ in the middle period that coincided with the apostolic age. He agreed with Saint Jerome, however, that they were no longer lawfully practiced after the promulgation of the Gospel, which he assumed was the case at the close of the apostolic age. He compared continued practice of ceremonial rites of the Old Law in the intermediate period to the honor given to the bodies of the faithful departed before they are buried.[27]

His reasoning was that if the rites of the Old Covenant were simply prohibited after the Passion of Christ, the impression would be that they were not actually from God and were no different from the rites of pagan religions. This would scandalize first-century Jews and lead them to conclude that the Gospel could not be a true revelation from God if it prohibited Jews from observing the Torah.[28] Thus, the ceremonial rites of the Old Covenant continued to be celebrated by the apostles, including Saint Paul (see Acts 16:3; 18:18; 21:21–26), to manifest faith in the continuity of the covenants and the fact that rites of the Mosaic Law were truly from God. However, after the Gospel was sufficiently promulgated, Augustine thought it was no longer fitting that the rites of the Old Covenant be practiced by Christians: "Gradually, therefore, and by degrees ... through the conversion of those Jews whom the presence of the Lord in the flesh and the times of the Apostles found living thus, all that activity of the shadows was to be ended ... Now, however, with the coming of faith, foreshadowed as it was by those early mysteries ... those former things have lost the life of their binding force. So, then, they are to be treated in such a manner as are the dead bodies of our kindred."[29]

Saint Augustine seems to have assumed that by the end of the apostolic age, all Jews of goodwill would have converted to Christianity, and thus the reason for the continuance of the apostolic practice would have ceased. Not all Jews converted, of course, and the Jewish people continued to exist as such. Therefore, if Israel's covenant has not been revoked, as *Nostra aetate* and Romans 11:29 state, it is not apparent why the reasoning applicable during the apostolic age would cease to apply to subsequent centuries and to our time.[30] The fact that the Church has required converts from Judaism to give up all Jewish practices proper to the ceremonial Law, parting from them as from a buried corpse, has surely made it harder for Jews to grasp the motives of credibility of Christ's claim to be the Messiah and Lord of Israel.[31]

Thomas Aquinas

Saint Thomas Aquinas takes the position of Saint Augustine in this controversy[32] and gives a new theological justification for the prohibition. Since the liturgical rites of Israel are sacred signs prefiguring the sacraments of the New Covenant and the coming of Christ, he argues that a Christian observance of such rites would imply that Christ and the messianic age had not yet come and thus would imply a sin against faith.[33]

Liturgical signs, however, express a wealth of meanings, which can vary according to the intentions of those who pray. Elsewhere Saint Thomas sees the sacramental rites of the Old Covenant as endowed not only with a typological meaning but also with a literal meaning of giving God legitimate communal worship that would sanctify the people of Israel through their exercise of faith, hope, and charity.[34] Thus it does not seem to follow, according to Saint Thomas' own principles, that continued observance of these rites must necessarily signify that Christ's paschal mystery is still future. The liturgical intention in participating in such rites could be both the literal sense of giving due and covenantal worship to God and the typological sense of prefiguring the paschal mystery that Christians believe has already been realized. We read the Hebrew prophets in the liturgy with a similar understanding that what was described as future has come to pass. Christians, therefore, can pray these prayers with many praiseworthy intentions, such as to praise God in union with the people of Israel and express solidarity with their prayer, worship, and longing, and to contemplate their marvelous typology prefiguring Christ.

Council of Florence and Benedict XIV

The reasoning of Saint Augustine and Saint Thomas was taken up by the Council of Florence in the Bull of Union with the Copts and the Ethiopians, *Cantate Domino*, which severely prohibited any continued celebration of aspects of the ceremonial Law of the Old Testament by Christians. A difficulty in interpreting this decree is distinguishing its doctrinal and its disciplinary aspects.

On the doctrinal level, the conciliar text states that after the promulgation of the Gospel, no one may base their hope for salvation on the rites of the Old Law and regard them as necessary for salvation, for they only prefigure and do not contain and apply the fruits of Christ's Passion. It concedes, following Augustine, that they could have been legitimately practiced until the promulgation of the Gospel, but not afterward.[35] This last stipulation, it seems, would pertain to discipline and be governed by prudential considerations. What constitutes sufficient promulgation of the Gospel is not defined, and the later magisterial development of invincible ignorance should be taken into account.[36]

This decree was directed to the particular situation of the Egyptian Coptic Church, in which at this time certain practices from the Jewish ceremonial Law were being observed by gentile Christians, such as circumcision and certain dietary restrictions.[37] Thus, it did not directly have Hebrew Catholics in mind. Despite its severe prohibition, the Council of Florence recognized that the Church could permit or require elements of the ceremonial Law of Moses, as was done by the Council of Jerusalem, for the sake of "ecclesiastical discipline".[38] This would be subject to the prudential judgment of the Church for that time and place. The 1983 Code of Canon Law contains no prohibition of circumcision or other ceremonial rites of the Old Covenant.

In the mid-eighteenth century, Benedict XIV qualified the teaching of the Council of Florence in the encyclical *Ex quo primum*, in which he declared that elements of the Jewish ceremonial Law could be observed for "just and serious reasons",[39] as was done by the Council of Jerusalem for the sake of peace between Jews and gentiles. In this document, Pope Benedict XIV approved a book of liturgical prayers (*Euchologion*) used in the Eastern rite by the Greek Uniates, in which certain elements of the ceremonial Law of Moses were present. Benedict XIV decided that such elements of the ceremonial precepts of the Mosaic Law could be observed *as long as there was some pastoral utility in their observance*: "Although the ceremonial precepts of the old Law have come to an end with the promulgation of the Gospel, and the new Law does not contain any precept which distinguishes between clean and unclean foods, nevertheless the Church of Christ has the power of renewing the obligation to observe some of the old precepts for just and serious reasons, despite their abrogation by the new Law."[40]

It is clear from this magisterial text that observance of elements from the ceremonial Law of Moses is not always sinful, nor need it liturgically imply that Christ has not yet come. The Church can even require the observance of some of these elements for gentile Christians if the needs of the time suggest it, as was the case in the Council of Jerusalem and in certain prayers of the *Euchologion*. The key principle, therefore, is that the Church can regulate their use according to her prudential judgment to serve pastoral needs. If the Church can even require such practices in certain circumstances, she can also permit them more broadly. Douglas Farrow writes:

> The documents in question [*Cantate Domino* and *Ex quo primum*] did have Gentile practices in view primarily; though their logic certainly applies to Jews, it is worked out in a context in which Christian Jews are almost out of mind. And when they return to mind—as they do today, thanks be to God—they require of the Church a new and different awareness of their needs, which have changed, as have those of Gentiles.... It is a matter of the Gentile learning again, in this neo-Marcionite and all too gnostic age of ours, to respect the earthiness of his salvation and to embrace the Jew as Jew; and of the Jew learning once again how to be both Jew and Christian, while glorying ... in the very freedom of which Paul spoke.[41]

Several significant historical factors have reshaped the ecclesial context in this regard, which include the Shoah, the promulgation of *Nostra aetate* at the Second Vatican Council, the disappearance of Christendom, and a new ecclesial context marked by much invincible ignorance and the need for a new evangelization.[42] We cannot consider the Gospel sufficiently promulgated even in the societies that once were part of Christendom. Today in many ways the situation is more like that of the apostolic age, in which Jewish Christians continued to practice such rites freely, than like the long period of Christendom in which such practices were prohibited.

I hold that there are at least five pastoral reasons why it can be beneficial for certain aspects of Jewish prayer and the ceremonial Law to be freely practiced by Hebrew Catholics (as well as Christians in general).[43] These reasons give to these prayers and practices a liturgical meaning transformed through faith in Christ.[44]

First, the practice of elements of Jewish prayer and worship, precisely insofar as they prefigure Christ and the sacraments, can make biblical typology come to life for Christians and aid them to see the vital connections between the mystery of Israel and the Church. For example, participation in a Hebrew Catholic Seder that points out the typology and its fulfillment in Christ[45] can help Christians understand the context of Israel's worship in which Jesus instituted the Eucharist.

Second, such practices can be helpful in fostering a reverential attitude to Jewish prayer on the part of Christians in general, thereby reducing anti-Semitism in the Church. Saint Augustine saw this as one of the reasons why the apostolic generation continued to make use of Jewish forms of worship, as in Acts 21:20–24.[46] If forms of Jewish worship were simply prohibited by the Church from the beginning, this would seem to put the Old Covenant on the same level as pagan religions and would denigrate their divine origin. It seems that the same considerations are just as relevant today after the Shoah as in the apostolic age.

Third, the maintaining of Jewish identity by Hebrew Catholics can be greatly aided by Hebrew Catholic forms of communal prayer. This would allow Hebrew Catholics to remain connected with the glorious heritage, religious life, and messianic aspirations of their people.[47] Without any shared liturgical practice, Hebrew Catholics generally lose their sense of Jewish identity in a few generations.[48]

Fourth, if the Jewish convert has no connection to the worship of the Jewish people, which results in the loss of Jewish identity, the Jewish community not unreasonably sees the conversion of Jews to Christianity as a vital threat to the survival of the Jewish people.[49] Precisely by helping to preserve the Jewish identity of Hebrew Catholics, the observance of Jewish forms of prayer could be seen by the Jewish people (and Christians) as a sign that conversion to Christianity is not necessarily contrary to the survival of the Jewish people.

Fifth, Jewish forms of prayer can be practiced by all Christians as a devotion to the life of Christ, who was "born of a woman, born under the Law" (Gal 4:4). The spiritual life of the Holy Family would have been expressed through and supported by the rich liturgical life of Israel. This would aid the faithful to see Yeshua as a Jew "born under the Law" and living a fully Jewish life.

Since the wall of separation between Jew and gentile is broken down, the ceremonial Law of the Old Covenant is not obligatory for Hebrew Catholics, for this would be an obstacle to table fellowship and to the primacy of the sacramental worship of the New Covenant. As the covenant with Israel and the New Covenant do not stand in competition with each other, for the latter is the messianic fulfillment of the former, so the sacramental rites of the two covenants do not stand in competition, but in a relationship of messianic fulfillment.[50] Since Hebrew Catholics are a very diverse group, whose religious backgrounds range from Orthodox to secular, the rule here should be freedom in Christ, as with other devotions and sacramentals in the life of the Church.

Mission of the AHC

In order to enable Hebrew Catholics to make a collective witness and to preserve their Jewish identity in the Church, Father Elias Friedman, O.C.D. (1916–1999), with Andrew Sholl, a Holocaust survivor, founded the AHC in 1979. Elias Friedman was a South African Jew who entered the Catholic Church in 1943 and became a Carmelite in the Stella Maris Monastery in Haifa, Israel. His major work, *Jewish Identity*, was published in 1987 by The Miriam Press, the publishing arm of the AHC.[51] In this work, he expressed the conviction that Hebrew Catholics need to enter into association with one another.[52]

Father Friedman gave a candid assessment of the obstacles facing such an association: "As they stand, few converts have any desire to enter into association with one another. They do not grasp the obligation which the possession of the 'election factor' imposes on them. Their sense of responsibility towards the destiny of their own people is feeble. Their historical identity has been disintegrated. The few that are inclined to assert their identity are discouraged and shrink back. Nothing less than the encouragement of the official Church could change the situation."[53]

To the objection that Hebrew Catholics are few in number, Father Friedman replied:

> In the last hundred and fifty years there have been plenty of converts. But so long as the régime of assimilation condemns them to absorption, the number of available converts at any given moment will always be small. A beginning must be made by changing the régime of assimilation with its cruel effects on the identity of the convert. Every Jewish convert needs to be registered as an Israelite at the moment of baptism and his descendants likewise. During his catechism he should be taught the doctrine of the Church concerning the identity of the Jewish people. After all, the existence of the "election factor" places an obligation on the Church to act in consequence by encouraging converts to associate in order to build their new identity in continuity with their past.[54]

Forty years later, these obstacles continue. I not infrequently encounter Hebrew Catholics at speaking events, and they are generally unaware of the existence of the Association and the importance of their Jewish identity and its witness in the Church. There are also obstacles within the Church. On one end of the spectrum are those who believe that Jews give up their identity when they are baptized. On the other end are those who hold that Jews are already in a salvific covenant and do not need to enter the Church.

David Moss has been the president of the Association for thirty years, from 1993 to the present. He has summarized the aims of the AHC as follows:

- To gather the Jews who have entered the Church and to help rekindle their *irrevocable* calling, providing a collective and unified witness to Jesus and His Church;
- To preserve the identity and heritage of the Jewish people within the Church;
- To provide pastoral support for those who have entered the Church;
- To provide support for Jews who are searching and inquiring about Jesus and the Church;
- To be an integral part of the *new evangelization*, contributing a vibrant and rich Jewish perspective;
- To be an eschatological sign of the *ingrafting*, which may have already begun;

- To help all Catholics understand the Jewish roots of their faith;
- To be a witness to the Jewish people that the cross is not a sign of persecution, but rather of *sacrificial love*, that Jesus is the *glory of Israel*;
- To be a witness of four millennia of *God's merciful providence and fidelity*, first to the People of Israel, next to the peoples of the world, and finally, to this world of the 21st century that is in a flight from God;
- And, finally, to hasten the day when *all Israel* shall proclaim:

> Blessed is He who comes in the Name of the Lord....

> The Church is now engaged in a dialogue with the Jewish people. This dialogue relates to the People Israel outside the Church. Fr. Friedman established the AHC to address the question and issues of the People Israel inside the Church.[55]

Another mission of the AHC is to promote love for the Jewish people (*ahavat Yisrael*), an appreciation for Jewish culture and heritage, and profound solidarity with Jews outside the Church. We are to combat anti-Semitism with philo-Semitism.[56] This "can help remove obstacles for the Jewish people to consider the Gospel as they come to see their identity and their heritage being preserved within the Church".[57] It can also be a witness to Messianic Jews that it is possible for Jews to live out their Jewish heritage and identity in the Catholic Church[58] while sharing fully in the Church's sacramental life, and especially in the mystery of the Eucharist, the sacrament of charity and communion in the Body of the Messiah.

Hebrew Catholics have a charism to bring out the profound continuity between God's covenant with Israel and its messianic fulfillment in the New Covenant. An important part of the activity of the Association is to promote studies of the Jewish roots of the Catholic faith, including Jewish history, tradition, theology, culture, feasts, the liturgical year, and the Hebrew language; to help develop means of celebrating Jewish traditions in the light of Christ; and to foster devotion to the saints of the Old Testament, including Mary, the daughter of Zion and mother of the Church, the apostles, and Hebrew Catholic saints. Finally, a collective Hebrew Catholic witness helps to manifest the bilateral constitution of the "Church as Jew and Gentile reconciled in Christ".[59]

NOTES

Introduction: Angela Costley and Gavin D'Costa

1. *Catechism of the Catholic Church*, no. 781 (henceforth *CCC*).
2. R. Kendall Soulen, *The God of Israel and Christian Theology* (Fortress Press, 1996), 28–34.

Chapter 1: Brant Pitre, The Jewish Roots of Jesus and Mary

1. Austin Flannery, O.P., ed., *Vatican Council II: The Conciliar and Post Conciliar Documents* (Liturgical Press, 1975), 759 (emphasis added). Here, the Council is quoting Augustine, *Quaest. in Hept* 2.73.
2. See Geri Parlby, "The Origins of Marian Art: The Evolution of Marian Imagery in the Western Church Until AD 431", in *Mary: The Complete Resource*, ed. Sarah Jane Boss (Oxford University Press, 2007), 115–18.
3. *CCC* 12 (facing plate). The icon is included in the Latin *editio typica*; see *Catechismus Catholicae Ecclesiae* (Libreria Editrice Vaticana, 1997), 14 (facing plate).
4. See John J. Collins, *The Scepter and the Star: Messianism in Light of the Dead Sea Scrolls*, 2nd ed. (Eerdmans, 2010).
5. See Brant Pitre, *Jesus and the Jewish Roots of Mary: Unveiling the Mother of the Messiah* (Image, 2018); *Jesus and the Last Supper* (Eerdmans, 2015); *Jesus and the Jewish Roots of the Eucharist: Unlocking the Secrets of the Last Supper* (Image, 2011). In what follows, I draw heavily on all three of these previous studies.
6. For studies of the Ark in Jewish Scripture and ancient Jewish tradition, see Choon L. Seow, "Ark of the Covenant", in *Anchor Bible Dictionary*, ed. David Noel Freedman, 6 vols. (Anchor Bible Reference Library; Doubleday, 1992), 1:386–93; James L. Kugel, *Traditions of the Bible: A Guide to the Bible as It Was at the Start of the Common Era* (Harvard University Press, 1997), 711–13, 733–36.
7. For an in-depth discussion with illustrations, see William H. C. Propp, *Exodus*, 2 vols. (Anchor Yale Bible 2-2A; Yale University Press, 1999, 2006), 2:372–92.
8. Cf. Gen 8:20; Ps 51:7; Francis Brown, S. R. Driver, and Charles A. Briggs, *A Hebrew and English Lexicon of the Old Testament* (Oxford University Press, 1952), 373.
9. Propp, *Exodus*, 2:380.
10. All emphasis to biblical quotations in this chapter is added by the author.
11. See Seow, "Ark of the Covenant", 389–90.
12. See Delbert R. Hillers, "Ritual Procession of the Ark and Psalm 132", *Catholic Biblical Quarterly* 30 (1968): 48–55.
13. Mordechai Cogan, *1 Kings*, Anchor Bible 10 (Doubleday, 2001), 280–81.
14. See Isaac Kalimi and James D. Purvis, "The Hiding of the Temple Vessels in Jewish and Samaritan Literature", *Catholic Biblical Quarterly* 56 (1994): 679–85; Menahem Haran, "The Disappearance of the Ark", *Israel Exploration Journal* 13 (1963): 46–58.
15. See Tudor Parfitt, *The Lost Ark of the Covenant: Solving the 2,500-Year-Old Mystery of the Fabled Biblical Ark* (HarperOne, 2008).

16. See Jonathan A. Goldstein, *II Maccabees*, Anchor Yale Bible Commentaries, vol. 41A (Yale University Press, 1983), 182–83, for an overview of the data, including the testimony of Eupolemus (second century B.C.) regarding Jeremiah's taking away the Ark (preserved in Eusebius, *Preparation of the Gospel* 9.39.5).

17. Josephus, *The Jewish War, Books V–VII*, trans. H. St. J. Thackeray, Loeb Classical Library 210 (Cambridge University Press, 1928), 69 (slightly adapted).

18. Tacitus, *Histories, Books IV–V, Annals Books I–III*, trans. Clifford H. Moore and John Jackson, Loeb Classical Library 249 (Harvard University Press, 1925), 191.

19. It is also apparent in the Apocalypse of John (see Rev 12:1–17), but we do not have the space here to discuss that passage. See Pitre, *Jesus and the Jewish Roots of Mary*, 60–70.

20. Michael Wolter, *The Gospel According to Luke*, trans. Wayne Coppins and Christoph Heilig (Baylor University Press, 2016), 1:80.

21. See Pablo T. Gadenz, *The Gospel of Luke*, Catholic Commentary on Sacred Scripture (Baker Academic, 2018), 45; Amy-Jill Levine, "Luke", in *The Jewish Annotated New Testament*, 2nd ed. (Oxford University Press, 2017), 111n35; 110n15; Wolter, *The Gospel According to Luke*, 1:83.

22. John McHugh, *The Mother of Jesus in the New Testament* (Darton, Longman, & Todd, 1975), 58 (emphasis added).

23. See Gadenz, *The Gospel of Luke*, 49–50; Pitre, *Jesus and the Jewish Roots of Mary*, 55–56.

24. For example, John T. Carroll, *Luke*, New Testament Library (Westminster John Knox, 2012); Beverly Roberts Gaventa and Cynthia L. Rigby, eds., *Blessed One: Protestant Perspectives on Mary* (Westminster John Knox, 2002); and François Bovon, *Luke*, 3 vols., Hermeneia (Fortress, 2002, 2012, 2013) do not mention any of the parallels between Mary and the Ark.

25. See Joseph A. Fitzmyer, *The Gospel According to Luke*, Anchor Yale Bible 28–28A (Yale University Press, 1983, 1985), 1:364, who admits the parallels but dismisses them as "subtle".

26. See Sarah Jane Boss, ed., *Mary: The Complete Resource* (Oxford University Press, 2007), 2. Cf. Raymond Brown, *The Birth of the Messiah*, rev. ed., Anchor Yale Bible Reference Library (Yale University Press, 1993), 328: "The evidence" for Mary as the new Ark in Luke 1–2 "is cumulative".

27. Gadenz, *The Gospel of Luke*, 49–50 (emphasis added), quoting Benedict XVI, Homily of August 15, 2006, in *Maria: Pope Benedict XVI on the Mother of God* (Ignatius Press, 2009), 79.

28. Hippolytus, *Discourse on Psalm 23* (second–third century A.D., quoted in Theodoret, *Dialogue* 1), in Philip Schaff, ed., *Nicene and Post–Nicene Fathers, Second Series* (Hendrickson, 1994; repr. Peabody), 3:177 (emphasis added; slightly adapted).

29. Athanasius, Homily from the Papyrus of Turin (fourth century A.D.), in Luigi Gambero, *Mary and the Fathers of the Church: The Blessed Virgin Mary in Patristic Thought* (Ignatius Press, 1999), 106 (emphasis added).

30. *CCC* 2676 (emphasis added).

31. Joseph Cardinal Ratzinger, *Daughter Zion: Meditations on the Church's Marian Belief*, trans. John M. McDermott, S.J. (Ignatius Press, 1983), 12.

32. For studies of the manna in Jewish Scripture and tradition, see Pitre, *Jesus and the Last Supper*, 149–59; Propp, *Exodus*, 1:582–601; Kugel, *Traditions of the Bible*, 616–21, 631, 776–77.

33. This was an especially popular hypothesis in twentieth-century scholarship. See, for example, Robert G. Boling, *Joshua*, Anchor Bible 6 (Doubleday, 1982), 191; John L. McKenzie, S.J., *Dictionary of the Bible* (Touchstone, 1965), 541.

34. Propp, *Exodus*, 1:596: "To judge from the following gloss, *mān* is a primitive form of the Hebrew interrogative pronoun *ma(h)*."

35. Ibid., 1:599–600.

36. Ibid., 1:600: "The statement that the Manna ceased when Israel entered Canaan, taken literally, would preclude identification with ordinary honey-dew" (Josh 5:11–12).

37. Ibid.

38. See James H. Charlesworth, ed., *The Old Testament Pseudepigrapha*, Anchor Bible Reference Library (Doubleday, 1983, 1985), 1:630–31 (emphasis added; slightly adapted).

39. See Pitre, *Jesus and the Last Supper*, 159–250.

40. See Frederick William Danker, *A Greek-English Lexicon of the New Testament and Other Early Christian Literature*, 3rd ed. (University of Chicago Press, 2000), 376.

41. See Pitre, *Jesus and the Last Supper*, 171–75.

42. See ibid., 193–250, for a full discussion.

43. See Rudolf Schnackenburg, *The Gospel According to St. John*, vol. 2 (Crossroad, 1990), 56–78, for the argument that "real food" and "real drink" more accurately reflect the Greek text.

44. Raymond E. Brown, *The Gospel According to John*, Anchor Yale Bible 29–29A (Yale University Press, 1966, 1970), 1:282–83.

45. Joachim Jeremias, *The Eucharistic Words of Jesus*, trans. Norman Perrin (SCM, 1966), 108.

46. Brown, *The Gospel According to John*, 1:285 (emphasis added).

47. Rudolf Bultmann, *The Gospel of John*, trans. G. R. Beasley-Murray (Westminster John Knox, 1971), 237 (emphasis added).

48. Johannes Beutler, S.J., *A Commentary on the Gospel of John*, trans. Francis J. Moloney (Eerdmans, 2013), 189–90 (emphasis added).

49. See especially James T. O'Connor, *The Hidden Manna: A Theology of the Eucharist*, 2nd ed. (Ignatius Press, 2005).

50. Ambrose, *On the Sacraments*, 4.24, in Saint Ambrose of Milan, *Theological and Dogmatic Works*, trans. Roy J. Deferrari, Fathers of the Church 44 (Catholic University of America Press, 1963), 305–6 (emphasis added).

51. Augustine, *Homilies on the Gospel of John* 26.13, in Saint Augustine, *Homilies on the Gospel of John 1–40*, trans. Edmund Hill, O.P., Works of Saint Augustine I/12 (New City Press, 2009), 460–61 (emphasis added).

52. *CCC* 1094.

53. See O'Connor, *The Hidden Manna*, 37–44, 48–68, for a discussion of the eucharistic theology of Ambrose and Augustine.

54. *CCC* 487.

Chapter 2: Angela Costley, The Ecclesiology of the Book of Acts: A Hebrew Catholic Perspective

1. The common authorship theory has been a mainstay of the interpretation of what is often called Luke-Acts and has been confirmed by many historical critics. See Adolph von Harnack, *Luke the Physician: The Author of the Third Gospel and the Acts of the Apostles* (Williams & Norgate; G. P. Putnam's Sons, 1909), 149–71; Wilfred L. Knox, *The Acts of the Apostles* (Cambridge University Press, 1948), 1–15; and Henry J. Cadbury, *The Making of Luke-Acts* (Macmillan, SPCK, 1961), 353–60, to name a few. Work has also been done on the unity of the two books' theology. For example, see Robert F. O'Toole, *The Unity of Luke's Theology: An Analysis of Luke-Acts* (Glazier, 1984), and Robert C. Tannehill, *The Narrative Unity of Luke-Acts* (Fortress, 1994). However, some scholars have disputed the joint authorship. See Patricia Walters, *The Assumed Authorial Unity of Luke and Acts*, Society for New Testament Studies Monograph Series 145 (Cambridge University Press, 2009), and Joseph A. Fitzmyer, "The Authorship of Luke-Acts Reconsidered", in *Luke the Theologian: Aspects of His Teaching* (Paulist Press, 1989), 1–26. The present author considers the two books to be companion pieces by the same author.

2. See Wilhelm M. L. DeWette, *Kurze Erklärung der Apostelgeschichte*, rev. and exp. Franz Overbeck (Hirzel, 1870), xxx, with whom Sanders enters into dialogue in Jack T. Sanders, *The Jews in Luke-Acts* (SCM, 1987), 39.

3. Alfred Loisy, *Les Actes des Apôtres* (Nourry, 1920); Ernst Haenchen, *The Acts of the Apostles: A Commentary* (B. H. Blackwell, 1971).

4. Ernst Haenchen, *Die Apostelgeschichte* (Vandenhoeck and Ruprecht, 1977), 163–66. See Sanders, *Jews*, 40–41 for a discussion of his views.

5. Haenchen, *Die Apostelgeschichte*, 163–66.

6. Gerhard Lohfink, *Die Sammlung Israels: Eine Untersuchung zur lukanischen Ekklesiologie*, SANT 39 (Kösel, 1975).

7. Ibid., 55.

8. Ibid., 60.

9. Hans Conzelmann, *The Theology of St. Luke* (SCM, 1982), 145–48; Augustin George, "Israël dans l'oeuvre de Luc", *Revue Biblique* 75 (1968): 481–525; and Joachim Gnika, *Die Verstockung Israels: Isaias 6, 9–10 in der Theologie der Synoptiker* (Kösel, 1961), 150–51. See also Lawrence M. Wills, "The Depiction of the Jews in Acts", *Journal of Biblical Literature* 110, no. 4 (1991): 631–33, for an overview of various scholarly opinions.

10. Jack T. Sanders, *The Jews in Luke-Acts* (SCM, 1987).

11. Ibid., 5, 37.

12. Ibid., 37.

13. Jack T. Sanders, "The Jewish People in Luke-Acts", in *Luke-Acts and the Jewish People: Eight Critical Perspectives*, ed. Joseph B. Tyson (Augsburg, 1988), 57.

14. Sanders, *The Jews*, 128; Sanders, "Jewish People", 67–75.

15. Sanders, "Jewish People", 67–75.

16. Ibid., 57–58; Sanders, *The Jews*, 305. On the depiction of the Jews as seditious in Luke, see Wills, "Depiction", 634–53.

17. Sanders (*The Jews*, 12) sees this as a tragedy for Luke, joining ranks with Robert Tannehill, who holds that Luke's attitude toward the Jews is not so much negative as it is a recognition of the sad situation of the people who were supposed to accept their Messiah and did not. See Robert Tannehill, "Israel in Luke-Acts: A Tragic Story", *Journal of Biblical Literature* 104, no. 1 (1985): 69–85.

18. Conzelmann, *Theology of St. Luke*, 145–213. At this point, it should be stated that other redaction-critical approaches have been taken to Acts to suggest that where we find positive references to Jews, or negative ones, perhaps the author is using sources from various points of view. Joseph A. Fitzmyer offers an introduction to this topic in *The Acts of the Apostles*, Anchor Bible 31 (Yale, 2010), 97–109. As Sanders points out, the idea goes back to Loisy, *Actes*, 60–120, but we would then have to ask why the redactor left the books in their current theological state. See Sanders, "Jewish People", 58.

19. Jacob Jervell, "The Law in Luke-Acts", *Harvard Theological Review* 64, no. 1 (1971): 21–22.

20. Jacob Jervell, *The Theology of the Acts of the Apostles*, New Testament Theology (Cambridge University Press, 1996), 34. In footnote 52, he states 18:6, but this is incorrect.

21. Ibid., 34–45. The extent to which Jews and gentiles mixed and the existence of so-called God-fearers like Cornelius (see Acts 10:22ff.) has been discussed at length by Jervell—see, for example, Jervell, "The Church of Jews and Godfearers", in *Luke-Acts and the Jewish People: Eight Critical Perspectives*, ed. Joseph B. Tyson (Augsburg, 1988), 11–20. I expand his ideas here.

22. For example J. B. Lightfoot, *The Acts of the Apostles: A Newly Discovered Commentary*, Lightfoot Legacy Set 1, ed. Ben Witherington III and Todd D. Still (InterVarsity Press, 2014),

214, and Luke Timothy Johnson, *The Acts of the Apostles*, Sacra Pagina (Liturgical Press, 1992), 241. In Session 11 of the Council of Florence, it is stated that the requirements were given so Jews and gentiles would have something in common until "no Jew would be met" because all were practicing Christians.

23. Jervell, *Theology of Acts*, 35.

24. See Fitzmyer, *Acts*, 557. The Greek has that God first took a people from the gentiles. This could also be read as referring to his selection of Israel through the election of Abraham, who was originally gentile but also the founder of the Hebrew people.

25. Jervell, *Theology of Acts*, 35.

26. Ibid.

27. Ibid.

28. Marilyn Salmon, "Insider or Outsider? Luke's Relationship with Judaism", in *Luke-Acts and the Jewish People: Eight Critical Perspectives*, ed. Joseph B. Tyson (Augsburg Publishing House, 1988), 76–77.

29. Ibid., 77.

30. Ibid., 79.

31. Ibid.

32. Sanders, "Jewish People", 58.

33. David L. Tiede, "'Glory to Thy People Israel': Luke-Acts and the Jews", in *Luke-Acts and the Jewish People: Eight Critical Perspectives*, ed. Joseph B. Tyson (Augsburg Publishing House, 1988), 25. For example, Isaiah 5:3 and 47:6, to be followed by oracles of salvation like 51:5–7.

34. Tiede, "Glory", 25.

35. It should be said that the theory that Acts is picking up on prophetic themes from the Old Testament is evident throughout the narrative. The apostles' actions and situation are often set within the context of Israelite prophecy, and the examples are taken from a variety of prophets from various stages in Israel's history. In Acts 2:16–32, for instance, Peter cites Joel 2:28–32 and tells those he is speaking to that the final days prophesized by him had arrived with Jesus, whom they have had killed, but who has now risen. In Acts 3:17–26, Peter also refers to Moses, the Jewish prophet of prophets, and he quotes Psalm 16:8–11 in Acts 2:25–28, attributing it to the prophet King David, arguing that David prophesied about the Resurrection of Jesus. In his speech at the Council of Jerusalem in 15:15–18, Peter also quotes Amos 9:11–12 as proof that gentiles would receive God's promises. Stephen's speech in 7:2–53 also contains a number of references to Israelite prophecy, especially Moses. In 28:23, Paul is preaching in Rome and specifically references Isaiah 6:9–10 and states that it is not unlike Israel to reject a prophet, following the realization that he has been unable to convince them about Jesus from the Law and the Prophets. As a summary of Luke's position, we might quote Peter in Acts 10:43; when Peter addresses Cornelius, he declares: "To him all the prophets bear witness that every one who believes in him receives forgiveness of sins through his name."

36. In Ezekiel, the promise of restoration is even held out to the whole people, as in Ezekiel 37 and the prophecy of the dry bones. It is also through the gentiles' acceptance of Jesus that Israel itself achieves glorification in Isaiah when the nations worship on its mountain, and it is arguably through the gentiles' acceptance of Jesus that Israel is ultimately glorified in Acts. Tiede states that while the rejection of God's reign continues to be at the heart of the narrative of Luke-Acts, at the very beginning of the narrative, it has been noted that Jesus will be the light to the nations, but thereby also the glory of God's people Israel (Tiede, "Glory", 46). The statement first comes in Luke 2:32 but is also found in Acts 13:47, which we saw earlier from Isaiah 49:6. See Tiede, "Glory", 26–28. He, too, suggests that "God's vengeance

and vindication have their times of wrath and restoration, and the Messiah has already been exalted to God's right hand as 'Leader and Savior in order to give repentance to Israel and forgiveness of sins' (Acts 5:31)." This results in the mission of that part of Israel that does follow Jesus as being the "light to the Gentiles" of Simeon's oracle, an idea not dissimilar from mine of a remnant.

37. Johnson, *Acts*, 46.

38. Ibid.

39. Philo, *On the Decalogue*, 46, quoted in ibid., 46.

40. For more on lists such as this in the ancient world, see Hans Conzelmann, *Acts of the Apostles*, Hermenia (Fortress, 1972), 14–15.

41. Fire is also the symbol of a covenant, as in the covenant made with Abram in Genesis 15:17–18.

42. I argue that the Council of Jerusalem seems to suggest that circumcision is not necessary for gentiles, yet the implication of this term is that these men have been circumcised. This might hold out an interesting prospect for Hebrew Catholic ecclesiology, since the creation of any kind of structure would be for Jewish Catholics, leaving open the question of whether there might be a similar situation if gentiles wanted to join a Hebrew Catholic rite—would their conversion also be to Judaism?

43. See Christopher Bryan, "A Further Look at Acts 16:1–3", *Journal of Biblical Literature* 107, no. 2 (1988): 292–94.

44. Salmon, "Insider or Outsider?", 78.

45. Bryan, "Further Look", 293.

46. Ibid.

47. See, for example, Paula Fredriksen, "Why Should a 'Law-Free' Mission Mean a 'Law-Free' Apostle?", *Journal of Biblical Literature* 134, no. 3 (2015): 637–650; and Emmanuel Nathan, "Two Pauls, Three Opinions: The Jewish Paul between Law and Love", in *Is There a Judeo-Christian Tradition? A European Perspective*, ed. Emmanuel Nathan and Anya Topolski (de Gruyter, 2016); Andrew S. Jacobs, "A Jew's Jew: Paul and the Early Christian Problem of Jewish Origins", *Journal of Religion* 86, no. 2 (2006): 258–86.

48. David B. Woods, "Interpreting Peter's Vision in Acts 10:9–16", *Conspectus* 13, no. 1 (2012): 171–214.

49. Mark Kinzer, *Postmissionary Messianic Judaism: Redefining Christian Engagement with the Jewish People* (Brazos, 2005), 68–71; D. A. Carson and D. J. Moo, *An Introduction to the New Testament*, 2nd ed. (Zondervan, 2005), 287; David H. Stern, *Jewish New Testament Commentary: A Companion Volume to the Jewish New Testament* (Jewish New Testament Publications, 1992), 257–61.

50. Woods, "Interpreting", 178.

51. Ibid., cf. Darell L. Bock, *Acts* (Baker Academic, 2007), 389, whom he cites.

52. See Jervell, "Church", 12–13.

53. Woods, "Interpreting", 186.

54. The issue over how much Jews and gentiles associated is a complicated one. Jervell, "Church", advocates for a kind of semi-Jew known as a God-fearer who was acceptable, while there is otherwise evidence of trade between Jews and gentiles and other forms of mixing. See Woods, "Interpreting", 181–86.

55. At this point, let it be said explicitly that this ecclesiology in no way denies that Old Testament prophecy has been fulfilled in Christ. Indeed, this ecclesiology *requires* that this latter theology be taken seriously. Nor is it a call to reinstitute the laws of *kashrut* for gentiles, as Tradition has decided this is not necessary. However, understanding the Church as Scripture does, in continuation with Israel of old, forces us to consider that the Church is not, in fact, gentile and to acknowledge the place of Jews in it and the importance of their own spirituality for the wider Church community. Jewish traditions once considered obsolete

might in fact still have a pastoral or pedagogical place, something acknowledged in *Ex quo primum* and also addressed in this volume.

Chapter 3: Scott W. Hahn, Christ as Temple in John: From Signs to Sacraments?

1. See, for example, Mary L. Coloe, *God Dwells with Us: Temple Symbolism in the Fourth Gospel* (Liturgical Press, 2001); Johannes Frühwald-König, *Tempel und Kult: Ein Beitrag zur Christologie des Johannesevangeliums* [Temple and Cult: A Contribution to the Christology of the Gospel of John], Biblische Untersuchungen 27 (Friedrich Pustet, 1998); Paul M. Hoskins, *Jesus as the Fulfillment of the Temple in the Gospel of John*, Paternoster Biblical Monographs (Paternoster, 2006); Alan Kerr, *The Temple of Jesus' Body: The Temple Theme in the Gospel of John*, Journal for the Study of the New Testament Supplement Series 220 (Sheffield Academic, 2002); Mark Kinzer, "Temple Christology in the Gospel of John", *Society of Biblical Literature Seminar Papers* 37, no. 1 (Scholars Press, 1998): 447–64; Lucius Nereparampil, *Destroy This Temple: An Exegetico-Theological Study on the Meaning of Jesus' Temple-Logion in Jn 2:19* (Dharmaram, 1978); Gunnar H. Østenstad, *Patterns of Redemption in the Fourth Gospel: An Experiment in Structural Analysis*, Studies in the Bible and Early Christianity 38 (Edwin Mellen, 1998); Antony Therath, *Jerusalem in the Gospel of John: An Exegetical and Theological Inquiry into Johannine Geography* (Intercultural Publications, 1999); and Stephen T. Um, *The Theme of Temple Christology in John's Gospel*, Library of New Testament Studies 312 (Sheffield Academic, 2006).

2. Coloe, *God Dwells with Us*, 216.

3. On the presence of sacramental symbolism in John, see Raymond E. Brown, "The Johannine Sacramentary", in *New Testament Essays* (Bruce, 1965), 51–76; Alf Correll, *Consummatum Est: Eschatology and Church in the Gospel of St. John* (Macmillan, 1958); Oscar Cullmann, *Early Christian Worship*, trans. A. Stewart Todd and James B. Torrance, Studies in Biblical Theology 10 (SCM, 1953); Frederick W. Guyette, "Sacramentality in the Fourth Gospel: Conflicting Interpretations", *Ecclesiology* 3, no. 2 (2007): 235–50; Francis J. Moloney, "When Is John Talking About the Sacraments?", in *"A Hard Saying": The Gospel and Culture* (Liturgical Press, 2001), 109–30; P. Paul Niewalda, *Sakramentssymbolik im Johannesevangelium? Eine Exegetisch-Historische Studie* [Sacramental Symbolism in the Gospel of John? An Exegetical-Historical Study] (Lahn-Verlag, 1958); and Bruce Vawter, "The Johannine Sacramentary", *Theological Studies* 17, no. 2 (1956): 151–66.

4. Benedict XVI, apostolic exhortation *Verbum Domini* (The Word of the Lord) (September 30, 2010), no. 40.

5. Ibid., no. 40 (emphasis in original).

6. Ibid.

7. See, for example, the brief reviews by Coloe, *God Dwells with Us*, 31–63; and Hoskins, *Jesus as the Temple*, 38–107; and longer treatments by G.K. Beale, *The Temple and the Church's Mission: A Biblical Theology of the Dwelling Place of God*, New Studies in Biblical Theology 17 (InterVarsity, 2004); and Jon D. Levenson, "The Temple and the World", *Journal of Religion* 64, no. 3 (1984): 275–98.

8. "The Temple was the embodiment of the covenant of David, in which the triple relationship between Yahweh, the House of David, and the people of Israel was established." Toomo Ishida, *The Royal Dynasties in Ancient Israel: A Study on the Formation and Development of Royal-Dynastic Ideology*, Beiheft zur Zeitschrift für die Alttestamentliche Wissenschaft 142 (W. de Gruyter, 1977), 145.

9. The necessity of water washings is not explicit in the Pentateuch's descriptions of the feast, but it was required by the logic of the laws of cleanliness in Leviticus 11–15 and elsewhere (see Num 19:11–12).

10. Although the texts cited are largely for the feast of Passover, celebratory eating was an important part of all the feasts, even when not mentioned in the biblical descriptions. All three pilgrimage feasts (Passover, Pentecost, Tabernacles) marked important agricultural events (barley, wheat, and fruit harvests, respectively).

11. See Therath, *Jerusalem in the Gospel of John*, 64–65; Hoskins, *Jesus as the Temple*, 69–89.

12. Therath, *Jerusalem in the Gospel of John*, xix.

13. See Correll, *Consummatum Est*, 44; Therath, *Jerusalem in the Gospel of John*, xiii–xix. For parts of the Gospel set in or near Jerusalem, see John 2:13—4:2; 5:1–47; 7:10—10:39; 12:12—20:31 (Jerusalem); 11:17–53; 12:1–11 (Bethany)—roughly three-quarters of the Gospel.

14. For a sustained treatment of the subject, see Gale A. Yee, *Jewish Feasts and the Gospel of John* (Michael Glazier, 1989). Concerning the structure of the Fourth Gospel, the feasts are only one of several structuring elements. For a review of almost all the major structural proposals, see George Mlakushyil, *The Christocentric Literary Structure of the Fourth Gospel*, Analecta Biblica 117 (Pontifical Biblical Institute, 1987), 17–85.

15. Cf. Therath, *Jerusalem in the Gospel of John*, 59.

16. Aileen Guilding, *The Fourth Gospel and Jewish Worship: A Study in the Relation of St. John's Gospel to the Ancient Jewish Lectionary System* (Clarendon, 1960).

17. See Hoskins, *Jesus as the Temple*, 2.

18. See the accounts of the Passovers of Kings Hezekiah and Josiah in 2 Chronicles 30–35; see also Scott W. Hahn, *The Kingdom of God as Liturgical Empire: A Theological Commentary on 1–2 Chronicles* (Baker Academic, 2012), 176–85.

19. Therath, *Jerusalem in the Gospel of John*, 60–61.

20. Raymond E. Brown, *The Gospel According to John I–XII*, Anchor Bible 29 (Doubleday, 1966), 121.

21. Lucius Nereparampil has devoted a monograph to the pericope (*Destroy This Temple*), and every major work on the Temple theme in John devotes extensive space to its exegesis.

22. Cf. Coloe, *God Dwells with Us*, 84; Kerr, *The Temple of Jesus' Body*, 101; and Therath, *Jerusalem in the Gospel of John*, 59.

23. Nereparampil, *Destroy This Temple*, 92–98; Kerr, *The Temple of Jesus' Body*, 96–97.

24. "The writer does not use our modern concept of incident, but that of a 'sign' (*semeion*) and thereby he means to point again to the double quality of an event at once visible and demanding a higher understanding in the context of faith." Cullmann, *Early Christian Worship*, 46.

25. See ibid., 76; and C. G. Lingad, *The Problems of Jewish Christians in the Johannine Community* (Gregorian and Biblical Press, 2001), 280–82.

26. Thus it is unnecessary to regard the mention of "water" in John 3:5 as intrusive in context and relegate it to a second hand, as Bultmann and others have done.

27. Some see in "water and the Spirit" a reference to natural birth (water) followed by spiritual birth (Spirit).

28. "The tactic of the Johannine discourse is always for the answer to transpose the topic to a higher level; the questioner is on the level of the sensible, but he must be raised to the level of the spiritual. An appreciation of the radical difference between the flesh and the Spirit is the true answer to Nicodemus." Brown, *John I–XII*, 128.

29. See Lingad, *Problems of Jewish Christians*, 298–99.

30. Mystagogy (literally "revelation of the mysteries") is the theological explanation of the mysteries that are communicated in the Church's sacraments.

31. The events of Jesus' second Passover as recorded in John take place in Galilee. Somewhat ironically, this section (6:1–71) constitutes the longest narrative in the Gospel that is *not* set in or near Jerusalem. Obviously, the entire chapter is too complex to interpret in detail within the scope of this essay. See Brown, *John I–XII*, 231–304.

32. In what follows, we are dependent primarily on James McCaffrey, *The House with Many Rooms* (Pontifical Biblical Institute, 1988). See also Kerr, *The Temple of Jesus' Body*, 268–313. Kerr finds Temple allusions not only in John 14:2–3, but in John 13 as well. He likens the foot-washing of the disciples to the Old Testament requirement that both priests and sacrificial animals have their feet washed when entering the sanctuary. Thus, John 13 is a preparation for entering the new Temple.

33. See McCaffrey, *House with Many Rooms*, 177–84; and Coloe, *God Dwells with Us*, 160–62.

34. McCaffrey, *House with Many Rooms*, 67–69, 73–75.

35. See, for example, Deut 12:5, 11–14, 18, 21, 26; Jer 7:12, 14, 20; 1 Kings 8:6–7, 21, 29–30, 35, 42. See also McCaffrey, *House with Many Rooms*, 185; and Coloe, *God Dwells with Us*, 164–67.

36. Coloe, *God Dwells with Us*, 163, quoting David E. Aune, *The Cultic Setting of Realized Eschatology* (Brill, 1972), 130.

37. See the discussion in Margaret Daly-Denton, *David in the Fourth Gospel: The Johannine Reception of the Psalms*, Arbeiten zur Geschichte des Antiken Judentums und des Urchristentums 47 (Brill, 2000), 78–79. See also Bertil Gärtner, *The Temple and the Community in Qumran and the New Testament: A Comparative Study in the Temple Symbolism of the Qumran Texts and the New Testament* (Cambridge University Press, 2005).

38. Coloe, *God Dwells with Us*, 154.

39. See Kerr, *The Temple of Jesus' Body*, 275–313.

40. See Cullmann, *Early Christian Worship*, 118. But Cullmann does not explain exactly how he arrives at this conclusion. Crossan comments: "Each of these works/words of Jesus were protosacraments, fragmented promises of the one great sacrament of the risen Lord who abides in the community of faith." Dominic Crossan, *Gospel of Eternal Life: Reflections on the Theology of St. John* (Bruce, 1967), 42.

41. Leo the Great, *Sermo* 74, 2, in *Nicene and Post-Nicene Fathers*, second series, vol. 12, ed. Philip Schaff and Henry Wace (Christian Literature Publishing Co.,1895), revised and edited for New Advent by Kevin Knight, https://www.newadvent.org/fathers/360374.htm.

42. "Jesus' fulfillment of the Jewish feasts and the Temple are both connected with the nature and content of God's provision for all his people. Jesus is and gives the true food and true drink that deliver believers from thirst and hunger. He accomplishes this by offering his flesh and blood for the life of the world and sending the Spirit to enrich believers with the salvific benefits of his sacrificial death. Thus, he simultaneously fulfills the Passover, feast of Tabernacles, feast of Dedication, and the Temple. Looking at the Temple in particular, he fulfills and replaces it as the place of sacrifice and the place from which God pours out his abundant provision upon his people." Hoskins, *Jesus as the Temple*, 196.

43. See R. Schnackenburg: "They [the Johannine communities] were churches in which liturgical and sacramental life was flourishing.... Their worship was the eschatological culmination of all worship practiced until then, transcending even the Jewish service of the Temple. Their pasch replaced and fulfilled the pasch of the Jews.... In the sacraments they possessed testimonies and vehicles of the continuing redemptive acts of Jesus Christ (1 John 5:6) and obtained living and abiding union with the Son of God and through him perfect communion with God (John 6:56).... It cannot be disputed that the Johannine Church experienced the word of Christ and the person of Christ as present in its solemn worship (comprising word and sacrament)." "Is There a Johannine Ecclesiology?", in *A Companion to John: Readings in Johannine Theology (John's Gospel and Epistles)*, ed. Michael J. Taylor (Alba House, 1977), 254–55.

44. "Already in the Old Testament we find that the cult was the primary means of communion between God and his chosen people. The cult of the new covenant has its foundation and its centre in the Eucharist which Christ himself instituted." Correll, *Consummatum Est*, 4.

"It was not Jesus' purpose to establish a new non-liturgical religion as a substitute for the old cult. Rather St. John saw the old cult as attaining its fulfillment and perfection in and through Christ. All that the old Jewish cult had stood for and expressed was fulfilled in Jesus, who himself was the centre of the new Christian cult." Ibid., 52.

45. "Although the Fourth Gospel does not refer to the Church as the Temple of God, it contains the theological basis for this Pauline title." Hoskins, *Jesus as the Temple*, 198.

46. Cullmann expresses it this way: "Since Christ is the center of all worship, all the media of the past ... (purificatory rites, washings, baptism of John) are replaced by the media of grace, in which Christ ... communicates himself ... in the sacraments of baptism and Lord's Supper." *Early Christian Worship*, 118.

47. Benedict XVI, *Verbum Domini*, no. 40 (some emphasis added).

48. See Matthew Levering, *Christ's Fulfillment of Torah and Temple: Salvation According to Thomas Aquinas* (Notre Dame, 2002), 83–145. For Levering, following Saint Thomas, the Temple is the locus of true worship that Christ's paschal mystery has transformatively fulfilled. But, significantly, "Aquinas's concept of salvation ... ends with neither Temple nor Church; rather ... it ends with communion, in the Mystical Body of Israel's Messiah, with God in the heavenly liturgy." Ibid., 127.

49. See Scott W. Hahn, *Kinship by Covenant: A Canonical Approach to the Fulfillment of God's Saving Promises* (Yale University Press, 2009), 176–213; and Hahn, *Kingdom of God*, 66–137.

50. For the Temple's central role in Second Temple theology, see John S. Bergsma and Jeffrey L. Morrow, *Murmuring Against Moses: The Contentious History and Contested Future of Pentateuchal Studies* (Emmaus Academic, 2023), 145–69; and Pilchan Lee, *The New Jerusalem in the Book of Revelation* (J. C. B. Mohr, 2001).

51. Baruch A. Levine, *Leviticus* (JPS, 1989), 215.

52. Ibid., 215–35.

53. Ibid., 216 (emphasis added).

54. Ibid., 215–35.

55. Bernard Lonergan, *Method in Theology* (Herder & Herder, 1972), 241, quoted in Francis Martin, *Sacred Scripture: The Disclosure of the Word* (Sapientia Press, 2006), 234 (emphasis added).

56. William M. Wright IV, *The Bible and Catholic Ressourcement: Essays on Scripture and Theology* (Emmaus Road, 2019), 224 (emphasis added).

57. The integration of sacrificial worship in heaven and on earth is further exposited in later Johannine tradition, especially in the liturgy of the Apocalypse. For an initial foray into this possibility, see Scott W. Hahn, *The Lamb's Supper: Mass as Heaven on Earth* (Doubleday, 1999).

Chapter 4: David Neuhaus, Understanding the Jewish Priesthood of Hebrews: Lessons for the Catholic Priesthood Today

1. The Second Vatican Council's *Presbyterorum ordinis* hardly mentions the Old Testament even though the discourses focusing on priest, People of God, and Temple are unintelligible without reference to the religious life of the people of Israel. *Sacrosanctum concilium*, the Council's document on the liturgy, begins, "The wonderful works of God among the people of the Old Testament were *but a prelude* to the work of Christ the Lord in redeeming mankind and giving perfect glory to God", stressing the newness of Christ's priesthood as compared to what went before him, a mere prelude. Vatican Council II, Constitution on the Sacred Liturgy *Sacrosanctum concilium* (December 4, 1963), no. 5 (emphasis added).

2. Jesus enters Jerusalem like a king (Mk 11:7–10 and parallels). In Matthew, Jesus is presented as a king from the beginning (2:2), and in John, his Crucifixion is an enthroning (19:19).

3. See Luke's presentation of the child Jesus in the Temple (2:46–47) and Jesus' use of parables in Mark 4, Matthew 13, and Luke 9–19.

4. See Jesus' identification with the figure of the prophet in Mark 6:4 and Matthew 13:57. In Luke, this is from the beginning of his ministry (4:16–19).

5. It is implicit in the words at the Last Supper when Jesus says: "This is my blood of the covenant, which is poured out for many" (Mk 14:24; cf. Mt 26:28; Lk 22:20).

6. A widely read treatise on priesthood, Jean Galot, *Theology of the Priesthood*, trans. Roger Balducelli (Ignatius Press, 1985), consecrates a good part of the discussion to refuting the claim that Jesus' priesthood is in continuity with that of the Old Testament, commenting: "Jesus refrains from letting the new priesthood be poured into the old framework of the Jewish priesthood.... He does not intend to be a priest after the Jewish manner and does not want the community which he is establishing to have a priesthood of this sort." Ibid., 37.

7. The structure of the epistle used in this article has been derived from the masterful work of Albert Vanhoye, *La Structure littéraire de l'épître aux Hébreux* (Desclée de Brouwer, 1963).

8. Cf. F.W. Farrar, *The Epistle of Paul the Apostle to the Hebrews* (Cambridge University Press, 1883); J. Moffat, *A Critical and Exegetical Commentary on the Epistle to the Hebrews* (Charles Scribner's Sons, 1924); W. Leonard, *The Authorship of the Epistle to the Hebrews* (Burns, Oates and Washburne Ltd., 1939); and C. Spicq, *L'Epitre aux Hébreux* (Librairie Lecoffre, 1952).

9. Mark Kinzer appropriately suggests that "new" is "more suitably translated as 'eschatologically renewed.' One is dealing with an 'old' or existing reality that is eschatologically transformed by the sovereign action of God." Mark Kinzer, *Searching Her Own Mystery: Nostra Aetate, the Jewish People, and the Identity of the Church* (Cascade Books, 2015), 58.

10. Ephraim Radner, *Leviticus*, Brazos Theological Commentary on the Bible (Brazos, 2008), 25.

11. This constant refrain in the prophetic literature in the Old Testament is echoed, for example, in Micah: " 'With what shall I come before the LORD, and bow myself before God on high? Shall I come before him with burnt offerings, with calves a year old? Will the LORD be pleased with thousands of rams, with ten thousands of rivers of oil? Shall I give my first-born for my transgression, the fruit of my body for the sin of my soul?' He has showed you, O man, what is good; and what does the LORD require of you but to do justice, and to love kindness, and to walk humbly with your God?" (6:6–8).

12. Jeremiah 31:32: "I dominated (*b'alti*) them/took them as a husband" is translated in Greek with the word "neglect/not care for" (*ameleō*).

13. Albert Vanhoye, "Universal Salvation Through Christ and the Validity of the Old Covenant", in Nicholas Moore and Richard Ounsworth, *A Perfect Priest* (Mohr Siebeck, 2018), 200–1.

14. Each of these four mediating figures is central to one of the four parts of the Christian division of the Old Testament (distinct from the three-part Jewish *TaNaKh*)—priest in the Pentateuch, king in the Historical Books, sage in the Wisdom Books, prophet in the Prophets.

15. Cf. Leviticus 4:5 and 6:22.

16. Walter Brueggemann, *An Introduction to the Old Testament* (John Knox Press, 2003), 67.

17. Gordon Wenham, *The Book of Leviticus* (Wm. B. Eerdmans, 1979), 19. Modern translations render the Hebrew *ṭama* "unclean" and *ṭahor* "clean"; here "impure" and "pure" are preferred.

18. The English sixteenth-century word "atonement", composed by Tyndale, translates the Hebrew magnificently: "at-one" with God.

19. Walter Brueggemann, *Theology of the Old Testament* (Fortress Press, 1997), 666.

20. In the Septuagint, the Tent of Meeting is the Tent of Witness, a variation in the translation of the Hebrew.

21. The Torah is constituted by five commandments with its center the command to fill the earth: "Be fruitful and multiply, and *fill* the earth and subdue it; and have dominion" (Gen 1:28).

22. On the concept of an architecture of holiness in time rather than in space, see Abraham J. Heschel, *The Sabbath: Its Meaning for Modern Man* (Farrar, 1952), 8–10.

23. Hebrews refers to failure to enter the Sabbath, referring to the entry into the land under the first Jesus (Joshua): "For if Joshua had given them rest, God would not speak later of another day. So then, there remains a sabbath rest for the people of God; for whoever enters God's rest also ceases from his labors as God did from his. Let us therefore strive to enter that rest, that no one fall by the same sort of disobedience" (4:8–11).

24. This priestly zeal associated with Phinehas is praised in Mattathias, father of the Maccabees (see 1 Mac 2:26) and in Jesus (see Jn 2:17).

25. Difficult to translate, the term is constituted of two words that refer to what is inhospitable to human existence—wasteland, emptiness, wilderness. The term appears only twice in the Old Testament: to describe the "nothingness" that precedes creation (Gen 1:2) and to describe the nothingness that is a consequence of sin (see Jer 4:23).

26. The third moment is re-creation, God's grace in his fidelity despite sin.

27. See Brueggemann, *Theology of the Old Testament*, 650–79.

28. Ibid., 665.

29. See Flavius Josephus, *Antiquities of the Jews* 3:180–87.

30. The plagues provoked by Pharaoh's increasingly hardened heart are an expression of the world plunged back into *tohu vavohu*.

31. John E. Hartley, *Leviticus*, vol. 4, *Word Biblical Commentary*, ed. David A. Hubbard and Glenn W. Barker (Word Books, 1992), 235.

32. Seeing God already featured: After accepting the Torah (Ex 24:3, 8), the representatives of the people eat, drink, and see God (see vv. 10–11).

33. All emphasis to biblical quotations in this chapter is added by the author.

34. Cf. Matthew 5:23–24: "So if you are offering your gift at the altar, and there remember that your brother has something against you, leave your gift there before the altar and go; first be reconciled to your brother, and then come and offer your gift."

35. Evocatively, the Hebrew word for "sacrifice" (*qorban/lehaqriv*) shares a root with the word "close"/"drawing close" (*qarov/lehiqarev*).

36. Pontifical Biblical Commission, *The Jewish People and Their Sacred Scriptures in the Christian Bible* (Libreria Editrice Vaticana, 2001), no. 46.

37. Brueggemann, *Theology of the Old Testament*, 699.

38. Ibid.

39. The *Catechism of the Catholic Church* explains: "We carry out this command of the Lord by celebrating *the memorial of his sacrifice*. In so doing, we offer to the Father what he has himself given us: the gifts of his creation, bread and wine which, by the power of the Holy Spirit and by the words of Christ, have become the body and blood of Christ. Christ is thus really and mysteriously made present" (1357).

40. *CCC* 1362.

41. Thomas Aquinas, *Summa theologiae*, trans. Fathers of the English Dominican Province (Christian Classics, 1981), III, q. 22: "Whether it is fitting that Christ should be a priest?" (henceforth *ST*).

Chapter 5: Bruce D. Marshall, Aquinas on the Jews and Judaism

1. On Aquinas' theology of Jewish election, see my essay "Religion and Election: Aquinas on Natural Law, Judaism, and Salvation in Christ", *Nova et Vetera* (English edition) 14, no. 1 (2016): 61–125, especially sections VI–VIII. More briefly, see my "Christ and Israel: An Unsolved Problem in Catholic Theology", in *The Call of Abraham: Essays on the Election of Israel in Honor of Jon D. Levenson*, ed. Gary A. Anderson and Joel S. Kaminsky (University of Notre Dame Press, 2013), 330–50. Some passages in the present chapter are adapted from

these two essays, which also include some bibliographic information on the now-extensive literature on Aquinas and the Jews.

2. *Super Epistolam ad Romanos lectura*, in *S. Thomae Aquinatis Super Epistolas S. Pauli lectura*, 8th ed., ed. Raphael Cai, vol. 1 (Marietti, 1953), (caput) 9, (lectio) 5 (no. 799) (henceforth *Ad Rom*). For a fuller list of God's special benefits to Israel, see *Ad Rom* 9, 1 (nos. 743–47). This and all translations are my own. For an English version of this text, see St. Thomas Aquinas, *Commentary on Romans*, trans. Fabian R. Larcher (Emmaus Academic, 2020). This translation follows the section numbers in the Marietti edition.

3. *Ad Rom* 11, 4 (no. 923).

4. Ibid., citing Deut 4:37.

5. *Ad Rom* 11, 4 (no. 924).

6. *Ad Rom* 3, 1 (no. 253).

7. *Ad Rom* 11, 4 (no. 927); cf. 11, 2 (no. 889) and 11, 3 (no. 909).

8. *Ad Rom* 11, 4 (no. 913).

9. *Ad Rom* 11, 2 (no. 890); cf. 11, 1 (no. 875).

10. *Ad Rom* 11, 4 (no. 916); cf. 11, 5 (no. 931).

11. *Ad Rom* 11, 2 (no. 878).

12. See *Ad Rom* 11, 3 (nos. 897 and 911).

13. *In Joh* 19, 1 (no. 2481), *in S. Thomae Aquinatis Super Evangelium S. Ioannis lectura*, 6th ed., ed. Raphael Cai (Marietti, 1972). As the allusion to Rom 11:18 here indicates, the "Ecclesia Iudaeorum" is the Jewish people going back to the patriarchs, not simply Jewish Christians.

14. *ST* I-II, q. 98, a. 4 co.

15. *Ad Rom* 9, 1 (no. 745; cf. no. 743); here, too, Aquinas cites Deuteronomy 4:37.

16. *ST* I-II, q. 102, a. 5, ad 1; cf. III, q. 70, a. 2 co.

17. For Thomas' version of the standard medieval distinction between moral, ceremonial, and judicial precepts in the Old Law, see *ST* I-II, q. 99, aa. 2–4.

18. *ST* I-II, q. 101, a. 4 co.

19. *ST* I-II, q. 105, a. 2, ad 10. There is thus an important sense in which it was correct to say, until the coming of Christ, that the true God was "the God of the Jews only (Rom. 3:29)". *Ad Rom* 3, 4 (no. 319).

20. In support of this, Thomas invokes, strikingly, Jesus' words to the apostles in John 15:15: "I have called you friends". *Ad Rom* 3, 1 (no. 250).

21. See *ST* I-II, q. 98, a. 4 co.; q. 101 a. 3 ad 2; q. 102 a. 6 ad 7–8.

22. As in Deuteronomy 9:6, cited in *ST* I-II, q. 98, a. 4 co.

23. See *In Joh* 8, 6 (no. 1240).

24. *Epistola ad ducissam Brabantiae*, in *Sancti Thomae de Aquino Opera omnia iussu Leonis XIII P. M. edita*, vol. 42, p. 375.23–25 (henceforth ed. Leonine). On the legal and social situation of the Jews in the thirteenth century and as Aquinas saw it, cf. John Y.B. Hood, *Aquinas and the Jews* (University of Pennsylvania Press, 1995).

25. *ST* II-II, q. 10, a. 12, ad 3. Thomas discusses the baptism of Jewish children in two other places and repeats verbatim the remark he makes here about the priority of natural and divine law. *ST* III, q. 68, a. 10, ad 2; *Quodlibet* II, q. 4, a. 2, ad 3 (ed. Leonine, vol. 25/2, p. 224.127–29).

26. *ST* I-II, q. 98 a., 4 co.; cf. I-II, q. 104 a. 2, ad 2.

27. *ST* I-II, q. 98, a. 4 co.

28. On the former, cf. *ST* I-II, q. 102, a. 5, ad 1; on the latter, *ST* III, q. 70, a. 2 co.

29. *ST* I-II, q. 104, a. 2, ad 2. This way of putting the point comes from Augustine, *Contra faustum* 22, 24, which Thomas invokes several times.

30. *ST* I-II, q. 104, a. 3 co. For the twofold *ratio* of the ceremonial Law, see *ST* I-II, q. 102, a. 2.

31. *Ad Rom* 3, 1 (no. 249).

32. In a sense, idolatry is the gravest sin, in that it "holds out divine honor to a creature" and thereby tries to overturn the whole order creation has to God. *ST* II-II, q. 94, a. 3 co.

33. On the many reasons why Christ needed to be circumcised, see *ST* III, q. 37, a. 1 co.

34. *In Joh* 4, 2 (no. 605), commenting on John 4:22: "Salvation is from the Jews."

35. On the former, see *ST* III, q. 1, a. 2 co.; on the latter, see *ST* III, q. 46, aa. 2 and 3.

36. *ST* III, q. 46, a. 1 co.; cf. (for the previous sentence) *ST* I, q. 19, a. 3 co.

37. See *ST* III, q. 16, a. 1 co.

38. *ST* III, q. 48, a. 2, ad 3.

39. "The preaching of the cross of Christ includes what seems impossible according to human wisdom, for example that God dies, that the omnipotent is subject to the hands of the violent." *I Ad Cor* 1, 3 (no. 47), in *S. Thomae Aquinatis Super Epistolas S. Pauli lectura*, vol. 1. He makes explicit the connection implied by conciliar Christology between the Virgin Mary as the Mother of God and the Cross as the slaying of God; see *In III Sent* d. 4, q. 2, a. 2, ad 1 (no. 72), in *S. Thomae Aquinatis Scriptum Super Sententiis*, ed. M.F. Moos, vol. 3 (Lethielleux, 1933).

40. *ST* III, q. 47, a. 5, ad 3.

41. *ST* III, q. 47, a. 4 co.; ad 3.

42. See *ST* III, q. 47, a. 5 co.; a. 6 co.; q. 46, a. 10, ad 1.

43. *ST* III, q. 47, a. 5 co.; cf. *In Joh* 8, 5 (no. 1227).

44. *ST* III, q. 46, a. 12, ob 3. While this statement comes from an objection to which Aquinas then replies, his reply (ad 3 here) does not question it. See endnote 24.

45. Vatican Council II, Declaration of the Church to Non-Christian Religions *Nostra aetate* (October 28, 1965), no. 4.

46. *ST* I-II, q. 104, a. 3 co; cf. *ST* I-II, q. 103, a. 4 co.

47. *Ad Rom* 14, 1 (no. 1087).

48. *ST* I-II, q. 103, a. 4 s.c.

49. *In I Cor* 1, 3 (no. 45).

50. *ST* I-II, q. 103, a. 4, ad 1.

51. *In Gal* 2, 3 (no. 86).

52. *In Gal* 5, 1 (no. 280).

53. *ST* I-II, q. 103, a. 4 co.

54. See *ST* I-II, q. 19, a. 8; q. 84, a. 4, ad 5.

55. *In IV Sent* d. 1, q. 2, a. 5, qla. 3, ad 3 (Moos ed., no. 317).

56. *Ad Rom* 14, 1 (no. 1087). The Council of Florence discusses these same issues, in much the same terms, in its decree *Cantate Domino*; see especially no. 12 (DH 1348). On Florence, see the essay in this volume by Robert Fastiggi, "Jewish Practices: The Council of Florence and Benedict XIV's 1756 Encyclical *Ex Quo Primum*". I cannot go into the precise relationship between this Council and the theology of Aquinas here.

57. *ST* II-II, q. 10, a. 11 co.

58. On this text, see my essay "*Quasi in Figura*: A Brief Reflection on Jewish Election, After Thomas Aquinas", *Nova et Vetera* (English edition) 7, no. 2 (2009): 477–84, which probably tries to make the passage bear more weight than it can really hold.

Chapter 6: Robert Fastiggi, Jewish Practices: The Council of Florence and Benedict XIV's 1756 Encyclical *Ex Quo Primum*

1. The Council of Trent, in its January 13, 1547 "Decree on Justification", states that "Christ ... merited for us justification by his most holy Passion on the wood of the Cross." See Heinrich Denzinger and Peter Hünermann, eds., *Compendium of Creeds, Definitions, and Declarations on Matters of Faith and Morals* (Ignatius Press, 2012), no. 1529 (henceforth *D-H*).

2. Unless otherwise indicated, all biblical texts are from the 1991 New American Bible.

3. There have been various interpretations about what Paul means by "works of the law". Because he does not exempt Christians from following the commandments of the moral law (see Rom 13:8–10; 1 Cor 6:8–11; 7:19), the "works of the law" are best understood as the cultic or ceremonial laws of Judaism such as "circumcision, dietary regulations, Sabbath observance, purity codes, and sacrifices". Scott W. Hahn and Curtis Mitch, *Romans*, Catholic Commentary on Sacred Scripture (Baker Academic, 2017), 50. Of course, the observance of the commandments of the moral law is not the basis for justification in Saint Paul, but failure to observe these commandments could result in the loss of justification (see 1 Cor 6:9).

4. When Paul speaks about "abolishing the law with its commandments and legal claims", he is not absolving Christians from following the commandments of the moral law. See Hahn and Mitch, *Romans*, 53, and Lawrence Feingold, *The Mystery of Israel and the Church*, vol. 3, *The Messianic Kingdom of Israel* (The Miriam Press, 2010), 237. It is best to understand the "commandments and legal claims" in this context as referring to the cultic or ceremonial laws of Judaism.

5. The "necessities" required of Christians of gentile origin reflect those things forbidden to the aliens living in Israel according to Leviticus 17–18. See the commentary on Acts by Richard J. Dillon in the *New Jerome Biblical Commentary*, ed. Raymond E. Brown, S.S., Joseph A. Fitzmyer, S.J., and Roland E. Murphy, O.Carm. (Prentice Hall, 1990), 752. These basic requirements also reflect what the Jewish Talmudic tradition identified as the Noachide Laws. These were the basic moral requirements that all human beings, as descendants of Adam and Noah, were expected to observe. See "Jewish Concepts: The Seven Noachide Laws", The Jewish Virtual Library, accessed June 30, 2023, https://www.jewishvirtuallibrary.org/the-seven-noachide-laws.

6. William S. Kurz, S.J., *Acts of the Apostles*, Catholic Commentary on Sacred Scripture (Baker Academic, 2013), 344.

7. The Law of Moses prohibited Jews from eating certain foods such as pork. It did not explicitly forbid Jews from eating with gentiles. There is some evidence, though, to suggest that at least from the second century B.C., eating with gentiles was forbidden by Jewish leaders. Some scholars, however, believe that only eating nonkosher food at gentile homes was forbidden. See Albert Vanhoye and Peter S. Williamson, *Galatians*, Catholic Commentary on Sacred Scripture (Baker Academic, 2019), 74–75.

8. As William A. Kurz, S.J., explains: "God has shown Peter in his vision (Acts 10:9–16) that he should not call any person profane or unclean. Here in his visit to Cornelius, Peter recognizes the main point of his food vision—that it applies more to persons than to food. He now realizes that people are not to be treated as unclean in themselves. Nor should he fear contamination by contact with them." Kurz, *Acts of the Apostles*, 173.

9. Although these Jewish Christians are said to come from James (Gal 2:12), they do not seem to represent the view of James as described in Acts 15:13–21. It is possible, though, that some Jewish Christians understood the decision of the Council of Jerusalem of Acts 15 to apply only to the gentile Christians and that they believed Christians of Jewish origin were still bound by Jewish laws.

10. Vanhoye and Williamson, *Galatians*, 77.

11. Ibid., 79.

12. Ibid., 80.

13. John K. Roth, "Judaism and Christianity: Christian Views", in *The Cambridge Dictionary of Christianity*, ed. Daniel Patte (Cambridge University Press, 2010), 660.

14. Augustine, *The City of God*, trans. Marcus Dodds (The Modern Library), book XVIII, 45, p. 657.

15. Lawrence E. Frizzell, "Jewish-Catholic Relations (Theological Dimensions of)", in *New Catholic Encyclopedia Supplement 2010 Volume 2 J–Z*, ed. Robert L. Fastiggi (Gale Cengage Learning, 2010), 603.

16. Ibid.

17. Augustine, *City of God*, book XX, 30, p. 760.

18. Ibid., p. 762.

19. Ibid., p. 760.

20. Roy H. Schoeman, *Salvation Is from the Jews: The Role of Judaism in Salvation History from Abraham to the Second Coming* (Ignatius Press, 2003), 310.

21. *CCC* 674.

22. Augustine, *City of God*, book XVIII, 46, p. 657.

23. Willehad Paul Eckert, "Church, Catholic", in *Encyclopaedia Judaica*, ed. Fred Skolnik, 2nd ed. (Thomson Gale, 2007), 4:710.

24. See Edward H. Flannery, *The Anguish of the Jews: Twenty-Three Centuries of Anti-Semitism* (Paulist Press, 1985), 28–89.

25. Ibid., 59.

26. Solomon Grayzel, "Church Councils", in *Encyclopaedia Judaica*, 4:716.

27. Ibid.

28. Ibid.

29. Flannery, *Anguish*, 56.

30. Ibid.

31. Ibid., 57–58.

32. Pinchas E. Lapide, *Three Popes and the Jews* (Hawthorne Books, 1967), 47.

33. Flannery, *Anguish*, 68.

34. Ibid., 67.

35. Jules Isaac, *Genèse de l'Antisémitisme* (Calmann-Lévy, 1956), 23, cited in Flannery, *Anguish*, 74.

36. Ibid.

37. *D-H* 480. Later popes would likewise forbid forcing Jews or others to convert. See Alexander II's 1065 "Letter to Prince Landolfo of Benevento" (*D-H* 698) and Innocent III's constitution *Licet perfidia Iudaeorum* of September 15, 1199 (*D-H* 772–73).

38. Although compulsory baptisms and forced conversion of Jews were forbidden, they still occurred. See Flannery, *Anguish*, 70–71, and Lapide, *Three Popes*, 57–58. Even when baptisms were not forced, Jews were often required to attend sermons or public disputations that criticized the Talmud and sought to persuade them with other arguments to abandon Judaism; see Lapide, *Three Popes*, 62–64.

39. See Flannery, *Anguish*, 76.

40. *D-H* 781. The ruling of Innocent III did not deal directly with the question of the baptism of Jewish children against the wishes of their parents. In 1639, Pope Urban VIII dealt with a case of a Jewish girl around age three who was baptized against her parents' wishes. The Holy Office forbade the baptism of Jewish children against the wishes of their parents, but if "they are in fact baptized, the baptism is valid, and the character is imprinted; the baptized daughter [therefore] should be brought up with Christians; [but] the woman who performed the baptism is to be sharply warned that in the future she should take care not to do such things ... especially since the bull of Julius III remains in force, which imposes a penalty of 1000 ducats and suspension on those who baptize the children of Hebrews against their parents' wishes" (*D-H* 1998). Pope Benedict XIV, in his February 28, 1747, instruction, *Postremo mense*, repeated the prohibition of baptizing Jewish children against their parents' wishes, and he cited *ST* III, a. 68, a. 10 to show that, according to the natural law, parents have natural rights over their children (*D-H* 2552). Benedict XIV, however, allowed for the baptism of

Jewish children without parental consent if the Jewish child "be found by some Christian to be close to death" (*D-H* 2555). This latter exception paved the way for the nineteenth-century case of Edgardo Mortara, a Jewish boy who was baptized by a Catholic woman who thought he was in danger of death. Because the baptism was valid and licit, the child, according to Italian law, was required to receive a Catholic education. When the parents refused this education, the Italian police removed the child from his parents' care, which led to an international storm of protest (see Flannery, *Anguish*, 169–70). The 1983 Code of Canon Law, canon 688.2, still allows for the baptism of infants in danger of death without the consent of the non-Catholic parents. Removing the baptized child who does not die from the parents' care, however, cannot be defended.

41. *Decrees of the Ecumenical Councils*, ed. Nicholas P. Tanner, S.J., vol. 1, *Nicaea I to Lateran V* (Sheed & Ward and Georgetown University Press, 1990), 145–46.

42. Ibid., 19.

43. *Sacrorum conciliorum nova et amplissima collectio*, ed. J.D. Mansi (Antonio Zatta, 1759), 2:1307.

44. Ibid., 7:397, 419 (Chalcedon); ibid., 11:946 (Trullo).

45. Flannery, *Anguish*, 88–89.

46. Tanner, *Ecumenical Councils*, 1:267.

47. Lateran IV had other canons requiring Jews to make adequate satisfaction for excessive loans that oppress Christians (canon 67); requiring Jews and Muslims to be distinguished from Christians by their dress (canon 68); and forbidding Jews from holding public office (canon 69). See ibid., 1:265–67.

48. *ST* I-II, q. 99, a. 5.

49. *ST* I-II, q. 104, a. 3.

50. *ST* I-II, q. 103, a. 4.

51. Ibid.

52. *ST* I-II, q. 103, a. 4, ad. 1. It is worth noting that in his reply to objection 1, Aquinas also allowed for circumcision during the time between Christ's Passion and the promulgation of the Gospel as long as it was done for reasons of health and not because circumcision was required.

53. See introduction to "Basel–Ferrara–Florence–Rome, 1431–1445" in Tanner, *Ecumenical Councils*, 1:453–54.

54. Norman P. Tanner, *The Councils of the Church: A Short History* (Crossroad, 2001), 71.

55. See the March 25, 1440, monition of the Council of Florence against the antipope Felix V in Tanner, *Ecumenical Councils*, 1:559–66.

56. See introduction to the Council of Florence, *D-H* 1300. See also the September 4, 1439, decree of the Council of Florence *Moyses vir Dei* against the Council of Basel, *D-H* 1309. This decree of Florence affirms the dependence of an ecumenical council on the pope.

57. This is the title and dating given to the council in *D-H* 1300–1353.

58. Tanner, *Ecumenical Councils*, 1:483.

59. Ibid.

60. Ibid., 484.

61. Ibid.

62. Ibid.

63. Ibid., 485.

64. Ibid.

65. This bull can be found in Tanner, *Ecumenical Councils*, 1:567–83, and also in *D-H* 1330–53, for the most significant portion. The Copts, Ethiopians, and Jacobites were Christians from Egypt, Africa, and the Middle East who did not accept the Council of Chalcedon of 451 and were called Monophysites (those who believe there is only one nature in

Christ rather than two). The Jacobites were named after a Syrian Monophysite bishop, Jacob Baradæus (c. 505–578).

66. *D-H* 1348.

67. Ibid.

68. Ibid.

69. Ibid. See also *ST* I–II, q. 103, a. 4., ad. 1.

70. *D-H* 1348.

71. See Joseph Gill, S.J., "Florence, the Council of", in *New Catholic Encyclopedia*, ed. Berard L. Marthaler, O.F.M. Conv., 2nd ed. (Thomas Gale, 2003), 5:772: "*Laetentur caeli* is an infallible document, the only one at the council."

72. Feingold, *Mystery of Israel and the Church*, 3:238n32.

73. *D-H* 1326.

74. *D-H* 3859.

75. *D-H* 3858.

76. Ibid.

77. John N.D. Kelly, *The Oxford Dictionary of Popes* (Oxford University Press, 1986), 297.

78. Flannery, *Anguish*, 158.

79. Cecil Roth and Claire Pfann, "Popes", in *Encyclopaedia Judaica*, ed. Fred Skolnik, 2nd ed. (Thomson Gale, 2007), 16:376.

80. The encyclical letter *A quo primum* can be found in *Magnum bullarium Romanum: Benedicti Papae bullarium tomus tertius* (Akademische Druk-u. Verlagsanstalt, 1966). An English translation can be found at https://www.newadvent.org/library/docs_be14aq.htm (accessed July 22, 2023).

81. The encyclical letter *Ex quo primum* can be found in *Magnum bullarium Romanum: Benedicti Papae bullarium tomus tertius*, 365–403. An English translation can be found at https://www.papalencyclicals.net/ben14/b14exquo.htm (accessed July 23, 2023).

82. Feingold, *Mystery of Israel and the Church*, 3:239.

83. Vatican Council II, Dogmatic Constitution of the Church *Lumen gentium* (November 21, 1964), no. 17, makes this observation: "Through her work, whatever good is in the minds and hearts of men, whatever good lies latent in the religious practices and cultures of diverse peoples (*in propriis ritibus et culturis populorum*), is not only saved from destruction but is also cleansed, raised up and perfected unto the glory of God, the confusion of the devil and the happiness of man."

Chapter 7: Roy Schoeman, Jewish Identity Within the Church— Two Jews, Three Opinions

1. I will use the term "Jew" in the contemporary colloquial sense, even though opinions among Jewish Catholics vary on the proper term to use. Some hold that the term "Jew" should refer only to one following the traditional Jewish religion, whereas a different term, "Hebrew" or "Israelite", should be used to refer to a member of the ethnic group who does not follow the religion.

2. In this chapter, the term "gentile" refers to anyone not of Jewish origin.

3. Although some Jews in the Church reject the traditional resolutions; cf. endnote 36.

4. I have adopted the term "Jewish convert" because it is the usual one, although many Jews in the Church, the author included, do not feel that it is appropriate, since the Church is post-Messianic Judaism, and think of themselves more as "completed Jews" or "fulfilled Jews".

5. See Acts 15:5: "But some believers who belonged to the party of the Pharisees rose up, and said, 'It is necessary to circumcise them, and to charge them to keep the Law of Moses.'"

This would have had a crippling effect on the early Church! It is also worth noting that the council addressed whether gentile Christians were bound under the Old Law but left open the question whether Jewish Christians might still be bound to it.

6. For a short overview, see Edward H. Flannery, S.J., *The Anguish of the Jews* (Paulist Press, 1985), 28–46. For fuller treatments, see Marcel Simon, *Verus Israel: Study of the Relations Between Christians and Jews in the Roman Empire, AD 135–425* (Littman, 1996); and James Parkes, *The Conflict of the Church and the Synagogue* (Hermon Press, 1974), 27–196.

7. As recorded in the *Jerusalem Talmud* (Berakhot 28bb–29a), the curse reads: "For the apostates let there be no hope, and uproot the kingdom of arrogance speedily and in our days. May the Nazarenes and the *'minim'* perish as in a moment. Let them be blotted out of the book of life ... and not be written together with the righteous." There is an extensive literature around the *Birkhat Ha-Minim*. See, for example, R. Travers Herford, *Christianity in Talmud and Midrash* (KTAV, 1995), 118–36 and 361–80.

8. Parkes, *Conflict*, 85–92.

9. Saint Clement, "Letter to the Corinthians", in *The Fathers of the Church*, ed. Roy J. Deferrari (Christian Heritage, 1946), 12–14.

10. An example is the Ebionite heresy, which asserted that adherence to Jewish ritual Law was still obligatory. For more on the dangers that Jewish-Christian beliefs posed to the early Church, see Parkes, *Conflict*, 95–106.

11. For instance, in his "First Homily": "Jews are dogs, stiff-necked, gluttonous, drunkards. They are beasts unfit for work.... The Jews had fallen into a condition lower than the vilest animals.... The synagogue is worse than a brothel and a drinking shop; it is a den of scoundrels, a temple of demons, the cavern of devils, a criminal assembly of the assassins of Christ.... I hate the Jews, because they violate the Law.... It is the duty of all Christians to hate the Jews." "John Chrysostom, Against the Jews. Homily 1", The Tertulian Project, accessed October 3, 2023, https://www.tertullian.org/fathers/chrysostom_adversus_judaeos_01_homily1.htm; and "John Chrysostom, Against the Jews. Homily 1", The Catholic Library Project, accessed February 25, 2025, https://catholiclibrary.org/library/view?docId=/Fathers-EN/Chrysostom.AdversusJudaeos.en.html;chunk.id=00000001.

12. Walter Laqueur, *The Changing Face of Antisemitism: From Ancient Times to the Present Day* (Oxford University Press, 2006), 48.

13. See Daniel Silver, *A History of Judaism*, vol. 1 (Basic Books, 1974); Bernard Martin, *A History of Judaism*, vol. 2 (Basic Books, 1974); Warren H. Carroll, *The Building of Christendom, 324–1100* (Christendom, 1987); and Flannery, *Anguish*, 66–121. For instance, "When the wave of Muslim expansion swept over Spain early in the eighth century, the conquerors found [the] Jewish enclaves ready to welcome almost any rule after the repressive, often brutal, policies of fanatically Catholic Visigoth kings." Silver, *History of Judaism*, 352.

14. Among the dozens that could be cited include Pope Innocent III, *Etsi non displiceat*, 1205; Pope Innocent IV (d. 1254), "Letter to the King of France" and *Si vera sunt*, 1239; Pope Gregory IX, *Epistle to the Hierarchy in Germany*, 1233; and Pope Paul IV, *Cum nimis absurdum*, 1555, instituting the ghetto in the Papal States. The last is available at https://ccjr.us/dialogika-resources/primary-texts-from-the-history-of-the-relationship/paul-iv (accessed October 3, 2023).

15. Such expulsions include from Bavaria, 1276; France, 1254, 1306, 1322, 1359, and 1394; Naples, 1288; England, 1290; Switzerland, 1294; Hungary, 1360; Austria, 1420; Spain, 1492; Portugal, 1496; Russia (except for the Pale of Settlement), 1791.

16. For example, the problem of the Marranos or *conversos* of the Iberian Peninsula. Although forced conversion was never endorsed by the Church, not infrequently, individual Christians or gangs of Christians would forcibly baptize an unwilling Jew, at which point he would be a Catholic in the eyes of the Church.

17. Cecil Roth, *The Spanish Inquisition* (Norton & Co., 1964); and Cecil Roth, *A History of the Marranos* (Sepher-Hermon, 1974). The popes' attempts to rein in the abuses were not consistently effective.

18. Paula E. Hyman, *The Jews of Modern France* (University of California Press, 1998), 17–18.

19. The loss of the Papal States under Pius IX has been attributed in part to the involvement of Jewish banks that loaned the Kingdom of Sardinia funds it needed for its war against the Papal States while cutting off "the flow of money that propped up the Papal States". Vittorio Messori, *Kidnapped by the Vatican* (Ignatius Press, 2017), 46.

20. In 1889, the Vatican secretary of state, Mariano Rampolla del Tindaro, wrote Pope Leo XIII: "The Masonic sect's close ties to the Judaic sect to the detriment of the Catholic Church are all too well known." David Kertzer, *The Popes Against the Jews* (Knopf, 2001), 189.

21. Walter Cardinal Kasper, *Dominus Iesus*, seventeenth meeting of the International Catholic-Jewish Liaison Committee, New York, May 1, 2001, https://www.bc.edu/content/dam/files/research_sites/cjl/texts/cjrelations/resources/articles/kasper_dominus_iesus.htm.

22. On a personal note, I have been banned by the bishop in one diocese in the United States from speaking at Catholic venues for encouraging Catholics to pray for the conversion of Jews.

23. "Original Manifesto of the AHC", Association of Hebrew Catholics, accessed August 11, 2023, www.hebrewcatholic.net/original-manifesto-of-the-ahc/.

24. Ronda Chervin, introduction to *Jewish Identity*, by Elias Friedman (The Miriam Press, 1987), 6–7.

25. *CCC* 674, citing Rom 1:20–26.

26. If one followed traditional Catholic teaching, this would entail the abandonment of Jewish ritual practices.

27. The Neocatechumenal Way is a catechumenate, not a rite (*Statute of the Neocatechumenal Way*, Title I, Art. 1, § 2), and the Anglican Ordinariates are examples of a pre-existent liturgy being incorporated into the Church. They do not constitute a rite but are personal ordinariates juridically equivalent to a diocese (Benedict XVI, apostolic constitution *Anglicanorum coetibus* [November 4, 2009]).

28. This significance is evidenced by *CCC* 674, cited above.

29. A high point of a recent trip to Israel was providentially stumbling upon, and "crashing", just such a Mass inside the Tomb itself in the Church of the Holy Sepulchre!

30. International Theological Commission of the Catholic Church, *Faith and Inculturation* (1988), chap. 1, para. 11, quoting John Paul II, *Slavorum apostoli* (June 2, 1985), 21, https://www.vatican.va/roman_curia/congregations/cfaith/cti_documents/rc_cti_1988_fede-inculturazione_en.html.

31. The Messianic Jewish movement is the movement for and largely by Jews to bring Jews to belief in Jesus as the Jewish Messiah. At that point, some enter Christian denominations, while others remain in communities of Jewish believers in Jesus. See Dan Cohn-Sherbok, *Messianic Judaism: A Critical Anthology* (Bloomsbury Publishing, 2000).

32. The Lemann brothers, later priests, canons, active participants at Vatican I, and close friends of Pope Pius IX.

33. Father Théotime de Saint-Just, *Les Frères Lémann Juifs Convertis* (Librairie S. François, 1937), 43–45 (translation by author). For the Messiah would have to have come when the Temple in Jerusalem, with its genealogical records, remained.

34. Ibid., 372.

35. At least universal in my extensive reading of and personal contact with hundreds of Jewish converts.

36. Eugenio Zolli, *Why I Became a Catholic* (Roman Catholic Books, 1953), n.p.

37. Jean-Louis Missika and Dominique Wolton, *Choosing God—Chosen by God: Conversations with Cardinal Jean-Marie Lustiger* (Ignatius Press, 1991), 42.

38. Christopher White, "Cardinal Lustiger: 10 Years After Death, Jewish Convert Still Looms over Church in France", *Crux*, August 4, 2017, https://cruxnow.com/global-church/2017/08/cardinal-lustiger-10-years-death-jewish-convert-still-looms-church-france.

39. Quoted in Roy H. Schoeman, *Honey from the Rock: Sixteen Jews Find the Sweetness of Christ* (Ignatius Press, 2007), 176; Trent Beattie, "Rosalind Moss' Unexpected Journey", *National Catholic Register*, December 8, 2011, https://www.ncregister.com/news/rosalind-moss-unexpected-journey.

40. See "Interview with Athol Bloomer", *The Hebrew Catholic*, no. 85 (Winter–Spring 2008), published by the Association of Hebrew Catholics, https://www.hebrewcatholic.net/interview-with-athol-bloomer/.

41. For example, Saint John Chrysostom, *Adversus Judaeos*, cited previously.

42. For example, Saint Ignatius of Antioch, *To the Philippians*, in *The Fathers of the Church*, ed. Roy J. Deferrari (Christian Heritage, 1946), 115; and Tertullian, *Adversus Judaeos*, in *Ante-Nicene Fathers*, trans. S. Thelwall, ed. Alexander Roberts, James Donaldson, and A. Cleveland Coxe; rev. and ed. for New Advent by Kevin Knight, vol. 3, chaps. 4–6 (Christian Literature Publishing Co., 1885), accessed October 3, 2023, https://www.newadvent.org/fathers/0308.htm.

43. *ST* I-II, q. 103, a. 3; see also Saint Thomas Aquinas, *Commentary on Saint Paul's Epistle to the Galatians*, 1.2.21.

44. For instance, David Moss, "AHC Interview of Archbishop Raymond L. Burke", Association of Hebrew Catholics, La Crosse, Wisconsin, August 5, 2010, https://www.hebrewcatholic.net/ahc-interview-of-archbishop-raymond-l-burke-2-of-5/.

45. For example, Cardinal Burke, "AHC Interview".

46. Joseph Cardinal Ratzinger, *Many Religions—One Covenant* (Ignatius Press, 1999), 27.

47. Joseph Cardinal Ratzinger, "The Heritage of Abraham: The Gift of Christmas", *L'Osservatore Romano*, December 29, 2000, https://www.ccjr.us/dialogika-resources/documents-and-statements/roman-catholic/pope-benedict-xvi/b16-00dec29.

48. Judaism, of course, acknowledges that the sacraments of Judaism, as given in the Old Testament and requiring animal sacrifice, ended with the destruction of the Temple in A.D. 70 but asserts that in its absence sacrifice, prayer, fasting, and almsgiving can substitute. For an excellent discussion of the transition from Temple to Talmudic Judaism, see Silver, *History of Judaism*, 255–78.

Chapter 8: Gavin D'Costa, Hebrew Catholics and the Nature of the Fullness of the Catholic Church

*Six modified paragraphs of this essay are drawn from "Hebrew Catholics: Constitutive of the 'Body of Christ'?", in *Covenant and the People of God: Essays in Honor of Mark S. Kinzer*, ed. Jonathan Kaplan, Jennifer M. Rosner, and David J. Rudoph (Wipf and Stock, 2023), 32–41. Used by permission of Wipf and Stock Publishers, www.wipfandstock.com.

1. See Fastiggi's and Marshall's essays in this volume and my own arguments about Tradition and Magisterium on this issue in Gavin D'Costa, *Catholic Doctrines on the Jewish People After Vatican II* (Oxford University Press, 2019), 27–63.

2. See the interesting treatment of this issue by Messianic Jew Mark Kinzer, *Searching Her Own Mystery: Nostra Aetate, the Jewish People, and the Identity of the Church* (Cascade Books, 2015) (I disagree with his otherwise excellent study on two counts: There is no structural supersessionism present in *Lumen gentium*, and the citation from the *Catechism* he provides does not support his case); and Antoine Levy, who also minimizes the Council's importance

in his "Bilateral Ecclesiology and Three-Dimensionality of the People of God", in Kaplan, Rosner, and Rudolph, *Covenant and the People of God*, 130–43.

3. See David Neuhaus' chapter in this book for a historical context to the doctrinal point I am tracing.

4. "Dogmatic Constitution on the Church", in *Commentary on the Documents of Vatican II*, ed. Herbert Vorgrimler, vol. 1 (Burns & Oates, 1967), 138–53; Giuseppe Alberigo and Joseph A. Komonchak, eds., *History of Vatican II*, vol. 4, *Church as Communion: Third Period and Intersession, September 1964–September 1965* (Orbis, 2003), 42–52.

5. All references to *Lumen gentium* are taken from the Vatican website, Vatican Council II, Dogmatic Constitution on the Church *Lumen gentium* (November 21, 1964), https://www.vatican.va/archive/hist_councils/ii_vatican_council/documents/vat-ii_const_19641121_lumen-gentium_en.html (henceforth *LG*), except where it is stated that they are taken from Norman P. Tanner, *Decrees of the Ecumenical Councils*, vol. 2 (Sheed & Ward, 1990). None of these terms appear in the First Dogmatic Constitution on the Church of Christ (1870) at Vatican I.

6. See Bruce Marshall's essay in this collection and a critique of his theological reading of Aquinas in Trent Pomplun, "Quasi in Figura: A Cosmological Reading of the Thomistic Phrase", *Nova et Vetera* 7, no. 2 (2009).

7. The official Vatican website uses "ratify", as does Abbott. Tanner uses "struck". Tanner is closer to the literal Latin, but "ratify" is possibly better, as it tallies with "fuller revelation". "Struck" rightly suggests something new.

8. Angela Costley's article in this volume develops this point with great clarity.

9. See my *Vatican II: Catholic Doctrines on Jews and Muslims* (Oxford University Press, 2014), 113–60.

10. *LG* 16, citing Romans 11:28–29.

11. Commission for Religious Relations with the Jews, "'The Gifts and the Calling of God Are Irrevocable' (Rom 11:29): A Reflection on Theological Questions Pertaining to Catholic–Jewish Relations on the Occasion of the 50th Anniversary of '*Nostra ætate*' (No. 4)" (December 10, 2015), no. 36, https://www.christianunity.va/content/unitacristiani/en/commissione-per-i-rapporti-religiosi-con-l-ebraismo/commissione-per-i-rapporti-religiosi-con-l-ebraismo-crre/documenti-della-commissione/en.html. This document has no doctrinal authority, by its own admission.

12. See Fastiggi's essay in this collection, which gives a similar positive answer to this question after engaging with Tradition and the Magisterium.

13. Admittedly, I need to parse the "slave and free" distinction properly before concluding the reading I am suggesting.

14. Vatican Council II, Declaration on the Relation of the Church to Non-Christian Religions *Nostra aetate* (October 28, 1965), no. 4, https://www.vatican.va/archive/hist_councils/ii_vatican_council/documents/vat-ii_decl_19651028_nostra-aetate_en.html.

15. Commission for Religious Relations with the Jews, "Guidelines and Suggestions for Implementing the Conciliar Declaration *Nostra Aetate*, No. 4" (December 1, 1974), https://www.bc.edu/content/dam/files/research_sites/cjl/texts/cjrelations/resources/documents/catholic/Vatican_Guidelines.htm.

16. For the papal Magisterium's teaching on this matter, see Pope John Paul II, Address to Representatives of the Jewish Community (Mainz, West Germany, November 17, 1980), https://www.bc.edu/content/dam/files/research_sites/cjl/texts/cjrelations/resources/documents/catholic/johnpaulii/Mainz.htm. The official Vatican website does not contain an English version.

17. Ibid. (emphasis added).

18. Ibid.

19. Ibid. (emphasis added).

20. Commission for Religious Relations with the Jews, "Notes on the Correct Way to Present the Jews and Judaism in Preaching and Catechesis in the Roman Catholic Church" (March 6, 1982), accessed February 27, 2025, http://www.christianunity.va/content/unitacristiani/en/commissione-per-i-rapporti-religiosi-con-l-ebraismo/commissione-per-i-rapporti-religiosi-con-l-ebraismo-crre/documenti-della-commissione/en2.html.

21. Commission for Religious Relations with the Jews, "We Remember: A Reflection on the Shoah" (March 16, 1998), http://www.christianunity.va/content/unitacristiani/en/commissione-per-i-rapporti-religiosi-con-l-ebraismo/commissione-per-i-rapporti-religiosi-con-l-ebraismo-crre/documenti-della-commissione/en1.html.

22. The essays by Lawrence Feingold and David Neuhaus in this collection should be consulted for this point.

23. Commission for Religious Relations with the Jews, "Gifts and Calling of God".

24. Philip A. Cunningham, "The Sources Behind 'The Gifts and the Calling of God Are Irrevocable' (Rom 11:29): A Reflection on Theological Questions Pertaining to Catholic-Jewish Relations on the Occasion of the 50th Anniversary of '*Nostra ætate*' (No. 4)", *Studies in Christian-Jewish Relations* 12, no. 1 (2017), note 59, https://doi.org/10.6017/scjr.v12i1.9792. Father Norbert Johannes Hofmann, who is a signatory of the document and secretary to the Commission, is another source: "Die Einzigartigkeit des jüdisch-christlichen Dialogs", in E. Zwick and N. Hofmann, eds., *Dialog der Religionen. Eine interdisziplinäre Annäherung* (Lit Verlag, 2013), 61. However, this accounts only for no. 15, not no. 43. I am grateful to Father Hofmann for his help. Cunningham cites the source: an interview by Oliver Maksan of the Catholic charity Aid to the Church in Need before a meeting of the Joint Commission for the Jewish-Catholic Dialogue with Cardinal Kurt Koch, "Jewish-Catholic Dialogue and the Dialogue Between the Holy See and Judaism", Jerusalem, May 9, 2013.

25. Commission for Religious Relations with the Jews, "Gifts and Calling of God", no. 15.

26. Ibid., no. 43 (emphasis added).

27. See D'Costa, *Catholic Doctrines*, 69–80.

28. Commission for Religious Relations with the Jews, "Gifts and Calling of God", no. 43.

29. Ibid., no. 40.

30. See Antoine Levy's essay in this volume on that question.

31. See, for background to this tradition, Roy H. Schoeman, *Honey from the Rock: Sixteen Jews Find the Sweetness of Christ* (Ignatius Press, 2007); and Shalom Goldman, *Jewish-Christian Difference and Modern Jewish Identity: Seven Twentieth-Century Converts* (Lexington Books, 2015).

32. See "Fr. Antoine Levy, O.P.", Association of Hebrew Catholics, accessed August 17, 2023, https://www.hebrewcatholic.net/fr-antoine-levy/.

33. Elias Friedman, *Jewish Identity* (The Miriam Press, 1987) is his most mature work, a chapter of which is found in this volume.

34. I prescind from the question of whether Levy's account of Kinzer is accurate.

35. In what follows, I retain the term "Hebrew Catholics" for consistency within my essay, although Levy uses the term "Jewish Church" in his title, which I think is misleading, given his own argument.

36. Levy's critiques of Kinzer are in some ways a Latin Roman Catholic critique of a low-church Protestant ecclesiology that permits autonomous churches without visible hierarchal ministry overseeing their unity.

37. Antoine Levy, O.P., *Jewish Church: A Catholic Approach to Messianic Judaism* (Lexington Books, 2021), 193.

38. Levy argues that this disunity was the fault of the Jewish nation's rejection of Yeshua—thus, supersessionism was the result of the Jewish no (ibid., 350–51); but at times he seems to allow for a more nuanced reciprocal causality regarding this primary schism.

39. Ibid., 353.

40. The same argument is found in Peter Hocken, *Azusa, Rome, and Zion: Pentecostal Faith, Catholic Reform, and Jewish Roots* (Pickwick Publications, 2016), 28–37; and Jean-Marie Lustiger, *The Promise*, trans. Rebecca Howell Balinski, Msgr. Richard Malone, and Jean Duchesne (W.B. Eerdmans, 2007), 19.

41. Levy, *Jewish Church*, 358n79.

Chapter 9: Antoine Levy, The Great Commission and Jesus' Messianic Secret: A Hebrew Catholic Perspective on the Challenge of the *Missio ad Ludaeos* in Contemporary Israel

1. As we will see further in this contribution, in order to be relevant, a contemporary reflection on the *missio ad ludaeos* must hold fast to these two principles: (1) The ongoing existence of Jews, together with their religious tradition, is crucial to God's providential design; (2) The acknowledgment of Yeshua as Messiah of Israel by Jews is equally crucial to the accomplishment of this providential design.

2. On all this, see Christopher Clark, *Politics of Conversion in Prussia, Missionary Protestantism and the Jews in Prussia, 1728–1941* (Clarendon Press, 1995).

3. On all this, see Michael R. Darby, *The Emergence of the Hebrew Christian Movement in Nineteenth-Century Britain* (Brill, 2010). The situation was similar in the United States, where Protestant missions ministering to Jews flourished beginning in the 1880s. The establishments of most Protestant missions, just as a majority of Jewish converts, were reluctant to contemplate a form of "Hebrew Christianity". The plea of Mark John Levy in favor of the observance of Jewish customs by converts in the 1920s remained an isolated voice.

4. See ibid., 62. Yaakov Ariel showed that in the United States, missionary activities were dealt with in a casual sort of way from the 1920s until the 1960s; see Yaakov Ariel, *Evangelizing the Chosen People: Missions to the Jews in America, 1880–2000* (University of North Carolina Press, 2000), 185–94.

5. As Rabbi Yechiel Eckstein, the founder of the International Fellowship of Christians and Jews, eloquently put it: "While Christians have sought to convert Jews to Christianity for almost two millennia, after the holocaust those attempts are regarded as especially pernicious threats to Jewish survival—indeed, a form of spiritual genocide. Christians may claim that it is their *love* for Jews that is motivating their missionary zeal and that to desist from witnessing to them is itself a form of anti-Semitism. However, for the most part, Jews will remain unconvinced. In the course of their history, Jews have literally been *loved to death* by Christians. To them, actions speak louder than words." Yechiel Eckstein, *What Christians Should Know About Jews and Judaism* (Word, 1984), 287.

6. Madeleine Comte, "De la conversion a la rencontre, Les religieuses de Notre-Dame de Sion (1843–1986)", *Archives Juives* 35, no. 1 (2002), 113 (translation mine).

7. Commission for Religious Relations with the Jews, "'The Gifts and the Calling of God Are Irrevocable' (Rom 11:29): A Reflection on Theological Questions Pertaining to Catholic-Jewish Relations on the Occasion of the 50th Anniversary of '*Nostra ætate*' (No. 4)" (December 10, 2015), no. 40, http://www.christianunity.va/content/unitacristiani/en/commissione-per-i-rapporti-religiosi-con-l-ebraismo/commissione-per-i-rapporti-religiosi-con-l-ebraismo-crre/documenti-della-commissione/en.html.

8. "Nicht Mission sondern Dialog", *Herder Korrespondenz*, Heft 12 (2018) (translation mine).

9. Commission for Religious Relations with the Jews, "Gifts and Calling of God", no. 40.

10. Ibid., no. 41.

11. See, for instance, Vernon C. Grounds' plea in favor of "Jewish evangelism": "Texts like these [Rom 1:4–16; 10:1–3, etc.] ... have inspired Christians to become tireless evangelists and missionaries carrying their Message literally to the ends of the earth and indiscriminately viewing every non-converted human being, pagan, Jew, Hindu, Muslim, animist and atheist alike, as a soul for whom the Savior died and with whom the Good News must be shared." The Jacob Rader Marcus Center for Jewish Archives, MS–603: Rabbi Marc H. Tanenbaum Collection, 1945–1992. Series C: Interreligious Activities. 1952–1992, Box 19, Folder 1, Evangelicals and Jews in an Age of Pluralism [Papers], 9–11 December 1980, 6–7.

12. The hesitations of the Protestant leadership were resented in many parts of the Evangelical world, not least among the "Jewish evangelists to the Jews". See, for instance, the critical stance adopted by Mitch Glaser: "The real question is ... whether Jewish evangelism should be included as part of the Great Commission. The problem is that Jewish evangelism has been the Great Omission of the Church." Mitch Glaser, " 'To the Jew First': The Starting Point for the Great Commission", lecture, Covenant Theological Seminary, 1984, copy at the library of the Caspari Center, Jerusalem.

13. See, for instance, the following declaration: "In our work among the more than 3 million Jews in the country of Israel, our goal is to help establish congregations which predominantly consist of Christian Jews. It is only natural that such believers have Hebrew as their main language, and that they integrate into their worship, services and holidays those elements of the Jewish traditions they find appropriate.... As with all missions, the mission to Israel's goal is to make itself unnecessary. Our goal is independent, self-sufficient and self-evangelizing congregations and groups." "To the Jew First: Statement About Christian Ministry to the Jewish People from the National Board of Directors, IV, The Norwegian Mission to Israel (February 1986)", *Mishkan* no. 2 (1986), 60.

14. In this regard, the "Willowbank Declaration" (1989) offers the most substantial presentation of the positions of contemporary Protestant "Jewish evangelism". It is issued by the World Evangelical Committee with the support of the Lausanne Committee. In it, one can read: "ARTICLE III.12. WE AFFIRM THAT Jewish people have an ongoing part in God's plan. WE DENY THAT indifference to the future of the Jewish people on the part of Christians can ever be justified." World Evangelical Fellowship, "Willowbank Declaration on the Christian Gospel and the Jewish People", April 29, 1989, https://ccjr.us/dialogika-resources/documents-and-statements/protestant-churches/int/wef1989apr29.

15. The same "Willowbank Declaration" states the following: "ARTICLE I.5. WE AFFIRM THAT God's forgiveness of the penitent rests on the satisfaction rendered to his justice by the substitutionary sacrifice of Jesus Christ on the cross. WE DENY THAT any person can enjoy God's favor apart from the mediation of Jesus Christ, the sin-bearer.... ARTICLE III.14. WE AFFIRM THAT much of Judaism, in its various forms, throughout contemporary Israel and today's Diaspora, is a development out of, rather than as an authentic embodiment of, the faith, love and hope, that the Hebrew Scriptures teach. WE DENY THAT modern Judaism with its explicit negation of the divine person, work, and Messiahship of Jesus Christ contains within itself true knowledge of God's salvation.... ARTICLE III.15. WE AFFIRM THAT the biblical hope for Jewish people centers on their being restored through faith in Christ to their proper place as branches of God's olive tree from which they are at present broken off. WE DENY THAT the historical status of the Jews as God's people brings salvation to any Jew who does not accept the claims of Jesus Christ."

16. Pope Saint John Paul II was the first to introduce this teaching: John Paul II, Address to Representatives of the Jewish Community (Mainz, West Germany, November 17, 1980), https://www.bc.edu/content/dam/files/research_sites/cjl/texts/cjrelations/resources/documents/catholic/johnpaulii/Mainz.htm. This stance was reiterated in the 1993 *Catechism of the*

Catholic Church (121), the 2015 Vatican document "The Gifts and Calling of God Are Irrevocable" (nos. 27, 33, and 34), and Benedict XVI's article "Gnade und Berufung ohne Reue: Anmerkungen zum Traktat 'De Iudaeis'", *Communio* no. 47 (2018), 403 (English edition: *Communio* no. 45 [2018], 181).

17. "The New Covenant in Christ is the culminating point of the promises of salvation of the Old Covenant". Commission for Religious Relations with the Jews, "Gifts and Calling of God", no. 27. See also no. 35: "Since God has never revoked his covenant with his people Israel, there cannot be different paths or approaches to God's salvation.... The Christian faith confesses that God wants to lead all people to salvation, that Jesus Christ is the universal mediator of salvation, and that there is no 'other name under heaven given to the human race by which we are to be saved' (Acts 4:12)."

18. "From the Christian confession that there can be only one path to salvation, however, it does not in any way follow that the Jews are excluded from God's salvation because they do not believe in Jesus Christ as the Messiah of Israel and the Son of God.... That the Jews are participants in God's salvation is theologically unquestionable, but how that can be possible without confessing Christ explicitly, is and remains an unfathomable divine mystery." Ibid., no. 36.

19. "The New Covenant can never replace the Old but presupposes it and gives it a new dimension of meaning, by reinforcing the personal nature of God as revealed in the Old Covenant and establishing it as openness for all who respond faithfully from all the nations." Ibid., no. 27; see also ibid., nos. 30 and 32.

20. "The term covenant ... means a relationship with God that takes effect in different ways for Jews and Christians." Ibid., no. 27.

21. "God entrusted Israel with a unique mission, and He does not bring his mysterious plan of salvation for all peoples (cf. 1 Tim 2:4) to fulfilment without drawing into it his 'first-born son' (Ex 4:22)." Ibid., no. 36.

22. See my *Jewish Church: A Catholic Approach to Messianic Judaism* (Lexington Books, 2021).

Chapter 10: Elias Friedman, Jesus and Jewish Identity: From Mosaic Judaism to the Church

*Excerpted from Elias Friedman, *Jewish Identity* (The Miriam Press, 1987), 52–65, with permission.

1. Kurt Hruby, "Le Concept et l'expérience historique de la nation", in *The Jerusalem Colloquium on Religion, Peoplehood, Nation and Land* (Truman Research Institute, 1970), 84.

2. Unless otherwise indicated, all biblical texts are from the 1970 New American Bible.

3. Eugene Fisher, *Faith Without Prejudice: Rebuilding Christian Attitudes Toward Judaism* (Paulist Press, 1977), 68.

4. Chrysostome Larcher, *L'actualité chrétienne de l'Ancien Testament d'après le Nouveau Testament* (Cerf, 1962), 246 (translator unknown).

5. Adolf Darlap and Heinrich Fries, *Histoire du salut et révélation*, vol. 1, *Mysterium salutis, dogmatique de l'histoire de salut* (Cerf, 1969), 201.

6. John Henry Newman, "The Principle of Continuity Between the Jewish and Christian Churches", in *Sermons Bearing on Subjects of the Day* (Longmans, Green, and Co., 1918), 207.

7. Ibid., 204–5.

8. Ibid., 210.

9. David Flusser, *Jewish Sources in Early Christianity* (Hebrew) (Hashomer Hatsa'ir, 1979), 455.

10. Willy Rordorf, *Sabbat et dimanche dans l'Église ancienne* (Delachaux et Niestlé, 1972), 178.

11. Newman, "Principle of Continuity", 206.

12. Ibid., 205.

13. Ibid., 200. Editor's note: The original text, reprinted here, has misattributed the citation from Hruby to Newman.

14. John Henry Newman, "The Christian Church, a Continuation of the Jewish", in *Sermons Bearing on Subjects of the Day* (Longmans, Green and Co., 1902), 190.

15. Ibid., 192.

16. Ibid., 195.

17. Charles Harod Dodd, *Le Parabole del regno* (Paideia Editrice, 1976), 113.

18. Editor's note: Although we leave Father Friedman at this point, the reasoning in his last few paragraphs led him elsewhere to give Catholics of Jewish origin or descent the title "Hebrew Catholic". "Hebrew" refers to the Israelite origin while avoiding the conflict over the use of the term "Jew", while "Catholic" refers to the fidelity of that person to the See of Rome and their Catholic faith. As Ronda Chervin puts it in the introduction to Father Friedman's book: "It follows that so-called 'Jewish converts' to Christian religions should not call themselves Jewish Christians, or Jewish Catholics, but instead Hebrew Christians, or *Hebrew Catholics*, for they are no longer under rabbinic law, but they should conceive of themselves as still part of the people of the election."

Chapter 11: David Neuhaus, The Catholic-Messianic Jewish Conversations

1. *CCC* 674.

2. Messianic Jews are those Jews who confess faith in Jesus (or Yeshua, his Hebrew name) and who form communities, mostly without affiliating with any church.

3. Orthodox Judaism insists that Jewish descent is matrilineal, but some streams of liberal Judaism also recognize patrilineal descent.

4. This argument was made by some Jewish believers in Jesus in the state of Israel, claiming their right to Israeli citizenship under the Law of Return, which guarantees citizenship to all Jews. The most prominent among these was the Carmelite brother Daniel Rufeisen, a Jew who had become a Catholic, who brought his case before the Israeli Supreme Court in the early 1960s.

5. The first Jewish believers in Jesus, as described in the New Testament, never renounced their Jewish identity and remained integrated within the Jewish community.

6. See Donald Lewis, *The Origins of Christian Zionism* (Cambridge University Press, 2010).

7. Jews joining the Church were traditionally obliged to renounce formally their Jewish identity and belonging.

8. See Kai Kjaer-Hansen, *Joseph Rabinowicz and the Messianic Movement* (Handsel Press, 1995).

9. In Israel, Jews who have embraced Christianity or who are Messianic believers sometimes face discrimination and hostility from their neighbors. One example of discrimination is that a Jew openly confessing faith in Jesus (whether Christian or Messianic) cannot receive automatic Israeli citizenship as foreseen for all Jews by the Law of Return (1950).

10. See Yaakov Ariel, *Evangelizing the Chosen People: Missions to the Jews in America, 1880–2000* (University of North Carolina Press, 2000); Daniel Cohn-Sherbok, *Messianic Judaism* (Cassell, 2000); and David A. Rausch, *Messianic Judaism: Its History, Theology, and Polity* (Edwin Mellen Press, 1982).

11. It is difficult to know precise numbers, as many members are not Jewish according to contemporary definitions of Judaism.

12. Mark Kinzer, *The Nature of Messianic Judaism* (Hashivenu Archives, n.d.), 5.

13. Dan Juster, *Jewish Roots: A Foundation of Biblical Theology* (Destiny Image, 1995), 148.

14. Mark S. Kinzer, "*Lumen Gentium*, Through Messianic Jewish Eyes", in *Israel's Messiah and the People of God: A Vision for Messianic Jewish Covenant Fidelity* (Cascade Books, 2011), 168–69.

15. See the fascinating study by John Connelly, *From Enemy to Brother: The Revolution in Catholic Teaching on the Jews 1933–1965* (Harvard University Press, 2012). The study insists on the role of Jewish Catholics in reformulating the Church's attitude toward Jews and Judaism. This contrasts with the role of some prominent Catholics of Jewish origin in the persecution of Jews in the medieval period, the most prominent being the Dominican Pablo Christiani.

16. See Canon VIII of the Second Council of Nicaea in A.D. 787, which requires all Christians to "depart from Hebrew practices, otherwise they are not to be admitted at all [to baptism or to Communion]".

17. Cardinal Jean-Marie Lustiger, *On Christians and Jews*, ed. Jean Duchesne (Paulist Press, 2010), 6.

18. John Paul II, Address to Members of the Jewish Central Council of Cologne (Cologne, Germany, May 1, 1987), https://ccjr.us/dialogika-resources/documents-and-statements/roman-catholic/pope-john-paul-ii/jp287may1.

19. John Paul II, Homily for the Canonization of Edith Stein (Vatican City, October 11, 1998), https://www.vatican.va/content/john-paul-ii/en/homilies/1998/documents/hf_jp-ii_hom_11101998_stein.html.

20. Among Jewish Catholics, some observe halakhic Jewish life; however, the majority practice little or nothing of Jewish tradition.

21. For an interesting discussion of the differences, see Emma O'Donnell Polyakov, "Jewish-Christian Identities in Conflict: The Cases of Fr. Daniel Rufeisen and Fr. Elias Friedman", *Religions* 12, no. 12 (2021), 1101, https://doi.org/10.3390/rel12121101.

22. The term is derived from the study of Bellarmino Bagatti, *The Church from the Circumcision* (Franciscan Printing Press, 1971).

23. Quoted in Nechama Tec, *In the Lion's Den: The Life of Oswald Rufeisen* (Oxford University Press, 1990), 168.

24. Elias Friedman, *Jewish Identity* (The Miriam Press, 1987), 65.

25. See an interview with David Moss, "Are Jewish Converts Still Jewish", Association of Hebrew Catholics, accessed March 4, 2025, https://www.hebrewcatholic.net/are-jewish-converts-still-jewish/. Moss prefers these believers to be known as Israelite or Hebrew Catholics in order to create a distinction with Rabbinic Judaism.

26. David Moss, "An Interview with Archbishop Raymond L. Burke on the Occasion of the AHC Conference of October 1–3, 2010", *The Hebrew Catholic* 88 (2010–2011): 30–35.

27. Elias Friedman, O.C.D., "Presenting the Association of Hebrew Catholics", accessed August 16, 2023, https://www.hebrewcatholic.net/wp-content/uploads/2013/07/Presenting-AHC.pdf.

28. "What Is Saint James Vicarate for Hebrew Speaking Catholics?", Studium Theologicum Salesianum, October 13, 2021, https://jerusalem.unisal.it/what-is-saint-james-vicariate-for-hebrew-speaking-catholics/.

29. Association of Hebrew Catholics, accessed May 9, 2025, https://www.hebrewcatholic.net/.

30. Rev. Jean-Baptiste Gourion, O.S.B. (later Bishop) and Rev. David Neuhaus, S.J., who both served in the role of Latin patriarchal vicar for Hebrew-speaking Catholics in Israel.

31. Kinzer, "*Lumen Gentium*, Through Messianic Jewish Eyes", in *Israel's Messiah*, 156–74.

32. David Neuhaus, "Gli Ebrei che credono in Gesù. Il Dialogo tra Cattolici ed Ebrei Messianici", *Civiltà cattolica* 4 (quaderno 3968) (October 24, 2015): 145–56.

33. Among Mark Kinzer's works are *Postmissionary Messianic Judaism: Redefining Christian Engagement with the Jewish People* (Brazos Press, 2005); *Searching Her Own Mystery:* Nostra

Aetate, *the Jewish People, and the Identity of the Church* (Cascade Books, 2015); and *Jerusalem Crucified, Jerusalem Risen: The Resurrected Messiah, the Jewish People, and the Land of Promise* (Cascade Books, 2018).

34. Among Antoine Levy's works is *Jewish Church: A Catholic Approach to Messianic Judaism* (Lexington Books, 2021).

35. Vatican Council II, Dogmatic Constitution of the Church *Lumen gentium* (November 21, 1964), no. 6.

36. See Kinzer, "*Lumen Gentium*, Gloriam Israel", chap. 3 in *Searching Her Own Mystery*.

37. *LG* 2.

38. *LG* 16.

39. Kinzer, *Searching Her Own Mystery*, 56.

40. *CCC* 839, quoting *Roman Missal*, Good Friday 13: General Intercessions, VI.

41. *CCC* 839, quoting Rom 9:4–5; 11:29.

42. *CCC* 840.

43. Commission for Religious Relations with the Jews, "'The Gifts and the Calling of God Are Irrevocable' (Rom 11:29): A Reflection on Theological Questions Pertaining to Catholic-Jewish Relations on the Occasion of the 50th Anniversary of '*Nostra ætate*' (No. 4)" (December 10, 2015), no. 43, http://www.christianunity.va/content/unitacristiani/en/commissione-per-i-rapporti-religiosi-con-l-ebraismo/commissione-per-i-rapporti-religiosi-con-l-ebraismo-crre/documenti-della-commissione/en.html.

44. Levy, *Jewish Church*, 5.

45. Ibid., 124.

46. Ibid., 130.

47. Ibid., 170.

48. Ibid., 195.

49. Ibid., 339.

50. Ibid., 353.

51. See the website of the Helsinki Consultation at http://helsinkiconsultation.squarespace.com/.

52. See the website of *Yachad BeYeshua* at https://www.yachad-beyeshua.org/.

53. See Richard Harvey, *Mapping Messianic Jewish Theology: A Constructive Approach* (Paternoster, 2009).

54. See David Rudolph, *Introduction to Messianic Judaism: Its Ecclesial Context and Biblical Foundations*, ed. Joel Willitts (Zondervan, 2013).

55. David Neuhaus, "Fulfilling the Torah: Living Torah in the Church", Helsinki Consultation, Oslo, June 22, 2013, https://www.catholic.co.il/?cat=&view=article&id=879&m= and http://static1.1.sqspcdn.com/static/f/1106451/23060673/1373203130257/Fulfilling+the+Torah-2013-+neuhaus.pdf?token=QNapR1%2B9jazidYEKobcv%2BKdqwLg%3D.

56. David Neuhaus, "A Catholic Jew Reflects on His Jewish Identity", unpublished full text of lecture delivered on June 25, 2011, at the Helsinki Consultation, Paris, June 24–28, 2011, http://static1.1.sqspcdn.com/static/f/1106451/23103232/1373737404187/Neuhaus.pdf?token=wc5QzqQ9JyCmW6lRjRRPSy975bw%3D.

Chapter 12: Lawrence Feingold, The Ecclesial Mission of the Association of Hebrew Catholics

1. Ronda Chervin, introduction to *Jewish Identity*, by Elias Friedman (The Miriam Press, 1987), 6. See also Friedman, *Jewish Identity*, 48–49, 171–73.

2. Vatican Council II, Declaration on the Relation of the Church to Non-Christian Religions *Nostra aetate* (October 28, 1965), no. 4. See also Vatican Council II, Dogmatic

Constitution on the Church *Lumen gentium* (November 21, 1964), no. 16. On this teaching, see Gavin D'Costa, *Vatican II: Catholic Doctrines on Jews and Muslims* (Oxford University Press, 2016), 113–59; and Lawrence Feingold, *The Mystery of Israel and the Church* (The Miriam Press, 2010), 3:229–31. For postconciliar teaching on this issue, see Gavin D'Costa, *Catholic Doctrines on the Jewish People After Vatican II* (Oxford University Press, 2019); and Lawrence Feingold, *Touched by Christ: The Sacramental Economy* (Emmaus Academic, 2021), 516–18.

3. See Thomas Aquinas' commentary on Romans 3:3, lectio 1, nos. 253–55.

4. John Paul II, "Discourse to Representatives of the Jewish People in Mainz" (Mainz, November 17, 1980). On the development this statement marks with respect to *Nostra aetate*, see the Commission for Religious Relations with the Jews, "'The Gifts and the Calling of God Are Irrevocable' (Rom 11:29): A Reflection on Theological Questions Pertaining to Catholic-Jewish Relations on the Occasion of the 50th Anniversary of '*Nostra ætate*' (No. 4)" (December 10, 2015), no. 39, https://www.christianunity.va/content/unitacristiani/en/commissione-per-i-rapporti-religiosi-con-l-ebraismo/commissione-per-i-rapporti-religiosi-con-l-ebraismo-crre/documenti-della-commissione/en.html; and D'Costa, *Catholic Doctrines*, 15–18.

5. Francis, apostolic exhortation *Evangelii gaudium* (November 24, 2013), no. 247. See also Francis, Address in the Synagogue of Rome (January 17, 2016); and the Pontifical Biblical Commission, *The Jewish People and Their Sacred Scriptures in the Christian Bible*, no. 65c (Libreria Editrice Vaticana, 2002), 161: "The New Testament takes for granted that the election of Israel, the people of the covenant, is irrevocable: it preserves intact its prerogatives (Rom. 9:4) and its priority status in history.... The Church is composed of Israelites who have accepted the new covenant, and of other believers who have joined them.... Far from being a substitution for Israel, the Church is in solidarity with it." See also the Commission for Religious Relations with the Jews, "Gifts and Calling of God", no. 27: "The New Covenant does not revoke the earlier covenants, but it brings them to fulfilment."

6. On the manifold implications of this teaching, see Mark S. Kinzer, *Searching Her Own Mystery:* Nostra Aetate, *the Jewish People, and the Identity of the Church* (Cascade Books, 2015), especially 1–24, 172–89; Bruce D. Marshall, "Elder Brothers: John Paul II's Teaching on the Jewish People as a Question to the Church", in *John Paul II and the Jewish People: A Jewish-Christian Dialogue*, ed. David Dalin and Matthew Levering (Sheed and Ward, 2008), 113–29.

7. See Exodus 19:5–6.

8. See Friedman, *Jewish Identity*, 86.

9. John Paul II, Homily for the Canonization of Edith Stein (Vatican City, October 11, 1998), https://www.vatican.va/content/john-paul-ii/en/homilies/1998/documents/hf_jp-ii_hom_11101998_stein.html. See also Jean-Marie Lustiger commenting to his parents on his conversion, in Cardinal Jean-Marie Lustiger, *On Christians and Jews*, ed. Jean Duchesne (Paulist Press, 2010), 14: "I am not leaving you.... I am not ceasing to be a Jew; on the contrary, I am discovering another way of being a Jew."

10. *Nostra aetate*, no. 4.

11. See *CCC* 528; Cardinal Jean-Marie Lustiger, *The Promise*, trans. Rebecca Balinski, Richard Malone, and Jean Duchesne (William B. Eerdmans, 2002), 95: "With the Christ-Messiah and through him, pagans ... receive the grace of entering into Israel's Election."

12. See Michael Wyschogrod, "Israel, the Church, and Election", in *Abraham's Promise: Judaism and Jewish-Christian Relations* (William B. Eerdmans, 2004), 183–84: "The fact that Paul asserts that in Christ 'there is neither Jew nor Greek, neither slave nor freeman, neither male nor female' (Gal. 3:28) does not rule out such a special role for the children of ancient Israel in the Church, just as the abolition in Christ of the difference between man and woman does not prevent Paul from insisting that women remain silent in the assembly. Even in Christ, men are men and women are women; only in an ultimate, perhaps eschatological,

sense are they one. The Church could have asserted the same of the difference between Jew and Gentile." See also Douglas Farrow, *Theological Negotiations: Proposals in Soteriology and Anthropology* (Baker Academic, 2018), 233.

13. See Friedman, *Jewish Identity*, 97.

14. Lustiger, *Promise*, 6.

15. Kinzer, *Searching Her Own Mystery*, 38. See also ibid.: "I have contended that the *ecclesia* should be conceived of as inherently twofold in character: it is a body of Jews and gentiles, with the Jewish disciples of Jesus remaining a visible communal presence within the one *ecclesia*, joining her to the Jewish people as a whole. I have called this model bilateral ecclesiology; it resembles closely the framework suggested by Cardinal Lustiger." See also Kinzer's earlier work in which he develops bilateral ecclesiology, *Postmissionary Messianic Judaism: Redefining Christian Engagement with the Jewish People* (Brazos Press, 2005), especially 151–79.

16. See Antoine Levy, *Jewish Church: A Catholic Approach to Messianic Judaism* (Lexington Books, 2021), 24: "For more than 1,500 years, Jews have been the only individuals that were asked to renounce the greatest part of their natural commitment to the people that had given them birth in order to become members of the Church."

17. See *Lumen gentium*, no. 13.

18. See Levy, *Jewish Church*, 24: "Paradoxically, what explains the small but fairly constant amount of Jewish members in the Church is not a definite and stable structure of transmission but an irregular stream of conversions."

19. I am presupposing the Scholastic distinction of three aspects of the Law of Moses into moral, ceremonial, and judicial precepts, as explained by Thomas Aquinas, *ST* I-II, q. 99. The moral precepts, as embodied in the Ten Commandments and their corollaries, have not lost their binding force. The ceremonial and judicial precepts, in contrast, have lost their obligatory nature in the New Covenant.

20. See Bruce D. Marshall, "Christ and Israel: An Unsolved Problem in Catholic Theology", in *The Call of Abraham: Essays on the Election of Israel in Honor of Jon D. Levenson*, ed. Gary A. Anderson and Jon D. Levenson (University of Notre Dame Press, 2013), 339–40: "We arrive, then, at what seems to be the basic theological problem about Christ and Israel.... God wills the election of Israel irrevocably, up to and including the end-time salvation of the descendants of Abraham, Isaac, and Jacob according to the flesh. But God no longer wills the practice of Judaism, indeed he apparently wills that it not be practiced. How, though, are the Jewish people going to make it to the eschaton without Judaism? The practice of Judaism is, it seems, indispensable for the Jewish people to remain, over time, distinct from the gentiles. Without it they would soon vanish, like the Hittites, into the sea of nations.... Visible distinction from the nations is, in other words, necessary for the election of Israel."

21. Wyschogrod, *Abraham's Promise*, 183. The text continues: "Had the Church believed that it was God's will that the seed of Abraham not disappear from the world, she would have insisted on Jews retaining their separateness, even in the Church."

22. See Levy, *Jewish Church*, 24: "In the absence of a stable structure that would secure the continuity of a living Jewish identity within the Church, it is difficult to see how membership in the Church could not be equivalent to its short-term disintegration. Due to intermarriage combined with the ban on Judaizing habits, the descendants of Jewish converts will be cleansed of the last traces of Jewish identity in the span of two or three generations."

23. Kinzer, *Searching Her Own Mystery*, 59.

24. See Hans Urs von Balthasar, *Martin Buber and Christianity: A Dialogue Between Israel and the Church* (Macmillan, 1961), 78: "The Church ... does not want its praise of God to derive simply and solely from the written word, but from the mind and heart of the Jews at prayer, from those who first formed the words, so that it can embrace them in its living tradition."

25. For a fuller exposition, see Feingold, *Touched by Christ*, 521–45.

26. See Melito of Sardis, *Sermon "On the Passover"*, nos. 36–42, trans. Richard C. White (Lexington Theological Seminary Library, 1976), 26–28.

27. See Augustine, "Letter 82 to Saint Jerome", in *Letters*, vol. 1 (1–82), trans. Wilfrid Parson (Catholic University of America Press, 1951), 401–3.

28. See Augustine's commentary on Acts 21:21–26 in ibid., 396–97.

29. Ibid., 401–3.

30. See Levy, *Jewish Church*, 71: "The idea that 'unbelieving' Israel had been rejected led theologians to view the forms of Jewish worship after Christ as dead and deadly. Still, in the same epistle, Paul categorically denies that Israel's lack of faith cancelled her election."

31. See Kinzer, *Postmissionary Messianic Judaism*, 224: "The message about Yeshua that came to Jews in the second century was radically different [than in the first century]. It spoke of how Israel's Covenant and way of life had been annulled in the Messiah, and it claimed that Jewish identity and practice were of no value or even prohibited. Any Jew who was loyal to the Covenant would conclude that such a message could not possibly come from the God of Israel. To reject such a purported Messiah would be an act of fidelity to God rather than infidelity!"

32. See *ST*, I-II, q. 103, a. 4, ad 1.

33. See *ST*, I-II, q. 103, a. 4. See also Matthew Tapie, *Aquinas on Israel and the Church: The Question of Supersessionism in the Theology of Thomas Aquinas* (Pickwick Publications, 2016). For Jewish critique of Aquinas' reasoning, see Michael Wyschogrod, "A Jewish Reading of St. Thomas Aquinas", in *Understanding Scripture: Explorations of Jewish and Christian Traditions of Interpretation*, ed. Clemens Thoma and Michael Wyschogrod (Paulist Press, 1987), 136.

34. See *ST*, I-II, q. 102, a. 2.

35. See Council of Florence, *Cantate Domino*, *D-H* 1348.

36. On invincible ignorance, see Pius IX, *Quanto conficiamur moerore* (August 10, 1863; *D-H* 2866); and *LG* 16. See also D'Costa, *Catholic Doctrines*, 38–46; and Feingold, *Touched by Christ*, 537–39.

37. See D'Costa, *Catholic Doctrines*, 37.

38. Council of Florence, *Cantate Domino*, *D-H* 1350. On the interpretation of this teaching of the bull *Cantate Domino* of the Council of Florence, see D'Costa, *Catholic Doctrines*, 44–54; and Gavin D'Costa, "The Mystery of Israel: Jews, Hebrew Catholics, Messianic Judaism, the Catholic Church, and the Mosaic Ceremonial Laws", *Nova et Vetera* (English edition) 16 (2018), 945–70. On the disciplinary nature of this prohibition, see Farrow, *Theological Negotiations*, 228–30, 245.

39. Benedict XIV, encyclical letter *Ex quo primum* (From the First) (March 1, 1756), no. 63.

40. Ibid. On *Ex quo primum*, see D'Costa, "The Mystery of Israel", 960–66; and D'Costa, *Catholic Doctrines*, 49–54.

41. Farrow, *Theological Negotiations*, 228–30.

42. See James P. Shea, *From Christendom to Apostolic Mission: Pastoral Strategies for an Apostolic Age* (University of Mary Press, 2020).

43. See Feingold, *Touched by Christ*, 540–45.

44. See Levy, *Jewish Church*, 263–96.

45. See "AHC Passover Haggadah", Association of Hebrew Catholics, accessed July 1, 2023, http://www.hebrewcatholic.net/the-ahc-passover-haggadah/. See also Archbishop Raymond Burke's appreciation after participating in a Hebrew Catholic Seder hosted by David Moss, in Moss' "Interview with Archbishop Raymond Burke", in *You Shall Be My Witnesses: Hebrew Catholics and the Mission of the Church* (The Miriam Press, 2012), 36–37.

46. See Augustine, "Letter 82 to Saint Jerome", 395–99.

47. See Farrow, *Theological Negotiations*, 233–34: "Jews have the responsibility to teach messianic Gentiles how to appropriate the Old Testament and to show non-messianic Jews

how to receive the New Testament. To this end, they may and (with the encouragement of the Church) ordinarily should maintain their identity as Jews by circumcision and by perpetuating inherited patterns of prayer and devotion and learning and living, insofar as these are conducive to maturity and to effective mission through Christian refashioning, though never in such a way as to impinge on their common sacramental and liturgical life with Gentiles. It must always be clear, as Matthew Levering has argued, that the Jewishness of Jews is fulfilled via their sacramental union with Jesus, in whom the demands of Torah have already been met and reconfigured in the Spirit for the whole Church."

48. See Friedman, *Jewish Identity*, 64: "Daniélou maintained that even if all Israel had embraced Christianity, the continuity of Israel would not have been threatened. How could he know? The history of Judaeo-Christianity belies his facile optimism.... In the personal experience of the author of these pages, to guarantee the continuity of Jewry's history, in the hypothesis of an entry en masse of Jews into the faith, steps would have to be taken and obstacles overcome."

49. See Friedman, *Jewish Identity*, 94: "The impression made on the Jew by the regime of assimilation was disastrous. It outraged him in the deepest fibers of his self-understanding. Secularists and religious Jews closed ranks in defense against the menace of the Christian Mission." See also ibid., 172: "If the existence of a Hebrew-Catholic community demonstrates to the Jews that the official Church does not intend to bring about the destruction of Jewry by assimilation, that would be a great gain for the Church."

50. For a study of the relationship of the sacramental rites of the Old Covenant to those of the New, see Feingold, *Touched by Christ*, 501–21.

51. On a personal note, I encountered *Jewish Identity* and the Association of Hebrew Catholics in 1990, one year after my wife and I became Catholic, and its formative influence on me helped me to connect with my Jewish roots and to see the importance of a Hebrew Catholic witness in the Church. I first met David Moss, president of the Association, in 2006, and we have worked closely together since then.

52. See Friedman, *Jewish Identity*, 171: "The Jewish convert should be encouraged to correct the deficiencies of his situation by common action with other converts. Together, they would endeavor to establish a policy for their own collective future and another for relations with Jewry. The ultimate object of their associating would be to petition the official Church to set up a Hebrew community, juridically approved by the Holy See."

53. Ibid.

54. Ibid., 172.

55. David Moss, "You Shall Be My Witnesses ... (Acts 1:8)", in *You Shall Be My Witnesses*, 49.

56. See "Studies", Association of Hebrew Catholics, accessed July 1, 2023, https://www.hebrewcatholic.net/studies/.

57. Moss, "You Shall Be My Witnesses", 48.

58. See ibid. Despite substantial ecclesiological differences, Hebrew Catholics can enter into fruitful dialogue with Messianic Jews. See the mission statement of the ecumenical fraternity *Yachad BeYeshua* at https://www.yachad-beyeshua.org/our-mission, accessed July 1, 2023.

59. Moss, "You Shall Be My Witnesses", 48.

CONTRIBUTORS

Dr. Angela Costley is a Hebrew Catholic theologian based in the United Kingdom. A graduate of Durham (B.A. Hons., P.G. Cert.) and Oxford (M.St.), she completed her Ph.D. at the Pontifical University, St Patrick's College, Maynooth, Ireland, in 2018. Her area of interest is discourse analysis, and her Ph.D. thesis, *Creation and Christ: An Exploration of the Topic of Creation in the Letter to the Hebrews*, was published in 2020 by Mohr Siebeck. She has also contributed to the successful Reading in Context series by Zondervan, has published in the Proceedings of the Irish Biblical Association, and has more recently published in New Blackfriars. A member of the board of directors of the Association of Hebrew Catholics, Costley is committed to deepening the Church's awareness of its Jewish dimension and securing recognition for the unique spirituality of Jewish Catholics. She currently teaches Sacred Scripture at Oscott College, one of England's Catholic seminaries.

Professor Gavin D'Costa is Invited Professor of Catholic-Jewish Dialogue at the Pontifical University of St. Thomas Aquinas, Rome, and Emeritus Professor of Catholic Theology at the University of Bristol, U.K. He is author of eight books, most recently *Vatican II: Catholic Doctrines on Jews and Muslims* (Oxford University Press, 2014) and *Catholics and Jews After Vatican II* (Oxford University Press, 2019). His work has been translated into seven languages. D'Costa has also published a book of poetry. His interests are in dogmatics and theology of religions, specifically the relation of Catholicism to Jews and Muslims. He is an advisor to the Roman Catholic Bishops in England and Wales on matters related to other religions and has worked with the World Council of Churches and the Pontifical Council for Interreligious Dialogue, Vatican City.

Dr. Robert L. Fastiggi, A.B. Dartmouth; M.A., Ph.D. Fordham, holds the Bishop M. Kevin Britt Chair of Dogmatic Theology and

Christology at Sacred Heart Major Seminary, Detroit, Michigan, where he has taught since 1999. He previously taught at St. Edward's University in Austin, Texas (1985–1999). He was the co-editor of the English translation of the forty-third edition of Denzinger-Hünermann, *Compendium of Creeds, Definitions, and Declarations on Matters of Faith and Morals* (Ignatius Press, 2012), and the executive editor of the 2009–2013 supplements to the *New Catholic Encyclopedia.* He also revised and updated the English translation of Ludwig Ott's *Fundamentals of Catholic Dogma* for Baronius Press (2018). He is a council member of the Mariological Society of America and a member of PAMI, the Pontifical Marian Academy International (Pontificia Academia Mariana Internationalis). Dr. Fastiggi and his wife, Kathy, have been married for forty years. They are the parents of three children: Mary, Anthony, and Clare.

Dr. Lawrence Feingold is Professor of Theology at Kenrick-Glennon Seminary in St. Louis, Missouri. He converted to Catholicism in 1989 together with his wife while engaged in realist marble sculpture in Pietrasanta, Italy. He is the author of *Touched by Christ: The Sacramental Economy* (2021); *The Eucharist: Mystery of Presence, Sacrifice, and Communion* (2018); *Faith Comes from What Is Heard: An Introduction to Fundamental Theology* (2016); *The Mystery of Israel and the Church* (2010); and *The Natural Desire to See God According to St. Thomas Aquinas and His Interpreters* (2010).

Elias Friedman, O.C.D., a Carmelite priest, was born in 1916 into a Jewish family in South Africa. He graduated from the University of Cape Town in 1938. In 1943, while serving as a doctor in the South African Medical Corps, he entered the Catholic Church. Four years later, he became a Carmelite and saw his first book, *The Redemption of Israel*, published by Sheed and Ward. He was ordained in 1953 and entered the Stella Maris Monastery on Mount Carmel in Haifa, Israel, where he resided until he passed away in 1999. The book from which we publish a chapter here, *Jewish Identity* (The Miriam Press, 1987), was the fruit of a lifetime of prayer, study, and more than forty years of religious life in Israel and was foundational in establishing the Association of Hebrew Catholics.

Scott W. Hahn is the founder and president of the St. Paul Center for Biblical Theology; author of over forty academic and popular titles, including *Kinship by Covenant* (Yale University Press, 2009) and *The Kingdom of God as Liturgical Empire: A Theological Commentary on 1–2 Chronicles* (Baker Academic, 2012). He holds the Scanlan Chair of Biblical Theology at Franciscan University of Steubenville.

Antoine Levy, O.P., is an adjunct professor at the University of Helsinki (Faculty of Theology) and the University of Eastern Finland (School of Theology). He is the co-founder of the Helsinki Consultation on Jewish Continuity in the Body of the Messiah, a forum of Christian and messianic theologians of Jewish descent (today, *Yachad BeYeshua*). He is the author of several books (*The Created and the Uncreated: Maximus the Confessor and Aquinas*, 2006—in French; *Jewish Church: A Catholic Approach to Jewish Messianic Theology*, 2022) and numerous articles in the fields of patristics, ecumenical theology, and philosophy. He is currently established in Jerusalem and conducts research at the University of Tel Aviv.

Bruce D. Marshall is Lehman Professor of Christian Doctrine in the Perkins School of Theology at Southern Methodist University (Dallas, Texas), where he has taught since 2001. He is the author of *Trinity and Truth* (2000) and *Christology in Conflict* (1987), and over one hundred articles and reviews in academic and popular journals. At present he is completing a book entitled *The Primacy of Christ: Faith, Reason, and the Cross*, and another book, with Professor Michael Root, entitled *Justification and Grace: Cross-Border Reflections*. He has served as Randall Distinguished Professor in Christian Culture at Providence College and is a past president of the Academy of Catholic Theology. In 2023, he held the Aquinas Chair in the Thomistic Institute at the Angelicum in Rome.

Rev. Dr. David Mark Neuhaus, S.J., teaches at the Seminary of the Latin Patriarchate of Jerusalem and at the Salesian Theological Institute in Jerusalem. He is also a researcher at the Jesuit Institute in Johannesburg, South Africa. His publications include *Justice and the Intifada: Palestinians and Israelis Speak Out* (edited with Kathy Bergen and Ghassan Rubeiz, Friendship Press, 1991); in collaboration with Alain Marchadour, *The Land That I Will Show You . . . Land, Bible and History*, which has been published in French (2006), English (2007), Italian (2007), German (2011), and Korean (2018); and *Writing from the Holy Land*, which has been published in French (2017), English (2017), and Italian (2018). He has published widely on Scripture, interreligious dialogue, and the Middle East.

Dr. Brant Pitre is Distinguished Research Professor of Scripture at the Augustine Institute Graduate School of Theology. He earned his Ph.D. in Theology from the University of Notre Dame, where he specialized in the study of Christianity and Judaism in Antiquity. He is the author of the best-selling books *Jesus and the Jewish Roots of the Eucharist* (Image, 2011), *Jesus and the Jewish Roots of Mary* (Image, 2018), and *The Case for Jesus* (Image, 2015). He is also author of *Jesus and the Last Supper* (Eerdmans, 2015), co-author with Michael P. Barber and John Kincaid of *Paul, a New Covenant Jew* (Eerdmans, 2019), and co-author with John Bergsma of *A Catholic Introduction to the Bible: The Old Testament* (Ignatius Press, 2016). He currently lives in Louisiana with his wife, Elizabeth, and their five children.

Roy Schoeman, a Jewish entrant into the Catholic Church, teaches at Holy Apostles College and Seminary in Cromwell, Connecticut. He has a B.S. from Massachusetts Institute of Technology and an M.B.A. from Harvard Business School. Prior to his conversion, he taught business on the faculties of Harvard Business School and Northeastern University. He writes, speaks, and teaches broadly on the theological and historical relationship between Judaism and the Catholic Church. In addition to his books and articles, he appears regularly on Catholic television and radio and the internet and speaks frequently at parishes, conferences, missions, and retreats throughout the United States and Canada, Central and South America, Australia, New Zealand, Ireland, and the United Kingdom. He also hosts a daily Catholic podcast and a weekly show on Radio Maria.

INDEX